BY YOUR LEAVE, SIR

Jack Barnes Sr.
with
Laurie Anne Blanchard

Copyright © 2015 Hollister Press

All rights reserved.

ISBN: 0692480935
ISBN-13: 978-0692480939

*To my wife Mona, and all of our children,
grandchildren, great grandchildren
and our great great grandchildren.*

*Love you all,
Poppa*

CONTENTS

1	Prologue	217	Chapter 25
5	Chapter 1	223	Chapter 26
13	Chapter 2	227	Chapter 27
19	Chapter 3	233	Chapter 28
25	Chapter 4	237	Chapter 29
35	Chapter 5	247	Chapter 30
45	Chapter 6	255	Chapter 31
51	Chapter 7	267	Chapter 32
59	Chapter 8	271	Chapter 33
65	Chapter 9	267	Chapter 34
73	Chapter 10	287	Chapter 35
79	Chapter 11	293	Chapter 36
91	Chapter 12	299	Chapter 37
101	Chapter 13	303	Chapter 38
113	Chapter 14	309	Chapter 39
121	Chapter 15	313	Chapter 40
129	Chapter 16	317	Chapter 41
137	Chapter 17	325	Chapter 42
149	Chapter 18	329	Chapter 43
157	Chapter 19	335	Chapter 44
167	Chapter 20	341	Chapter 45
175	Chapter 21	345	Chapter 46
185	Chapter 22	349	Chapter 47
193	Chapter 23	355	Chapter 48
209	Chapter 24	361	About the Author

ACKNOWLEDGMENTS

It's been 70 years now, since the End of World War II. However, to me, the memories are still sharp and poignant. While the names have been changed to protect the innocent, I want to thank my friends who experienced it with me, my family who has heard these stories for 70 years now and my wife who has listened to me talk about this book for the last 35 years or so while I worked on it. This book wouldn't have made it to press without the help of my daughter and writing coach Laurie Blanchard, my son Jack, who pried the draft of this book out of our hands, my editor Aaron Reimer, my cover editor Eilonwy, and Ravastra Design Studio's beautiful work on the cover.

Lastly, and most importantly, my eternal gratitude and heartfelt love goes out to the love of my life, my wife Mona, who has listened to me talk about this book for the last 35 years or so while I worked on it, and put up with my thousands of hours in the office.

PROLOGUE

The year was 1942, three months after Pearl Harbor and three months before high school graduation. I was seventeen and scheduled to join the Navy at that time.

I had just taken Marie, a fellow classmate who was a cheerleader on the football team, back to her home. I went to games just to watch her bounce. She had refused my request to go steady, complaining I lacked imagination. I bitterly regretted not developing a line of bull, and vowed that never again would this happen.

At that moment my Model A Ford blew a tire. I let the car coast to a stop, got out and locked the door. There was no spare.

The highway was dark, traffic was light, and then it began to drizzle. Rain drops soon coursed down my forehead and dripped off the end of my nose as I huddled beside my disabled vehicle. This night just kept getting worse.

In the distance, I could hear the powerful engine of an approaching car. Seconds later, a late model Pontiac roared around the curve. The driver saw me, hesitated, and then slammed on the brakes. The smell of burning rubber hung in the air as I ran toward the car. The passenger leaned back and opened the rear door for me. The car was rapidly accelerating before I could get the door closed. The driver turned around and grinned at me over his shoulder. I wasn't sure what to think when I realized he, and his front seat passenger were boys even younger than me.

"Hey, thanks for the ride; it was getting wet out there. Are you going into Placerville?"

"Why not? We don't have anything better to do," came the cheerful reply from the driver.

My stomach developed a sinking feeling. "How did you manage to get a new Pontiac?"

"We borrowed it," the passenger contributed with a short laugh.

I was just about to ask them to drop me off on the side of the road, when I heard the magic words.

"You want to drive it?"

Wow! My recent concerns diminished considerably. This car was reputed to be able to hit over a hundred miles per hour. The driver interpreted my astonished silence as acceptance, and pulled the car to the side of the road. Well, what could go wrong in the short distance to Placerville? The rain hadn't reached here yet, so we decided to find out how fast this car really would go. My foot floor-boarded the throttle at the first, long straight-away, the speedometer began to rapidly unwind. Seventy—eighty—ninety—and then something in the rear-view mirror was distracting my concentration—flashing red lights!

For the second time that night, I eased over to the roadside and parked. My heart beat wildly as my suspicions were confirmed; this was not a speeding ticket! State patrolmen with drawn pistols approached from each side of the car, and aimed flashlight beams into our faces.

"Get out, with your hands on top of your heads!"

Doors were opened, and we were not too gently removed, frisked, handcuffed, and shoved into the back seat of the patrol car. One officer carefully opened the trunk of the Pontiac. The way he was acting, we expected to see him pull out a body. He seemed to spend a long time back there and finally returned to the patrol car, and picked up the radio microphone.

"We have the car," was his terse report, "everything looks intact. We are leaving for the Placerville jail."

The other officer drove the Pontiac, and on the way back I asked this officer, "Can you tell us what is going on?"

"It's a Sacramento affair," was his noncommittal reply, and wouldn't say anything more.

We arrived at the jail and were placed in separate cells, where we were allowed one phone call, and I had to face the humiliation of reporting my new lodgings to my parents.

The next morning, a man I somehow felt was from the OSS interviewed each of us separately. The first familiar face was Barry Miller, the young, deputy district attorney of El Dorado County.

Barry was an airport acquaintance, and we shared a love of flying.

"Hey! Am I glad to see you." I said through the bars of the cell. "What have I gotten involved in?"

"Jack, start at the beginning, and tell me everything that happened last night."

My recitation carried through to my being here in a jail cell.

"Barry, please tell me what it's all about?"

"Well, here it is, Jack. The Pontiac belongs to an Army captain from the Sacramento Army Depot, and has some highly explosive and very hush-hush ordinance in the trunk. The captain stopped to pick up cigarettes and forgot to take his keys. Evidently, the two boys borrowed the car for a joy ride. The military assumed enemy agents had hijacked it and broadcast a statewide alert. The car was spotted outside Placerville, and of course you know the rest. Your problem is you're the oldest, and you were driving."

A sick feeling was spreading throughout my body.

"Barry, I have it all set up to go into the Navy when I graduate in June. If I have an arrest record they won't take me."

"I'll see what I can do. *If* your Ford is where you say it is it'll help." He gave me a look that told me my Ford had better be there.

The next visitors were my parents, who were very upset about my being in jail. Mother was weeping and dad was angrily pacing the floor.

"Well, how does it feel to be a jailbird?" he demanded. "I suppose you know you made the morning newspaper." The words had the impact of a solid blow.

This possibility hadn't occurred to me, and dad's attitude was upsetting. My mind had been picturing myself as a falsely accused innocent—expecting sympathy.

Up until then, my nature had been that of a shy, sensitive, high school student, who wouldn't have dreamed of talking back to his father. The stress of being arrested, the lack of sleep and the feeling of shame over the situation were not helped by dad's attitude. Something inside me seemed to snap.

"What's the matter?" I defiantly replied. "Are you worried about your social standing?"

Wow! Did that produce a reaction! Dad was a big, husky, fruit rancher, in top physical condition. His face got so red, I quickly stepped back, secretly glad the bars were between us.

"If you ever get out young man, you and I are going to have a discussion in the barn."

"No, we aren't going to have any barn discussions," I recklessly continued. "I'm not coming home!"

"And just where do you plan to go?"

"I'm going directly into the Navy—now!"

Mother was openly sobbing, and dad was beginning to cool down.

"What about your high school diploma?" he asked. "You only have a couple months to go."

"To hell with the diploma—if the ship sinks, I won't need it anyway."

Mother's sobs were increasing and each one stabbed like a knife. It was a shame she got caught in the middle.

"Well, we'll see about that," dad growled through clenched teeth, and took mom's arm to lead her out.

They had already signed for me to enter the Navy after graduation, and I wondered if dad could retract the signature?

I retired to the bunk, aghast at what had occurred. I'd really burned my bridges.

Barry arrived the next morning with good news. By going directly into the Navy, all charges would be dropped and the arrest record expunged.

Well, there sure wasn't anything to lose. My dad and I weren't speaking, I'd blown it with Marie, and after the newspaper item, everyone in town probably was thinking of me as a car thief. Somehow, my life had spun out of control and I was just following along to see what was going to happen next!

ONE

"You'll be sorry." This was the refrain that greeted us as we descended the bus steps and formed a line in the reception area of the San Diego Naval Training Station. The fact that these remarks were generated by "old salts" of only a few days did nothing to raise my drooping spirits.

Events moved rapidly from this point. A chief petty officer introduced himself as our new company commander. Company 238 was formed, lined two abreast, and raggedly marched to the indoctrination and supply center.

The basic facts of Navy life were explained in about fifteen minutes. They dealt mostly with money. We were to receive twenty-one dollars a month, out of which was to be deducted nearly everything received except the basic clothing allotment. Should any of the articles be lost or stolen, replacements would also be deducted. We were issued under clothing, shoes, a hat, uniforms, a seabag and a hammock.

Our next move was to line up before a battery of barbers for our initial Navy haircut. My dark blond hair was medium long with a natural wave, and the thought of a complete loss was disturbing. Maybe if I were extra friendly with the barber he would understand.

As my turn came up, so did my hopes. The barber was friendly. He even asked if I would like to keep my nice wave. After my happy affirmative, he suggested holding my hands in my lap—palms up.

In thirty seconds there it was, hair, wave and all—in my hands. I now had a regulation, half-inch haircut and the barber didn't even attempt to hide his smirk. To add insult to injury it was posted on the wall— this shearing would be deducted from our first twenty-one dollars.

Loaded with full seabag and hammock, Company 238 staggered to the two-story, concrete barracks—our new home for the next six weeks. Morning began at daybreak with the brassy blare of reveille. We had just a few minutes to make beds, shave, shower, shine, and be out in front for muster. The formation marched, still raggedly, to the mess hall for our first Navy breakfast. We couldn't believe what the mess cooks were throwing on our trays as we progressed down the serving line; white navy beans and a piece of toast with a lumpy, thick, brown liquid poured over the top. This must be the infamous "shit-on-a-shingle" we had been warned about. A cup of the blackest coffee I had ever seen was served last. The food was edible. However, many never got beyond the coffee.

Training commenced immediately after breakfast, and continued much the same for the next six weeks: calisthenics, marching, signaling, rowing, use of gas masks, military courtesy, and seemingly anything else the company commander could think of.

At mail call it was a surprise and relieved to receive two letters, one from my grandmother and the other from my mother. Perhaps I hadn't been completely drummed out of the family. My grandmother's was a sweet newsy letter, and didn't mention my difficulties at home.

Mother got right to it. She and dad must have really had a discussion. He had been to the newspaper and forced them to print a correction, stating I was a hitchhiker, not a car thief. Dad also located a spare tire for the Model A, and now had the car in the barn waiting for my first leave.

She went on to say that dad was ashamed of the way he behaved, and I should be too. Finally, she firmly added that they would be looking for a letter each week and were expecting me home on my first leave.

Wow! I loved my parents and suddenly it felt as if a big load of gloom had been removed. My answer was started immediately.

No liberties were to be granted until graduation, and, at first, we were so tired by the end of the day we wouldn't have gone to San Diego if we could. The options available in the evening were washing clothes by hand, writing letters, and telling improbable stories about our civilian love life. This soon began to pall, and, even worse, a pecking order began to develop in the barracks, with an older man dominating the immature, younger ones.

This upset me, mainly because I was on the receiving end. During an evening's reconnaissance, the discovery of the station gym provided a possible solution. A classy middleweight was in charge of the boxing program and although it was for ship's company of the training station, the next evening I fell in with the rest.

I was just getting acquainted with the light bag when the trainer growled, "What are you doing in this class, recruit?"

I stopped hitting the bag and told him the truth. "A Texas redneck is giving me a bad time and when we get to it, I want to be sure I know what I'm doing."

He scowled. "Tough luck— this class is full."

"He is saying all sailors from California are fruits."

The trainer's voice took on an angry tone.

"I'm from California." He hesitated then said, "Go find a pair of gym shoes."

It was three rounds every evening, along with a workout on both punching bags. The instructor clearly pointed out my weaknesses—with a right to the jaw, and a left to the body. I had better improve fast or the needed skills would come too late.

One evening, following a left hook and a right cross that connected solidly, the instructor decided to let me box with the other trainees. Three rounds with someone in my own skill range was a lot more encouraging than three with him, and I began to really anticipate each evening.

There was a full-length mirror for shadow boxing, and one evening I realized the image I was punching was different in some way. My blond hair had grown out enough to comb and my battered chin gave my face a determined expression. At the beginning of boot camp, I had just completed a growth spurt at six feet two inches, and was really skinny at a hundred and forty-five pounds. Now five weeks later, my body was seven pounds heavier and moving with confidence.

Oddly, the problem in the barracks that started it all disappeared just as I was looking forward to straightening a few things out. I believe my tormenter found out where I was spending every evening.

In the earlier part of our training, we had all been given a series of tests to determine our aptitude for different training schools. With four years of automotive mechanics in high school, and a natural affinity for machinery, I knew I had done well on the aviation mechanic tests, and had high hopes of making the school in Florida. At the conclusion of training it was a waiting game, with frequent trips to the bulletin board to see if we had been assigned. During the waiting period, we drew clean-up duties at the station.

The day before we were scheduled for our first San Diego liberty, two of us drew a detail to move a large, truckload of empty cardboard boxes to the station dump. There were more boxes to be moved than one trip could easily accommodate, but we wanted to get this over with and overloaded the truck. The other sailor drove, and I climbed in back of the truck, secure because I had wooden siding around me to hold on to.

As the truck gained speed, the wind started lifting the boxes. I was afraid a bunch would go flying out and we would get in trouble. It seemed the only way to keep the boxes in the truck was to climb up on top and hold them down with my body weight. From the driver's position, he couldn't see that I was up there, spread-eagled on top. Everything was going fine until the driver turned a corner too fast. The boxes and I took a short, wing-less flight to the concrete pavement.

I woke up three days later in the U.S. Naval hospital. My broken left arm was set in a cast, the back of my head wrapped in thick white bandages to protect a skull fracture, and I had a king-sized concussion. I later learned my head had been packed in ice as they tried to control the swelling of my brain and there had been talk of a medical discharge—if I survived!

Unfortunately, it would be at least six weeks before a possible return to duty, and of course the school draft I wanted would be long gone.

Life at the naval hospital wasn't very demanding. The day after they finally let me out of bed, I checked out the grounds and discovered the hospital was located at the edge of beautiful Balboa Park. I ended up spending the mornings there, walking at first, and later when my headache subsided, and jogging to keep in shape. The afternoons were spent in the recreation room where ping-pong was the main game. Luckily I was right handed and it was my left arm that was broken. We played for hours. There wasn't much else to do except play cards, and lust after the nurses. I never had been much for playing cards.

A young, tall, slim, navy nurse with short hair and an exciting figure had just been assigned to the hospital. She broke my game concentration whenever she glided by. Ever since the injury to my head, all I thought about were women and money, and it seemed as if a stranger was taking over my mind. Perhaps what the neurologist warned regarding personality changes following severe head trauma could have been true.

After four weeks of steady afternoon ping-pong, competition became as scarce as money. Somehow my pay records had gotten lost in the shuffle. There were not a lot of places to spend it, but it was frustrating not knowing when I would get paid.

Meanwhile, the first contingent of wounded from the battle of the Coral Sea in the South Pacific arrived. These were old salts, and the main interests of the mobile ones were booze and gambling. The hospital was a little short on booze, so the recreation room was converted into a little Reno. When the card and dice games were shut down, they played ping-pong for money.

Ping-pong got a lot more interesting as soon as real money was being bet. I deliberately didn't play any better then was necessary to win and was able to keep a steady stream of challengers. My finances were improving so rapidly that I no longer cared if my pay records caught up… That is until I met Monte.

Monte was an older, balding, first class yeoman, who came off a ship that sank. Monte didn't swim and nearly sank as well. The doctors were still trying to separate him from the fuel oil he had swallowed in his near death experience.

Monte was a steady winner at the adjoining ping-pong table, but up to now we had never met. The line of challengers at each table diminished until only Monte and I remained; we stood facing each other.

"Shall we make this interesting?" Monte asked with a bland expression.

"Might as well," my reply was equally nonchalant. Although Monte was about fifteen years older than me, after watching his play I was confident I could beat him.

The bet was substantial, however, with plans for a big bet later I managed to lose by a couple of points. Monte graciously allowed me an opportunity to recoup, and the stakes were doubled. I played a little better and managed to win this one. The least I could do was allowing Monte one more chance.

"Let's settle it this game, Monte impatiently began pulling greenbacks out of his pocket, and then added the contents of his wallet to the pile on the table. I felt fortunate to find enough in my wallet to match his bet. This game was definitely all-out.

Word of the shoot-out had spread, and patients were lining both sides of the table. Monte's first serve was so hot I didn't even attempt a return.

Uh-oh! Monte had also been sandbagging.

I moved back several feet and manage to return the next serve. From there on, it was kill shots, reverse English, sneak serves and anything else we had in our repertoire. I played as if my life savings were on the line, as indeed they were, and Monte seemed equally inspired. The final point to win the tie game was a fluke, as Monte's serve ticked the edge of the table and kept right on going.

I had lost and with the caliber of the play everyone witnessed, there wouldn't be any more eager challengers for either of us.

My face must have revealed my disappointment.

"Don't feel bad, Jack, you played a hell of a lot better than I expected." Monte finished stuffing my money into his wallet and walked over. "Matter of fact, for a while there I was afraid you had me sucked in, instead of the other way around. Come on, I'll buy the cokes."

I followed Monte to the lounge, and when we were comfortably seated, Monte asked about my arm. This seemed to open a door and before I realized it, I was telling him about the missed school in Florida and even about my difficulty with girls. When I finished my sad story, Monte slowly leaned back in his seat, an intent expression on his face. He looked around to be sure we couldn't be overheard and then began to speak softly.

"Look, you may have lost some money today, but I'm going to give you some information that's worth a hell of a lot more. This man's Navy is really just a big paper ship. The officers think they are sailing it, the warrants and chiefs think they are, when really the yeomen have the last say. We are the ones that put names, dates, and numbers down in records, and we are the ones who can adjust them."

I leaned forward to catch every word. This was getting interesting.

He knew he had my attention and continued.

"You say you want to go to the school in Florida. Wait until you see where you are assigned. If you don't like it go see the yeoman in charge of assignments. Be sure he is alone, be humble, tell him what you want, and have a folded five dollar bill in the palm of your hand."

I was sure I must have looked stunned, and I was just beginning to contemplate the possibilities when Monte switched to a topic even more fascinating.

"As far as making out with women," Monte continued, leaning back with his fingers interlocked behind his head. "I'm going to give you what it took me fifteen years in the Navy to find out."

Monte then began to give me information every young man would kill to have at his fingertips. In this instance fingertips were to be taken literally. My eyes opened wider and wider as Monte got to the intimate details. When he reached the area of wine over bar whiskey as an aphrodisiac, I interrupted.

Monte, how am I even going to get into a place that sells the stuff, with an ID that says I am only seventeen?"

He looked at me for a moment like a teacher who is disappointed in a prize pupil. "Jack, you haven't been listening. Who makes out new ID cards when one is lost?"

"Yeomen?" I asked hopefully.

"Right, don't forget to have a five dollar bill with you."

By the end of our conversation, my head was reeling from an overload of input—who would have thought being a successful lover could be so complicated? Monte's last words covered my money shortage.

"Don't worry Jack, the missing pay records have arrived, and this payday apprentice seaman pay goes from twenty-one to fifty. You have it made."

TWO

While putting in time at the hospital recovering from the head trauma and resulting personality deviation, a group of Free French sailors had completed basic training. They also were waiting assignment. Only one of them spoke English and French was not widely understood.

I had two years of high school French quite recently, and upon return from the hospital wanted to improve my accent. However, when I approached the group in French I was unprepared for their reaction. First an incredulous stare—then laughter. Apparently, my French teacher's accent had been even worse than I feared. When the laughter subsided, we did find we could communicate, albeit with humorous reactions to my every phrase. Soon I realized they were seriously trying to convey an important message to me. They wanted me to be their interpreter that evening on liberty in San Diego. The one who spoke English was in sickbay.

This was to be my long delayed, first liberty since joining the Navy, and my plans had been made for months. They sure hadn't included a half-dozen French sailors! I conveyed this to them as politely as possible, and couldn't believe their response; they became highly agitated. There was one club in town with most of the female action, and they doubted their ability to get the message across.

This began to sound even more interesting than my planned liberty. However, there was the barrier of getting into the club with an ID card showing me woefully underage. When this difficulty was pointed out, their final offer was they would pay all expenses for the liberty, and would loan the uniform and ID of the one in sickbay. Their only requirement was to be available for interpretation during the evening. It was too good to pass up.

The uniform fit fairly well and was more picturesque than my own. Out the main gate that evening, burst seven excited bodies in Free French Navy uniforms. My control of the situation was established by shepherding them onto the correct downtown bus. It was dinnertime and we were all tired of Navy chow. My mental dossier of the best restaurants from reports of previous returnees suggested the dining room of the Cortez Hotel, especially as I wouldn't be paying for the meal. It was the best, most expensive, and where the officers dined. Into the prestigious Cortez dining room we trooped, where even in a city used to uniforms, we created quite a stir.

When the maitre d' attempted to seat us at two separate tables, my new personality took over.

"*Non!*" I explained, in my best French accent. "I am le only one weeth le English, so naturellement we must dine together."

This brought more attention as tables were repositioned.

As soon as we were seated, a glance at the menu confirmed there was good news and bad news contained within. The good news was the entrees were in French, the bad news was they were very expensive. The waiter, who seemed a little condescending about moving the tables, now came for our orders. A glazed look crossed his eyes as each order was rapidly delivered with a faultless, Parisian accent. The maitre d' glanced over, saw his man was in trouble, and stepped into the breach. We started again and it soon became apparent the maitre d' was also in trouble. He had been nice about the tables, so I interpreted for him the desires of his French customers.

For all this trouble, my order for the filet mignon seemed appropriate—no matter what it cost. Having never tasted champagne, I generously ordered it for all. The meal was really superb, and after the second glass of champagne, my limbs quit shaking. I almost forgot I was only seventeen, illegally in the uniform of another country, and with an ID identifying me as Ravel Deveraux, twenty-one, from Paris.

The champagne helped to prepare my hosts for the shock of the bill and we eagerly looked forward to the Paris Club, the evening's *piece de resistance*.

As we lined up at the club entrance, the bouncer was at the door checking ID's. He also didn't seem to be able to communicate in French and finally threw up his hands in disgust, letting us all in.

This was extremely exciting for me, having never been in a nightclub before. I quickly glanced around, paying particular attention to the bar, the dance floor, and band stand. There were booths and tables on both sides of the dance floor where the five-piece band was just finishing a set. The French seemed to have gained courage from the early part of the evening and soon had tables together right at the dance floor.

I'd noticed as we came in, several of the booths and bar seats were occupied by attractive young ladies. I'm sure the French did also because we were no sooner seated and served our first drink, when they started placing orders. Marcel wanted the cute blond at the bar, Jean indicated a brunette across the dance floor in a booth with three other girls. Claude was trying to get my attention. I quickly gulped another glass of champagne as I realized I was expected to set up each of the French, with the girl of his choice. This was above and beyond our original deal. Little did the French realize, they had chosen the failure of Placerville as their front man. I seriously considered bolting for the door.

Fortunately, the champagne hit bottom about then and my new personality rose with the bubbles. Well, Marcel had ordered first so up to the bar I went, reminding myself to think French. I introduced myself with a French accent to the cute blond, as Ravel from Paris. I explained I was the only one of this valiant group of U. S. allies that spoke English, my compatriot Marcel, he thinks she is the most beautiful girl he has ever seen and prays she will join him at the table. She went for it, and held onto my arm all the way back. I introduced Marcel; he gave her his chair and quickly pulled up another. More and more I was feeling an exhilarating sense of power—like I really was Ravel from Paris and anything was possible. Seventeen years of inhibitions were vanishing with each glass of champagne and my newfound persona was heady stuff.

One down and five to go! My next stop was the booth with the brunette for Jean. I used much the same approach only this time invited all four young ladies, and they also accepted. There really was something about the French!

In the transition from booth to table, I couldn't help admiring firm thighs and sculptured cheeks revealed by the tight sheath dress of the statuesque blond I was following. Could the front be as exciting as the rear?

I introduced the brunette to Jean, the other two to the French, helped find chairs for the girls and seated the blonde named Cleo next to me. The front was indeed as exciting as the rear. This one was definitely a keeper.

"*Bon soir ma cherie, comment allez-vous?*"

"I'm sorry, Ravel; I don't speak French."

"I'm sorree, also, ma chere, you arre so lovelee, I theenk you must be from Paree."

"Oh, Ravel, what a nice thing to say. I love your accent when you speak English."

The band had just finished a break, and now was playing some of my favorite dance music.

"Cleo, ma chere, may I 'ave the plaizure to 'old you een my arms while we danse?"

"Of course, Ravel."

She slipped right into my arms and followed beautifully. I was glad mother had insisted I take dancing lessons. What a dilemma! I didn't dare let her suspect I wasn't French. I didn't know the penalty for wearing the uniform of another country. I wanted to make points on my own, and yet two more Frenchmen were expecting delivery. Finally, I confided to Cleo.

"Ma chere, I am le onlee 'ope of my reemaining compatrriots frrom acrross le sea finding gerls, ave you anee suggestions?"

Cleo gave it a moment's thought and then answered, "Ravel, because you are French, I may be able to do something."

When the music ended, she went to a booth on the other side of the dance floor and talked to two girls there with two marines. In a few moments, she returned with the girls, leaving behind the unhappy marines.

As Cleo and I blended together on the next slow dance, she complimented me on how well I spoke English, and how much more romantic French sailors were than Americans. She told me sailors in San Diego had such a bad reputation, she wouldn't be seen with one. I whispered into her ear, "Onlee le Frrench know le language d'amour."

This triggered an involuntary, erotic response, which was most pleasant. We were dancing very closely with her arm around my neck and her lovely ear close to my lips.

I whispered, "*Cheri, je t'adore.*"

It happened again, a definite, seductive, pelvic rotation. Wow! I tried the same words in English; nothing much, just, "Oh Ravel!"

I tried other French endearments. They all worked. This girl was programmed, at least subconsciously, for French amour. I was unhappy when the music stopped at this exciting moment of discovery.

The party's tempo quickly accelerated with the arrival of more girls, and I must admit the French do have style. They add something to American dance steps, which in the case of a fast jitterbug, became a floorshow.

The language of love must be truly international, as my services as an interpreter were no longer required. Each dance with Cleo was more exciting than the last. I ran through every French phrase of endearment I could think of, and even made up a few. The results were driving me out of my mind. I knew there wasn't time to take her home tonight. I also knew if I showed up for a date later in an American sailor uniform, I was a dead duck. She loathed American sailors and it was very unlikely I would have another chance at a French uniform.

Cleo and I were dancing very closely. My last phrase not only produced a seductive, involuntary reaction, she lifted her lips for a lingering, passionate kiss. I know this was the last dance before we hurried back to the station, and I'd probably never see her again. Out of desperation, came inspiration! I remembered the fiasco with Marie for not being imaginative enough and the vow I took thereafter.

"Cleo, ma chere," I breathed heavily.

"Yes, Ravel?"

"Eef I tell you somezing, weel you will guard eet with your life?"

"Oh, yes."

"Cleo, I am rellee a secret agent, ere on the special assignment. I will soon need a beauteeful gerl to accompanee me as a covair. Could I possiblee ask you to help? I must warn you eet might be dangerous."

"Oh, Ravel, it sounds exciting; call me any time."

"Merci, Cleo, all France thanks you—reemember I may be wearing some other uniform as a disguize. Maybe even a Merican one. Now cherie, eet ees time we must say au revoir."

After getting Cleo's address and phone number, I rounded up the reluctant French; we kissed the girls a fond adieu and returned to the training station. I was relieved the guard at the main gate wasn't too careful about the ID's of returning liberty parties.

As I lay in my bunk before drifting off to sleep, General Sherman's phrase crossed my mind. "War is hell."

THREE

The next morning, I checked the bulletin board for assignments. Sure enough, down near the bottom was a draft for sea duty aboard a destroyer, and my name was on it! I probably wouldn't have had the confidence to follow yeoman Monte's suggestion, but since the head trauma, this new personality occasionally took over, and I was beginning to like the results.

I took a five dollar bill, folded it into a small square with just the five showing, went to the administration building, located the yeoman in charge of assignments and expressed to him my great desire to attend the aviation machinist mate school in Florida, and not to go to sea on a destroyer. I had the five in the palm of my hand resting on his desk, and as I glanced around to see if we were being observed, I removed my palm from the bill. When I swung my head back the five was gone.

"Well, let's see what we can do," muttered the yeoman as he pulled out the next Florida school draft which hadn't yet been posted. He removed the last name, added mine, and consigned some soul to sea duty.

Five days later, I was on a troop train headed for Jacksonville, Florida. I was overjoyed to make the school, but desolate I didn't have time for a date with Cleo and the exciting possibilities it held.

There may have been worse methods of travel during this first year of the war, but I just couldn't think of any. The troop train consisted of what we called cattle cars with bunks, rudimentary sanitation, and dining facilities, pulled by an antique, coal-burning locomotive spraying hot cinders the full length of the train. It was slow to begin with, and having the lowest priority of all rail traffic compounded this. We waited on the siding for all other trains to pass.

By the time we reached Texas, our undress blue uniforms were gritty from all the cinders, and not having shower facilities sure didn't help. As we pulled into Fort Worth we were shunted onto a siding as usual, and then informed there would be an eight-hour delay before we continued on.

This was too much! Visions of a good meal, a cooling draft, maybe even a shower, swam before my eyes. The chief in charge of our two cars did his best to keep us aboard. Unfortunately for him, there was no way to lock the doors. I glanced at Mike, a slim, dark haired, fellow trainee with an adventurous spirit, and received a nod in reply. We didn't need to say anything, just quickly cleaned up as best we could, slipped on our dress blues, and were out the back door while the Chief was guarding the front.

Mike and I removed our presence from the rail yards as quickly as possible and soon reached the business district, where we couldn't believe what we were seeing. Young, attractive girls were everywhere; in pairs, in groups, in cars—it was a smorgasbord. Even more unbelievable, they were friendly, very friendly! The ones on foot smiled and waved, and a nearly new 1941 Ford convertible with two lovelies inside pulled to the curb beside us.

"Want a ride, sailors?" the dark haired driver called.

"Sure do," we replied in chorus.

"Well, hop in." The driver smiled.

The blond girl on the passenger side, slipped into the back seat with Mike and I took her place in the front.

"Where would you fellas like to go?" the driver asked me.

"Anywhere you're going will be just fine," I replied, "we have eight hours to kill."

"There aren't any more where you came from, are there?"

"Yes," I replied, "but I really don't think you're going to need them." Both girls laughed.

"Sailor, if you can keep fifteen Texas girls happy, I won't look for any more." The driver had a wicked grin.

I realized I might be getting in over my head.

"Where are the rest?" I asked in a slightly subdued voice.

"At the hotel, waiting for me to deliver some fellas. The chaperone of our floor took sick, and we're going to have one big bash before she gets back."

"Who's we?"

"The Rainbow Girls, this is our convention and it's been a little dull up to now."

When I mentioned there was a whole trainload of sailors sitting in the rail yard, they got all excited. They already had the food and drink, and they thought it was right hospitable of the Navy to supply the fellas. The driver headed back to round them up.

There were six escapees in the first group we came to and she wanted them all. We put the top down and by using it as a seat we got them all aboard. They were from our draft, and thought it was our idea to pick them up. I wasn't about to say anything different.

The driver pulled up in front of what was most likely the best hotel in Fort Worth, and we unloaded. It took some doing to get us all into the elevator to the seventh floor, where the party was already under way in the largest suite I'd ever seen. There was a regular buffet on the table and lots of cold beer and soda pop. A record player was going full blast. About fifteen girls and four soldiers were already there, and the additional sailors were an instant success.

I was having a mental struggle between getting better acquainted with the driver of the car or with the buffet and beer. Having fared so badly on the train, the buffet was about to win, when the driver came over and apologized for being such a poor hostess. She allowed she was going to make up for that right here and now, and demonstrated that Texas girls do know how to make a fella feel better.

I found out her name was Lucinda, just call her Lu, from Goose Creek, Texas. She was the same age as me, and her daddy had lots of whatever they raise in Goose Creek—I think she said doggies. There was no doubt in my mind, with her jet-black hair and aristocratic Spanish features she was a most striking girl.

Well, after two trips through the buffet and several cool ones, I was feeling much better. The next slow record, Lucinda got up close, and if what followed was a sample of Texas style dancing—they really had something going there. When Lu molded her seductively slim body to mine, wild things started to happen.

As the dance ended she asked, "Jack, is there anything else you would like to do?"

Well, her close dancing had produced some perspiration, and that sure reminded me I hadn't had a shower in a week. I was too shy to tell her what else it had done.

"Lucinda, the thing I need most right now is a shower."

I wasn't sure if she had something else in mind, but the next thing I knew I was luxuriating in the ceramic tile shower of her suite across the hall. I had just finished washing my hair and soaping up good, when I felt a cool draft on my back and heard the bathroom door close. I was facing the back of the shower, there was only a curtain, and I heard Lucinda's voice.

"Jack, its only Texas hospitality to scrub a guest's back."

Well, who was I to argue with local customs, and besides this girl knew how to scrub a back.

About this time we heard the front door open, and Mike and Lucinda's roommate gave a call. This brought the back scrubbing to an end, and of course when Mike found out about the shower he had to have one too, complete with a back scrub from Lucinda's roommate.

While Mike's cleanliness was being assured, Lucinda and I were getting comfortable on the big bed in her bedroom. All I was wearing was the towel, and I was beginning to believe this was the big moment I'd been waiting for. Mike was prolonging his back scrub, and anyway, they had a separate bedroom. I had been hearing a lot of banging going on out in the hall, and then someone was pounding on the door of our suite. Lucinda reluctantly rose, went to answer, and through the open bedroom door I could see a MP and an SP standing at the entrance.

The SP demanded, "Are there any sailors in there?"

Instead of answering, Lu asked. "Why do you want to know?"

The SP lowered his voice and replied, "The troop train is pulling out four hours early. We have rounded up all the sailors except two, and if they don't get back immediately they will miss the train."

Mike came out of the shower with a towel around his middle, in time to hear these last words. Well, we admitted we were the two lost sailors. The Shore Patrol waited while we dressed, and Lucinda and I returned to her room for our goodbyes. The opportunity had passed, and I don't know which of us felt worse. I promised to come to Goose Creek on my first leave, and then it was time to go.

The Shore Patrol drove us to the rail yard as quickly as possible however; the train had already pulled out. Right at this point we were in a rather delicate situation; either we were AWOL, or were the innocent victims of a change in schedule. I was glad we had been cooperative with the Shore Patrol, and as I explained the situation in the best possible light, he made the decision to help. One telephone call and he had received authorization to issue travel vouchers and meal tickets on the first passenger train to Jacksonville. By blind, incredible luck, this turned out to be the streamliner, with berths, porters, and a dining car. This fast passenger train had right-of-way over all traffic.

At the first call to dinner, Mike and I secured a good window seat in the dining car, and as the meal tickets were good for anything we order, we ordered well. Midway through the meal we slowed for a congested rail yard, and Mike asked with a grin, "Jack, do you see what I see?"

The white-coated waiter was refilling my coffee cup as I glanced out the window. There, parked on a siding as usual, was our cinder covered troop train. As we slowly passed, we were looking at them and they were looking at us. We recognized several of the earlier party participants, noticed their surprised reaction, and in the last car we were staring into the angry eyes of the chief. He was looking at the remains of an excellent dinner, thick, white tablecloth, and a waiter at our beck and call. We were looking at a hot, dirty, chief, who would probably strangle us if he could get his hands on us. We smiled, nodded our heads, and the passenger train picked up speed.

We arrived in Jacksonville one full day before the troop train and felt like old hands when the dirty, tired remnants of the school draft staggered in.

FOUR

It was just as well we had the good train trip, because the next news was sure upsetting. It seemed that new incoming trainees drew mess cooking for three months before starting classes. This was three times a day, seven days a week, without a break. Even though the Naval Air Station at Jacksonville is really a beautiful place with the tree lined, St. Johns River winding through, it didn't soften those three months of confinement.

What really hurt was our customers in the mess hall were already in school and had liberty every weekend. We had to listen to glowing tales of the girls at Jax Beach, the beauty of St. Augustine, and a rumor there would be five thousand WAC's (Women's Army Corps) in training at Daytona Beach. I was getting cabin fever, and over two months remained before I would be eligible for liberty.

Remembering the advice of yeoman Monte at the hospital, I contacted the yeoman assigned to ship's company and laid out my difficulties.

"No problem," commented yeoman Fred, "Nothing that can't be solved for as little as five dollars—in advance of course."

I crossed his palm with paper, and he explained. "The base drum and bugle corps are a volunteer group, mostly students, with liberty every weekend—even for mess cooks."

"That's great," I countered, "but what if I don't play a drum or bugle?"

"Anyone can play the bass drum," replied Fred. "I happen to know the drummer ships out next week— follow him around this week and learn the beats."

"Thanks, I will. Oh, by the way, Fred, when they made out my ID card, they made a mistake and showed me as seventeen instead of twenty-one. Can anything be done about it?"

"No problem. Leave your old one here, and I'll have another to go with it this afternoon." I dug out another five.

The drum and bugle corps marched Wednesday and Friday afternoons. I marched beside the bass drummer learning the beats, and still made it back to the mess hall in time to serve the evening meal.

The next Wednesday, the bass drummer was gone, and I hesitantly strapped on the big bass drum. After the first few blocks I began to gain confidence, and before we stopped I was pounding merrily away. When we finished, I got the leader aside and explained if I was going to pound the drum, he would have to get me off mess duty Wednesday and Friday evenings, along with the weekends. The base Commander was really proud of his drum and bugle corps and my wishes were granted.

The way it worked out, I was off from the end of Friday's march until breakfast, Monday morning.

I had been watching the snare drum, and decided it really wasn't much more difficult than the bass drum; it sure was lighter. I got Mike aside, pointed out the advantages of becoming a musician, and mentioned the ID card situation. He quickly got the message, and went into apprenticeship on the snare.

It wasn't long before two eager young sailors were headed to Jacksonville for their first liberty.

Jacksonville seemed to have a lot in common with San Diego. A beautiful city—with sailors everywhere. The girls definitely weren't interested in the fact two more sailors had joined the pack. The movies were the same ones we had already seen on the base. The only thing left to do was catch a bus to the famous Jax Beach.

This turned out to be a flat strip of sand, where cars drove right on the beach. There were restaurants, honky-tonks, an amusement park, and lots of sailors. Beer drinking seemed to be the popular pass-time. About the only beer served was Jax beer. Rumor had it the beer was brewed right here, and served as fast as it came out of the vat. Judging by the taste, I couldn't argue.

By mutual consent we returned to the base early, not at all impressed by the wonders of Florida. What was even worse, we had to answer innumerable questions from our fellow mess cooks who wouldn't get liberty for months and hoped to live vicariously through our experiences. I know we were a disappointment to them.

The next meeting of the drum and bugle corps brought a ray of hope. Slim, a southern boy from Pensacola heard about our liberty fiasco and volunteered to show us the real Florida next weekend!

Slim was as tall as me and even skinnier. He had an easygoing personality, and a southern drawl so thick that at first I thought it was a foreign language. It wasn't until I saw Slim in action I realized his drawl could charm birds out of trees, and any southern girl within hearing.

Slim had one serious liability; he was extremely goosey! If he was deliberately or even accidentally touched on a certain portion of his rear anatomy, he would let out a blood-curdling shriek, jump straight up in the air and throw his arms back wildly. I saw it happen once while the band was marching and it was as if a bomb had exploded. One snare drum was damaged and a drummer had to fall out with a bloody nose.

Slim told us to bring shaving kits and Saturday morning we were hitchhiking south on the coast highway. We lunched at St. Augustine, which had everything from a massive Spanish fort to horse-drawn cabs. Best of all, there were pretty girls and very few sailors. I was sure this was where Slim was leading us for the weekend, but no, after lunch we continued south.

Daytona is a resort city with superb beaches, fancy hotels, and friendly people. There was a small Naval Air station a few miles from town, and this had been the extent of the military in the area. As we walked down a tree-lined street, it became obvious a new element had been added. About one-third of the pedestrian traffic were WACs in uniform.

"Slim," I asked, "did you know about this invasion before we left Jacksonville?"

"Well, ah did heah the rumor, and thought it was worth checking out."

Things were definitely looking up. Slim, who was leading with Mike and I closely following, turned into an apartment complex, and inserted a key into one of the doors. Inside were a compact living room, kitchen, bedroom and bath. I noticed a Navy uniform hanging in the bedroom closet. Both Mike and I believed this was Slim's secret hideout, however, it turned out to be his brother's, who was stationed at the small air station. Slim didn't think his brother would be in this weekend, so it looked as if we would have a place to sleep. Slim checked the refrigerator and returned with a cold six-pack.

Comfortably sprawled on the sofa and chair, a couple of beers each for inspiration, we planned our conquest of Daytona Beach. The first and biggest decision was whether to conquer the civilians, or military? Slim allowed he knew a civilian girl who had two pretty friends, but he added they were still in high school, and had early curfews.

We then mentally pursued the military, and what might materialize at the USO dance. We decided to hedge our choice by stocking the apartment with food and drink, just in case a party might develop later.

The time was nine-thirty. We plotted an immediate course for the USO dance, which was held in the park recreation building, a low rambling affair surrounded by palm trees, tropical shrubbery, and park benches. As we approached through the park we could hear the music. When we got closer we knew there was a large crowd by the fact all the outside benches were filled. Not only were people sitting, they were standing in groups.

The entrance doors to the recreation building were wide open, and we could see the dance floor was packed. It took a minute before it registered in my numbed mind, what I was seeing was almost all women—WACs to be exact.

By this time we had merged into the outer group, and what was happening was alarming. We were the center of attention of approximately one hundred full-grown females, and they all had a predatory look in their eyes. Even, Slim, the cool, southern, bon vivant, was spooked. We scurried into the recreation building before—we didn't know what—could occur.

The dance was in full swing, with a scattering of sailors and some soldiers from a base further south. This was the grand total of the men.

The rest were WACs; dancing together, standing in groups, sitting in chairs around the dance floor, and seemingly all looking at us expectantly.

The music had just finished from the last dance, and we three huddled together, trying to decide what to do next. We never had time to reach a consensus before the music started again, and three WACs asked us to dance. Mine was smaller than I would have chosen, had I been choosing, but she did have other attributes. I never knew a girl could be so pathetically eager to please.

Her attitude helped to restore my shattered male confidence. We finally got our two different heights and styles of dancing to merge, and by the end of the dance had established an easy rapport. I found out her name was Robin, she was from upstate New York, was nineteen, and she has been a WAC three weeks.

"Robin," I asked, "what in the world is going on? I can't believe all the girls I'm seeing."

"This is just the tip of the iceberg," was her unhappy reply. "There are five thousand of us here for training. They have us in all the resort hotels, and you are the first man I've spoken to since I've been here!"

I think I detected a quiver in her voice. About then the music started again and she commented, "You had better get us to the dance floor soon, unless you want to dance with two at once."

I glanced up to see a determined WAC bearing down on us. Retreating quickly to the dance floor with Robin, I watched for Slim and Mike. When I located them, I asked Robin if they were still with her two original friends. They were, so we danced by each couple with the suggestion we meet outside after this dance. All were agreeable and soon we were under one of the palms enjoying the cool tropical breeze. Robin introduced her friends and I introduced Slim and Mike.

We debated our next move. I believe all of us were a little uncomfortable here at the dance. Slim suggested a party at the apartment, as I'd hoped. There was no hesitation from the girls. I believe if we had suggested a nude swim in the ocean, they would have agreed. Something about all those girls together had completely destroyed their self-confidence.

We hadn't walked a block before we were arm in arm, and soon we reached the apartment. As Slim inserted the key he hesitated; we could hear soft music and laughter. Slim removed the key and rapped lightly. The door opened, and there stood an older version of Slim, with his arm around a lovely young thing in civilian clothes. The two brothers seemed happy to see each other, and we all were invited in.

Slim's brother and his date had been sampling the goodies we had stocked earlier, which now, with a magnificent gesture, he offered to us. Well, not to worry, there was plenty for everyone. Slim and Mike were mixing drinks for the WACs and I stuck to my usual beer.

Slim's brother had the radio turned to soft, romantic music, the lights were turned down low, and it was time to get better acquainted. After the second beer, I felt completely relaxed and was thoroughly enjoying myself. We had all shed unnecessary parts of our uniform. The girls were down to skirts and blouses, fellas to tee shirts and trousers. The shoes disappeared first. Slim's brother and his girl had the sofa, and the rest of us were seated on the carpet using the wall as a backrest, which left room in the center for one or two couples to dance. After a couple more drinks had been served, someone turned out the remaining light, and Robin and I got even better acquainted. Our hands were as busy as our lips, and I was really beginning to believe tonight was the night.

Sound effects in a close, dark, situation like this can be most informative. The one getting attention was the click of the bedroom door, as it was locked from the inside. I was sure Robin didn't miss the significance. She couldn't have any doubt of my immediate desire. When the click of the lock signified the bedroom was now available, I gently encouraged Robin toward the door. She hesitated.

"Jack, I'm scared," she whispered. "I'm afraid you'll hurt me."

Blast! What terrible timing. This was the first indication I might have a problem—and just when I thought the big moment had arrived. I did my best to reassure Robin, and felt I was making progress when we heard the door lock again. Someone had beaten us to the bedroom. I was reconciled to keeping Robin reassured until the bedroom cleared, when suddenly it happened!

"*Aie-e-e-e!!!*"

I recognize the horrible shriek of Slim when he is goosed. This was immediately followed by the crash of a box spring and mattress plunging through the bed frame, and then the wild screams of a terrified WAC.

The volume of the screams was increasing, when Slim's brother flipped on the light in the living room. Three couples in various stages of disarray stared at each other—aghast!

Seconds later a naked WAC came running out of the bedroom, clutching a bundle of clothes to her chest. Slim stood in the doorway wearing only a sheepish grin. Slim's brother, Mike and I realized what had happened, and soon were howling with laughter. Not so the girls. The two WACs indignantly gather about their companion as she quickly pulled her clothes on.

"Crazy sex fiend—that's what he is—crazy sex fiend!" the one WAC kept sobbing.

Slim's brother tried to explain to the girls about Slim's gooseyness, but to no avail. The minute Slim's WAC was dressed, the three girls stormed out of the apartment.

Well, I was still batting my usual zero, and Robin's last remark wasn't doing much for my self-confidence. I helped Slim reassemble the bed, and his brother and girl friend retired—still chuckling.

We flipped a coin for the sofa; Mike won. It really was his night! Slim and I toughed it out and slept on the carpet.

Our hosts hadn't made an appearance when we got up the next morning, so we left a note thanking them for their hospitality.

Breakfast was first on the agenda, and we headed for the nearest coffee shop. As we cut through the park, the fragrance of magnolia, gardenia, and orange blossoms wafted through the air.

The coffee shop was about half full of WACs, and as we located a table we were already receiving friendly smiles. I decided with very little effort I could learn to like this place.

We decided to explore the beach in our few remaining hours, and didn't even get out of the coffee shop before we had three guides. I think they must have been eavesdropping on our conversation.

These were really nice girls, only they seemed starved for masculine attention. It all came out as we slowly wended our way toward the beach.

There were almost five hundred women in the resort hotel they were assigned—no men at all! A few of the women there had been ladies of the night in civilian life, anyway; all the women seemed to be able to talk about were men and sex. This steady, erotic conversation was demoralizing these girls, and what they seemed to really desire was a friendly, normal relationship. This wasn't exactly what we three had in mind, but as there wasn't time for much else, we relaxed and enjoyed the day. We even bought lunch.

Toward evening, we told the girls goodbye, and were fortunate to catch a ride toward Jacksonville. Unfortunately, the ride terminated at a deserted stretch of highway, when the driver turned off into his private lane.

It was dusk and there was little, to no highway traffic. We were standing beside the empty highway when I saw little white lights going on and off out in a meadow.

"Mike, do you see what I see out there?"

Mike turned to check where I was looking, and then he became intrigued. "I've never seen anything like that before," he agreed.

"Yo' po' Yankees don't know nuthin' at all, them's fiahflies," Slim announced.

I noticed an empty bottle by the roadside and the thought occurred to me that if I could catch the fireflies and put them into the bottle, I would have the equivalent of a flashlight. I glanced down the road, no traffic, so I picked up the bottle and ran out to the center of the meadow. I put the bottle down, used my hat for a net and started chasing fireflies.

I caught the first one, put it in the bottle and make a plug of grass for a cap. When Mike saw I was actually catching them, he couldn't resist joining the chase. Slim couldn't believe it. He kept yelling we were going to miss our ride as he sounded off about weird Yankees. Before long, we had about a dozen in the bottle and it was glowing pretty good.

It was nearly dark and we decided we had better get back before Slim deserted us. When we returned to the highway we were surprised to find cars parked, in each direction. I heard Slim explaining to another southerner,

"These po' dumb Yankees never seen fiahflies before." He added that the two white ghosts the drivers had seen running around out in the meadow were us in our white uniforms chasing them. I guess we had created quite a spectacle, and the superstitious drivers had to have an explanation before they would continue on. We proudly showed off our bottle of fireflies. I found they glowed better with a good shake. The southern drivers shook their heads in disbelief. They all felt sorry Slim was stuck with the likes of us, and wanted to know where he was going. Slim said, "Jacksonville," and presto, we had a ride. The driver felt so sorry for Slim, he drove us all the way to the Naval Air Station.

Slim disgustedly departed for his barracks, and Mike and I returned to ours. The minute we got inside, we found a delegation of mess cooks waiting for a report on our weekend. Well, we made up for the dry report of last week. When we got to the part about the five thousand WACs, and their behavior, I believe the temperature in the room went up ten degrees.

FIVE

I'd just completed Wednesday's drum and bugle corps march, and because it lasted longer than usual I was late for the evening meal. Jogging toward the mess hall, I casually noticed the back of an officer walking ahead on the sidewalk. I pulled off to the edge of the sidewalk and jogged right on by. I quickly discovered this wasn't the right thing to do.

"Sailor!"

"Yes Sir," I replied as I came to a halt, turned around and delivered a salute.

"Do you ordinarily pass an officer in this manner?"

I recognized the Base Commander with a rank of Lieutenant Commander.

"I don't know, Sir. This is the first time this situation has come up."

"Are you being impertinent, young man?"

"Not at all, Sir, I just don't know what I've done wrong."

"You mean you don't know the proper way to approach an officer from the rear?"

I struggled to keep a straight face.

"Apparently not, Sir. How should I have done it?"

He glared at me suspiciously.

"You approach to within three paces, and you say, "By your leave, Sir."

I couldn't believe it—had I missed something in boot camp?

"Then what happens?" I asked.

"The officer then gives permission for the enlisted man to pass, and he salutes as he passes."

"What does the enlisted man do if the officer doesn't say anything?" I innocently asked.

"What's your name, Sailor?" he angrily demanded. "You're on report."

"Jack Barnes, Sir."

"Barnes, you be at Captain's mast at ten hundred hours tomorrow."

"Yes Sir," I saluted and proceeded on at a slower pace. I knew the mess hall had closed.

The next morning, I appeared at Captain's mast, which was conducted by the Lieutenant Commander and the master-at-arms, with a yeoman to keep records. Charges were read by the master-at-arms, and the sentencing done by the Lieutenant Commander. I was third in line and listened to the charges as my name came up.

"Violation of military courtesy and insubordination. How do you plead?"

I knew that if I plead not guilty, it would go to a court martial and I had visions of a firing squad, so I plead guilty.

"Thirty days, prisoner at large," intoned the Commander. "Report to the master-at-arms."

I located the master-at-arms shack, and sat there until he returned from Captain's mast. The master-at-arms was a mean looking bosun's mate with an armful of hash marks.

"Might as well get started now," He rummaged around in a big sack until he found a white jumper with big red PAL letters stamped on the back.

"Wear this for the next thirty days, and report here every four hours. If you are late your sentence starts all over again."

The full significance of my fate didn't hit me until later. This meant no more Daytona Beach, also no more full night's sleep. On deeper reflection I realized the Base Commander wasn't going to want a PAL marching in his beloved drum and bugle corps. An idea began to form in my mind.

It took a couple days to adjust to the weird hours I was keeping, and to get over feeling sorry for myself. I had been so busy with my other activities I'd been neglecting my workouts. I sure didn't have this excuse now, so back to the gym and jogging I went.

The gym was supplied with weights, punching bags, boxing gloves and a boxing ring. There wasn't a boxing instructor, so I contented myself with workouts on the light and heavy bag. The second day I was lifting weights when I heard someone really talking to the light bag, and it was answering back. There is real rhythm and skill in keeping the light bag going and I'd never heard anything like this before. I looked to see who the pro was and recognized Sammy, one of the mess cooks. In his gym shorts he was all muscle, and I guessed he would weigh in as a heavyweight. I drifted over to watch and it was a show in coordination.

When he finished he recognized me and asked, "Hey, Jack, do you box?"

"Not really," I replied. "I was just getting a feel for it in San Diego when I shipped out."

"Say, that's great. I was hoping someone would come in to spar with. I'm getting rusty."

Against my better judgment, I went along with it, and I wasn't greatly encouraged when he tossed me a head guard and didn't take one himself.

The first round was a feeling-out process. It began to look as if I had the faster reflexes and the reach. He had the weight and experience. The second round I discovered he had the third ingredient—a punch that would fell an ox.

I foolishly let him get inside, and even when I knew he was pulling his punches I felt like I was being kicked by a mule. The third round I attempted to keep him at a distance, and threw my left hook, right-cross combination. I scored with the hook, missed with the right, and suddenly I was seeing stars. When the round ended Sammy showed me how to cover up after missing with a right, and thanked me for the workout. I didn't feel he had received much, and I had a strong suspicion Sammy was a lot better than he was letting on. He finally admitted he had fought sixteen professional fights, won fourteen, twelve by knockouts, one draw and one loss. I considered myself lucky to be alive.

This was an added incentive to get into better shape, and I really concentrated on it. When Sammy couldn't find anyone better, we sparred together, and soon even I could see improvement.

Every morning after breakfast and before my ten-hundred hour PAL report, I jogged for miles along the bank of the St. Johns River. It was on the station, secluded, with beautiful wooded banks.

I was jogging back one morning when I saw a detail marching my way. This in itself wasn't unusual, but there was something strange about this group. They were wearing skirts! This was my introduction to the women's branch of the Navy—WAVES.

About twenty WAVES had just finished basic training and been assigned to the Naval Air Station. I jogged right on by and that evening discovered they were hanging out at the canteen, an informal lounge with a juke box, serving sandwiches, pop, ice cream and beer.

I was coming from the serving counter with a cold beer in hand when a WAVE, regally enthroned at a nearby table, motioned me over. Two younger WAVES accompanied her. There was an empty chair so I slid into it with, "Hi, I'm Jack Barnes."

They introduced themselves and the one who had arrogantly summoned me asked the inevitable question.

"What do those big, red, PAL letters on your back stand for?"

I had become tired of this question, probably because I wasn't proud of being a "Prisoner At Large." It was surprising these WAVE trainees, as well as my fellow mess cooks, didn't know the meaning of the PAL letters.

My new personality suddenly surfaced, and I replied, "Professional At Love."

This produced an astonished silence. The one who asked the question drew her thin lips into a straight line. She was a tall angular woman with sharp features; raven black hair and a superior attitude. I would guess she was in her late twenties, one-way or the other. She knew she was going to lose face with the two younger WAVES unless she quickly put me in my place.

"And what does a PAL do?" She sniffed condescendingly.

"Just what the name implies," I responded with a straight face. "You have probably heard of the black belt in karate, well the PAL is the seal of excellence in another area."

The two younger WAVES were listening to this exchange with wide-open eyes.

"Why do you have the letters stamped on your back?" She demanded suspiciously.

"I'm really not too happy about that." I conceded. "When the Base Commander found you girls were coming, he thought it was the only fair thing to do, you know, a way to keep the amateurs and professionals separated."

I would have given anything to have a movie of the expressions crossing her face. Skepticism, indignation, each had its turn as she tapped her cigarette stained fingers angrily on the table. She wouldn't accept being called an amateur—professional had an unpleasant connotation. She was almost certain I was lying, and yet my answers were so outrageous she couldn't think of a way to disprove them. She tossed her black hair disdainfully as she searched for the ultimate put down.

I glanced at my watch, saw it was nearly time for my PAL appearance before the master-at-arms' and said, "Sorry I have to leave, girls, but my presence is required by someone very close to the Commander and I don't want to jeopardize my PAL rating." With this I hurried to make my mandatory four-hour muster.

The next evening when I stopped by the canteen, I found I had become a character. Even some of my fellow mess cooks were looking at me a little strangely! The two naive, younger, WAVES of the evening before were sitting together, and immediately invited me to join them. They were still rejoicing about the put-down of their older companion, who has been superior and condescending to all the other girls. These two had told everyone what the PAL letters meant, and there had been a raging debate in the WAVE barracks ever since. The other girls had been curious since I jogged by the first morning.

Soon more WAVES, all with PAL questions, joined us. The difficulty with telling improbable stories I discovered was what to do for an encore. I finally confessed I'd already said too much, and if they repeated what they heard I could lose my PAL rating. I saw Mike come in and I was glad for an excuse to get away from the inquisition.

"Hi, Mike, did you make it to Daytona last weekend?"

"Sure did, Jack. Phil came with us."

"Did you take in the USO dance?"

"You bet."

"Were the girls there?"

"Yeah, but we ignored them. Three who were really ready picked us up. They had the place, the booze, and even a car."

"No foul-ups this time?"

"Not this time. I think Slim told his WAC to keep her hands off a certain place."

Mike grinned as he headed for the serving counter. Somehow his report failed to cheer me up. I felt so dejected I headed back to the barracks. Here I was, probably the only virgin on the station, confined, while my buddies were making out like bandits at Daytona. Every time I got close something went wrong—the shore patrol broke in, Slim got goosed, the girl got scared, or something. Was I never going to get a chance to practice those dynamite sexual instructions I had received from Monte, there at the naval hospital?

Earlier I had received a letter from home mentioning my friend Chet had joined the Navy, and was now in boot camp. I had dropped him a letter, and now I had a reply. He mentioned he would have his first San Diego liberty in two weeks, and asked if I had any suggestions?

To get my mind off Mike's glowing report, I started to answer the letter. I thought of Cleo, and an improbable scenario begins to develop in my mind. I told Chet about my wild night in a Free French, naval uniform, and told him if he would follow the enclosed instructions explicitly, he would probably have the greatest liberty of his life. I told him to call the phone number I was enclosing, to identify himself as an American comrade-in-arms, of Ravel Deveraux, of Paris, and to tell Cleo he had an important message from Ravel. I then composed the important message for him to deliver.

Ma Cherie Cleo,

How often you have been in my thoughts since I was so abruptly called away on this secret mission. I wasn't even allowed to call you. Alas, I am forlorn.

The mission was a success, but only due to the brave actions of le bon Chet, to whom I'm entrusting this document. I owe him my life, and I have no way to repay him. Je suis desolate.

Should he be successful in reaching America and delivering this to you, be not deceived ma cherie; I know your contempt for American sailors. This is le grand freedom fighter, preparing for another mission—perhaps his last!

If you can think of any way to reward him for saving my life, I will forever be in your debt. I know you have the large heart. Until we meet again, Vive La France! Vive La Cleo! Au Revoir. Ravel."

P.S. Burn this letter immediately. Should it fall into the wrong hands, all our lives could be en peril.

My last words to Chet were that the least he could do was let me know how it came out.

Wednesday, a special drum and bugle corp. march was scheduled for some high brass guests, from Washington. I had been cheating by wearing my regular jumper for marches, but I was feeling so low this time I deliberately pulled on the soiled jumper with the big PAL, letters, and arrived after the band had formed. The leader took one look at me and turned as white as his uniform.

"Jack, get another jumper immediately!"

"Can't, boss, I'm a 'Prisoner At Large' and I have to wear this jumper for a month—Commander's orders."

"Who can play the bass drum?" the leader shouted, looking hopefully at the group.

There was smothered laughter and a few indignant protests. We all know the big bass drum set the beat, and the band couldn't march without it. The leader made a desperate decision.

"All right, Jack, we'll put you in the middle. Try to duck down and stay out of sight."

We started the march with me camouflaged by surrounding marchers. We could see the Officers' Club ahead with the big brass reclining in the easy chairs on the veranda. The Base Commander was standing, beaming proudly. Our drums and bugles shifted to our very best march. The adjoining marchers drew a little closer to me as the leader signaled for me to duck lower. I was almost on my knees then!

As we drew abreast the impromptu reviewing stand, I deliberately reared back to my full six feet two and dramatically twirled the drumsticks with each violent blow on the big, bass drum! This forced my marching companions to give me room, and then I was on center stage. Out of the corner of my eye I could see the shock register on the Commander's face, as he viewed the big red PAL letters emblazoned on my soiled jumper. Several of the honored guests were laughing outright, others were tight lipped. The leader, marching backward so he could watch, had a terrified, stricken look.

The Commander's yeoman was waiting for us as we completed the march with orders for both the leader and I to report to the Commander immediately. The leader was so upset, all the way over he kept mumbling, "Why Jack, why?" I didn't believe he really expected an answer.

The Commander's ashen face and glazed eyes were more terrifying than if he was wildly ranting. He paced from one side of the office to the other.

"Collins, how could you humiliate me so, letting this disreputable sailor march in our band?" I could see perspiration on the leader's face.

"Sir, I didn't know he was a PAL until he showed up, just as the march was about to start. Commander, he is the only one who can play the bass drum—we can't march without it."

The Commander turned his ashen face on me, and pointed his finger as though it was a pistol.

"You did this deliberately, sailor!" he accused in an icy voice. It was now my turn for perspiration.

"Oh no, Sir," I innocently protested. "I just didn't know what to do. If I didn't show up, the band couldn't march. You sentenced me to wear this jumper for thirty days—what should I have done, Sir?"

The Commander pondered my facial expression suspiciously, and I could feel him wavering. Finally he reached a decision, strode to his desk and jotted a note.

"Take this to the master-at-arms," he said in an emotionless voice, his head still bowed so he wouldn't have to look at me. I accepted the note, an quickly departed. As I headed for the master-at-arms shack, I glanced at the note. It rescinded my sentence, immediately.

My hunch was right. The drum and bugle corps meant more to the Commander than an insignificant PAL.

The master-at-arms had an angry glint in his eye as I reported.

"You're thirty minutes late, sailor; this means your time starts all over again."

I handed him the note, and watched his expression change to bewilderment.

"I don't know how you pulled this off," he glared threateningly. "Your sentence is suspended. Turn in the PAL jumper, and sailor, I don't want to ever see you here again!"

"Sure boats," I condescendingly replied. "Next time you are in trouble, let me know. I'll put a word in for you."

SIX

Monday, our long awaited aircraft mechanic school commenced. We were told that, upon graduation, the top third of the class would receive promotion to Aviation Machinist Mate Third Class, and go on to flight engineer training. They didn't mention what would happen to the remaining two-thirds.

I buckled down for the final six weeks, and at graduation Mike, Sammy and I were in the top third. We received the new rating, and were scheduled to commence our flight engineer training. This began with an indoctrination course on the slow, graceful, amphibious, PBY Catalina flying boat. I discovered our final operational training flight would consist of an actual submarine patrol, from Jacksonville, Florida to Key West, from Key West to Charleston, South Carolina, and back to Jacksonville.

Early in the morning the new crew met at the PBY, on a ramp above the St. Johns River. The two pilots and navigator were young, Marine Second Lieutenants, the radio operator and I were Third Class Petty officers, and the two waist gunners were seamen. A food carton was loaded aboard, and we soon followed. I noticed this was one of the early PBYs, which were not truly amphibious. The landing gear was only temporarily mounted, and as soon as we taxied into the water, the beach crew pulled some pins and removed the gear. This meant we could only land on water.

I was busy as we taxied out to the center of the river. Everything looked good, and the take-off run began. I had a ringside seat from my engineer's tower, and it was exciting. Water flew in all directions as we picked up speed, the hull rising, then skimming along the surface. We were air-borne, and little lights were lighting up on my panel. I retracted the wing floats, made some minor adjustments, and the patrol began.

We cruised just off the coast, watching the clear water for the dark hulk of an enemy submarine. We had only six depth charges mounted beneath the wing, and if we missed with them we might as well go home. In a short time we were passing St. Augustine, where I could see the Spanish fort in the background. A little further and I recognized the beach at Daytona.

Mark, the radio operator, was also the cook, and he had the range in the galley fired up. Before long, he was passing out tender steak sandwiches and hot coffee. When we passed Miami, and headed for Key West, the crystal clear water reflected delicate shades of blue and green. We landed at the Naval Base where we spent the night, and next morning departed for Charleston. This was our longest leg, and by the time we arrived I was tired of the cramped, engineer's compartment.

We secured the PBY to a float, and checked into the transient barracks. None of the enlisted men had been to Charleston before, so we decided to see what the town had to offer. We located a good dining room, enjoyed an excellent meal, and then explored the main drag of town.

Charleston was a typical Navy city, with sailors everywhere. The main street seemed to be lined with bars and tattoo parlors. As we walked along we noticed groups of British sailors with their distinctive uniforms. Someone had mentioned there was a Limey cruiser in the harbor.

Neither Mark nor I had ever been in a tattoo parlor before, so we stopped at the next one. We could hear the electric needle operating on someone behind a curtain, and noticed the walls of the empty front room were lined with samples of the artist's craftsmanship. There was everything from eagles, serpents, and nude women, to flags of every country with a Navy. We looked it all over, and then joined the other two members of our crew in the gin mill next door.

The place was about half full, with a circular bar, and the bartender in the middle. Across from us, at the other end of the bar, were three drunken British sailors. One of them was a large, heavy-set man, older than the other two, with coarse features and a foul mouth. We couldn't believe some of the things he was saying about the United States.

I felt my hackles rise with the first slur against my country, and I noticed Mark and the two seamen were reacting the same way. If this had been going on for a while, I was surprised a fight hadn't started by now. I called the bartender over, and asked, "Hey, what gives?"

"I'm not happy about this situation either," confided the bartender, "but I can't call the Shore Patrol until something happens. The big guy is a brawler. One of his mates said he nearly killed a Yank back home over a girl. Anyway, he hates the United States with a passion."

We tried to ignore him and enjoy our drinks, but it became increasingly difficult to tune out this British sailor's hatred towards our country and all U.S. sailors to boot. He sure was carrying a grudge against the American who stole his girl back home in England.

We began to discuss ways to shut him up, but all of our scenarios ended with us being potentially hurt or thrown in the brig and really this S.O.B. wasn't worth it. At this point one of the two of us who had been in the tattoo parlor half kidding came up with a suitable punishment for the American hating British sailor. A few drinks later, with continual insults coming from across the room, the idea began to have serious merit. We called the bartender back over.

"Hey, Mac, another round here, and a double for the loud Limey. Don't let him know who is buying, and keep them coming!"

The bartender looked at us for a moment, and then gave a conspiratorial wink.

The loud one seemed surprised to receive a free drink; the other two seemed disappointed not to. When the first drink was gone the bartender replaced it with another, and I noticed he didn't charge us for it. When the third free one arrived, and none for the other two British sailors, they became angry and left. Not the loud Limey; as long as there was free booze he'd drink it, and curse the bloody Yanks at the same time. The next drink began to get results. He definitely was slowing down, and the invectives were slurring. It was time to move in.

Mark and I moved over, took the stool on each side and ordered another round. We attempted to strike up a conversation.

"How's it going, Mac?"

"ScrewyoubloodyYanks!"

The fact his words all ran together, we took as a good sign. When the loud one was drinking his last one, Mark suggested, "Hey, if you hate the United States so much, you should get a British flag tattoo, then no one can mistake you for a Yank."

While he was mulling that one over, I suggested, "There is a place right next door. Let's finish our drinks and check it out."

The last drink did it, and, with Mark and I guiding, we wove our way to the tattoo parlor. The two seamen brought up a rear guard action.

Fortunately, the parlor had no customers, and we unfolded our drunken companion into the chair behind the curtain. Our two seamen stood in the doorway, effectively blocking it. By this time we had his British hat and jumper off, and the trousers were similar to ours.

A small, wizened, proprietor appeared from the quarters in back, and asked, "What can I do for you, sailors?"

We explained, "Our mate here wants a flag, so there can be no doubt about his nationality."

I pointed to the sample of the American flag with God Bless America, beneath.

"That should be about right," I said, and peeled off the four, five-dollar bills we had jointly contributed.

"Just put it right across his chest."

The proprietor went into the tattoo parlor where his client was passed out.

"Hey," the proprietor protested as he returned, "I'll lose my business license if I tattoo anyone who is drunk."

I peeled off two more fives, he went back in, and we soon heard the sound of the electric needle. The two seamen blocking the entrance explained to those wanting to enter, that their mate was having a very private part of his body tattooed and he wanted privacy.

It seemed like forever before the job was completed. We had visions of the Limey awakening, and the possible consequences. Finally we got the jumper and hat back on him, not remembering the tattoo artist would recognize the British uniform. When he did he got a shocked, panicky, look on his face.

The second we were out the door he locked it behind us, and turned out the lights. We supported the unconscious Limey part way down the block, where we eased him down with his back against a wall, then crossed the street where we could watch without being seen.

In a short while some British sailors came by on their way back to their ship, and took their shipmate with them. We headed back to the transient barracks without much money, but with a patriotic sense of accomplishment.

We were having breakfast the next morning at the transient mess, when an excited seaman came charging over to the table next to ours, and started telling his mates what was happening on the base.

"Inspections are being held on all ships and shore installations. Two British officers and a British enlisted man, together with American Shore Patrol, are going down each line of men checking every sailor. Seems a British seaman who hates Americans looked into the mirror this morning and saw an American flag with *God Bless America* beneath it, tattooed across his chest. They say he went completely berserk, and now the British are in a big flap, and it could become an international incident. The Brit said he can recognize the ones who did it; I think they are headed over here next." He paused completely out of breath.

Sheer panic struck our table; a bench was overturned as we made a dash for the PBY. Fortunately our officers were arriving, and they seemed surprised at the eagerness of our departure. We were still watching over our shoulders as we taxied out for takeoff. I expected a red recall light any minute.

On our flight back to Jacksonville, we were so busy grinning at each other we could have missed an enemy submarine.

SEVEN

Upon our return from the operational training flight, I saw that Mike, Sammy and I were all scheduled for aerial gunnery school at Purcell, Oklahoma.

Our first day at the gunnery school got off to an inauspicious start. The program was heavy on physical conditioning, which included calisthenics, running, boxing and wrestling. An American-Indian Lieutenant was in charge, and we soon discovered he was something else. I believe he viewed this as an opportunity to even the score with the white man. The two classes taking the course at the same time, one Navy, one Marine, were combined for physical training.

The first morning we mustered in our gym clothes, and the Lieutenant made a speech about how in the next month, he was going to convert us from our present miserable condition, into real fighting men. To prove his point, our first activity was a two-mile run. He led the way and we strung out behind. The trail was practically an obstacle course, going up one hill and down another, crossing a creek, through a wood lot, and back to where we started. Well, after the first quarter mile the field began to thin, and towards the end there was only the Lieutenant and I left. Neither of us was really breathing hard. It was obvious to me; he had been running this course every day for no telling how long. I had been running a longer distance every day at Jacksonville.

He didn't seem too happy about my finishing by his side. The object of this maneuver was to demonstrate our miserable condition, and it was also obvious he was breathing harder than me. Soon the rest came straggling in and we were lined up in the gym, two rows facing each other—marines on one side, sailors on the other. Boxing was next, and the man opposite us was to be our opponent.

The Lieutenant demonstrated a few basic maneuvers, and then we put on the large gloves. Our last instruction was "no shirking." He would be watching to be sure we were giving it our best. I drew a rough appearing marine about my height and twenty pounds heavier. I treated him gently!

Each match was three minutes long, and then we moved on to another opponent. The second opponent had a tender nose and that kept him on the defensive. The third marine knew what it was all about and we had an interesting three minutes. I glanced down the line to see how Sammy was making out, and was surprised he appeared as ineffectual as his opponent. Well, back to work, one more opponent and we shifted to wrestling.

The next day we started the gunnery portion of the school. This began with skeet shooting and after a demonstration on the care and use of a Remington twelve-gauge pump and the proper way to lead the target. We each got twenty-five shots. The round clay target came out of a low box in any of three directions, and we didn't know which. The purpose was to improve coordination, and to learn to lead the target. The instructor dropped the comment he would buy a case of beer for the first group with a perfect score. His beer was safe from me, eighteen out of twenty-five was my best, and I'd shot skeet.

Our next class was a lecture on machine gun sights, and specifically the ones used in the Arco and Sperry ball-turrets. We moved to simulators, which were a little on the order of a Link trainer with gun controls, a gun sight, and passing model targets. After a week of this, we would get to use the real thing with live ammunition.

The week passed quickly, the physical activities fit right into my regular program, and the only sour note was the Lieutenant in charge. He seemed obsessed with his superiority over the enlisted men in the two classes. His last edict was because we were not trying hard enough in boxing, the next shirker would go three rounds with him. This was supposed to strike fear into our hearts, and accelerate the bruises in boxing. What he didn't know was the sailors and marines had gotten together, and agreed to keep all punches below the head. No more bloody noses and black eyes!

All the officers at the school seemed preoccupied with boxing, and the Friday night smoker was the big event of the week. This consisted of three, three-minute rounds, with as many matches as boxers could be inveigled into participating. There was a lot of beer drinking and considerable betting, especially when it was a marine against a sailor.

The first Friday night Mike, Sammy and I attended, and none of us were impressed with the talent. Sammy had kept his boxing ability under wraps for some reason.

We had liberty over the weekends, and had to be back by midnight Sunday. There hadn't been a payday yet, and I wasn't feeling flush enough to go anywhere. My first weekend was spent on the base, where I had lots of company. I believe the frank talk from the school doctor regarding Paul's Valley fever and the local girls may have had something to do with it, as it sure got my attention.

Monday started much like the last week. My score was slightly higher on the skeet shooting. We moved to real turrets bolted on the back of flatbed trucks, and fired at canvas targets mounted in the firing range. Each turret had a belt with a numbered amount of fifty caliber shells. The bullets were each painted with a color that comes off as it pierced the canvas. At the end of the firing the hits are counted, and we are each graded by the number we scored. I was pleased with my count.

The Lieutenant was becoming more abusive in boxing each day, and none of us could figure out what his problem was. Friday, in the evening's smoker there was one good bout between a marine and a sailor. It was a close decision, and I noticed a lot of money changing hands in the officers' area.

The beginning of our last week arrived, and events started happening immediately. In boxing I was next to Sammy, and I noticed he was again putting up only a token performance. The Lieutenant noticed also, and told Sammy if it happened again he had to go three rounds with him. Sammy's next bout was just as lack-luster. The Lieutenant lost control, stopped all bouts, grabbed a pair of gloves, and told someone to tie the laces. He was really going to teach Sammy a lesson. Before they could start Sammy came to life, yelling, "Hold it! What about an enlisted man hitting an officer?"

The Lieutenant took off the gloves, pulled off his shirt with the brass on the collar, put the gloves back on and said, "Now, it's just man to man."

The round started and it was something to see. The Lieutenant really was after Sammy and Sammy was riding with every punch. It looked like he was being worked over, yet none of the Lieutenant's punches were landing solidly. Sammy was bobbing, weaving, ducking, covering up, and still hadn't thrown a punch. I could tell when the Lieutenant realized he had been sucked in, and changed from a slugger to a boxer; however, it was too late! He let Sammy get inside, and I knew what was coming. The solar plexus punch only traveled six inches and even with the big gloves it stopped the Lieutenant's breathing. For minutes the Lieutenant was bent over, gasping for breath, unable to straighten up. I hoped Sammy hadn't killed him.

Sammy had already taken off his gloves, when finally the Lieutenant got a breath of air, staggered into his office, and slammed the door.

Sammy was the hero of the day, and everyone wanted to congratulate him. As we are walking to the gunnery class I accused Sammy of setting the whole thing up, and asked, "Why'd you do that, Sammy?"

He replied, "Wait until Wednesday and I'll explain."

Of course, what happened was all over school in an hour, and was the favorite topic of conversation for the rest of the week.

Mike had really been getting good at skeet, bringing in scores above twenty. No one was particularly excited when he had twenty-two without a miss, then twenty-three. When he made twenty-four, all other shooting stopped. Mike took a deep breath, got an easy going-away shot and broke number twenty-five. Everyone in our group cheered except the instructor. He had to buy the beer.

This week we were firing from moving turrets on the back of trucks at a moving target which was a big yellow sleeve towed by an airplane. There was a tracer every fifth round so we could see if we were getting too close to the tow plane. The score this week would count the most toward our final grade. Only a portion of the class got to fire each day and the rest observed. I didn't fire until Thursday, which was also the day the disbursing officer arrived for our long awaited payday.

Wednesday, Sammy got me aside and explained his plan. He and I were going to get into an argument in the PX that night. While drinking beer, harsh words were going to be exchanged, and Mike was going to leap in before blows could be struck. I was going to challenge Sammy to a match at the smoker Friday night, and he would accept. Sammy believed our Navy class could get four to one odds from the marines and officers, after the publicity of the K.O. of the Lieutenant.

It was cold-blooded skullduggery, and I realized Sammy had depths none of us suspected. Apparently Sammy learned more in New York than just boxing. Sammy went on to say that we knew each other's moves so well that we could put on a completely rehearsed fight, and no one would know otherwise. He also pointed out I would be a wealthy hero when I knocked him out.

Sammy cautioned me not to bring anyone else in on this deal until Friday, except Mike. This caution would reduce chances of a leak. I explained the plan to Mike, he liked it, especially the part about four to one odds.

When evening came, we three took a table at the PX where they served three point two beer. After a few beers, Sammy and I got into a loud argument.

"You skinny drink of water; you couldn't punch your way out of a wet paper bag!" Sammy angrily shouted.

"You muscle bound ape, just because you sucker-punched the Indian doesn't make you a fighter, you got lucky. You're so slow, I'd cut you to ribbons!" I shouted just as loudly.

I had a glass of beer in my hand and although the script didn't call for it, I threw it in Sammy's face! I'd always wanted to do this, and now was too good an opportunity to let pass by—and get away with it.

I saw the shock on Sammy's face and then he started over the table after me. I was glad Mike leaped in and grabbed him, shouting, "Settle it in the ring Friday night!"

Others were picking up the chant. Mike was having trouble holding Sammy back, so I shouted, "I'll be there if fat boy has the guts to show up." And I angrily stalked out.

Thursday morning, this was the chief topic of conversation. Even the officers were getting interested. The disbursing officer arrived, and we had pay call instead of physical activity. Sammy and I both gave Mike our pay, plus whatever money we had left, to take to the PX bartender who handled the local betting. Mike told him if he could get four to one odds on me, he would cover up to two thousand. Most of my friends thought I'd cracked up to challenge Sammy. I told them not to place any bets right then.

This was my day to fire at the sleeve, and as the target was towed over, I got set up beautifully. I picked up the rear of the sleeve in the ring sight and got in a full burst, working my way to the front. Unfortunately, I traversed a little too far, and hit the towrope. Down came the sleeve, and the tow plane had to fly back to the airport at Norman to pick up another target.

The downed sleeve was recovered, and I found I had one of the top scores.

By evening, our five hundred plus was covered with a big demand for more. We passed the word to the rest of our class to put it all on me, at not less than four to one. For those that refused to believe it, I just said, "Go ask Sammy."

Sammy and I went jogging separately, met at the back of the station in the wood lot, and there rehearsed the fight. Once we had it down pat we jogged back separately. Friday we completed the last of our classes, and by evening the betting had accelerated. The marines were completely tapped, and the officers were so eager they were offering five to one odds. I was wounded to think there was so little regard for my boxing ability. I heard the Lieutenant that Sammy had sucker-punched had bet a bundle on Sammy.

The smoker was overflowing, with standing room only. There were three preliminary bouts and we were the main event. Sammy and I were ready as the third preliminary ended and the referee was announcing ours as the main event and a grudge match. Sammy got a big cheer from the marines and officers as he was introduced, and I got one from the navy. It was easy to tell who had bet on whom.

When the bell rang for the first round, we sparred cautiously. Sammy jabbed with a left; it was short. I jabbed with a left; it scored. Sammy threw a left and right; they both scored. I threw a left hook and right cross combination; they both scored; but Sammy kept boring in, a left, a right, I was hurt! The marines and officers cheered wildly. I clinched, and shook my head to get it clear, and the referee broke it up. Sammy charged back in with lefts and rights, and it looked bad when the bell sounded.

The second round was similar to the first, only Sammy was even more aggressive; it was a miracle I finished the round. The crowd was in a fever of excitement; the marines and officers were already counting their winnings.

The third round started the same way, and then halfway into the round, I threw a wicked right hand lead. It caught Sammy squarely on the button. He was staggered—the crowd was staggered. I followed up my advantage with hard lefts and rights. Sammy, trying to cover up, backed against the ropes. I went to work on the body. Sammy was in pain; it was brutal! When he covered up below, I went to the head, and when he staggered away from the ropes, I brought up a haymaker from left field. The crowd went wild; they saw it coming. It connected squarely, and Sammy went down like a poled steer, with his face in the canvas. No one expected him to get up, and he didn't. The fight was over!

The marines and officers were stunned; Sammy was still lying there. I went to help him up and he staggered to his corner. The referee poured water over Sammy's head and I saw his left eye wink. We shook gloves, and the crowd applauded such good sportsmanship. We dressed and headed for the barracks, where Mike had the collected bets. There was over six hundred dollars for each of us.

Saturday morning, our class boarded the bus for the trip to the Oklahoma City railroad station. I was relieved to be getting off the base, as we had nearly all the money of everyone remaining. The marines in the bus next to us were giving us dirty looks. Both the officers and marines were suspicious because the navy backed me exclusively. Their latest thinking was that I really was a pro that was rung into the fight, and all the sailors knew it. I was anxious to get out of town before they came up with something closer to the truth. I knew if they had any excuse at all, they would pull us off the bus and get their money back. Every minute seemed an hour as they glared at our bus.

We arrived at the train station in Oklahoma City and caught the passenger to San Diego, where we were to be assigned to a B24 squadron for training.

EIGHT

A bus from the Kearney Mesa Naval Air Station was waiting as we arrived in San Diego. Here, we were to get our final training as flight engineers on the PB4Y2, a single-tailed, Navy version of the B24 bomber.

When we arrived at the air station, I took one look at the monster with the big tail, and immediately felt ill. The vertical stabilizer and rudder must have been at least three stories high. I knew in a crosswind it would make landings very hazardous. We started an immediate thirty-day flight engineer training course on the bomber I had developed such an aversion too. My only consolation—we were scheduled for a two week leave upon completion of the course. On second thought, I hoped it was a consolation. It would mean facing dad for the first time since that scene in the jail cell. The letters from home had been filled with warmth, and I had missed them all more than I cared to admit.

I managed to struggle through the flight engineer course, and as soon as it was completed I was on the highway with my thumb out. My biggest problem was getting a ride out of the San Diego area. The highway was lined with servicemen trying to reach Los Angeles.

Five rides and a day and a half later, I arrived at Placerville. I was stiff from sitting so long, so I decided to walk the last two miles to the ranch.

As I ambled along this road I'd walked so many times as a kid, it brought all kinds of memories flooding back. The last mile was on ranch property, and each turn had a special significance. There on the right, flowed Hangtown Creek. I remembered the depression, and how we survived by stripping our old Star automobile and connecting a massive water pump to the engine. My grandfather, my dad, and I hydrauliced this creek and its banks for gold. To a very young boy, it was an exciting way to earn money.

My job had been to keep the sluice boxes clear of the larger rocks the hydraulic nozzle washed in. The big excitement came at the end of the week when we cleaned the gold from the sluice box riffles.

Granddad had the best hand with a gold pan, and all the family would gather around as he reached the black sand. Soon the yellow streak of flakes would begin to appear in the pan, and if it had been a good cleanup, the small nuggets would follow. I remembered this was the way we survived the depression, while each year our young pear orchards came closer to production.

The lower orchard was visible on the right, and the mature trees looked immense. I noticed they haven't been pruned yet, and wondered why.

It didn't seem so long ago I watched dad and granddad clear this narrow valley floor with a team of mules. Yes, there was the old stump puller still sitting on a bank. I remembered watching the mules pull that long boom around in circles as it slowly tightened the cable attached to the round drum and to a stump. The leverage of the boom would overcome the tenacity of the stump, and out it would pop.

A little further on I came to the gold mine which was going to make us all rich, only the seam petered out about the time we got the small, ball mill installed. The tunnel was still there into the hillside, with the track leading to the remains of the mill. Then I could see our two-story ranch home with the two tall cedar trees in the front yard.

The first one to spot me was Missy, my collie. She stood poised on the high front porch overlooking the road and suddenly leaped off, clearing the steps completely. The next thing I knew I had fifty pounds of excited collie in my arms.

Missy's commotion had alerted those in the house and I could see the front porch start to fill up. I noticed my grandparents were there also. My walk broke into a run, and in a moment I had joined them on the porch. The women got a little carried away with hugs and kisses. Soon I was shaking hands with granddad, and then, last, there was dad— standing to one side.

Somehow he didn't look so big and fearsome any more. He looked more like a lonesome man who was glad to see his missing son. I started to shake hands, and then he extended his arms and held me like he used to when I was a little boy. I relaxed and felt like I'd truly made it home.

We wandered into the house, where I could smell all kinds of good things cooking. I noticed proudly hanging in the front room window, a flag with a blue star. I couldn't get over how much my little thirteen year old sister had changed in the year and a half I've been gone. I could see she was going to be a striking beauty. They all couldn't get over how much I'd changed. I was twenty pounds heavier and shaving every day.

After the first round of questions was answered, mom went to the kitchen to check on dinner. In a few minutes, I followed and for the second time I was being held like a little boy.

"Jack, if you knew how many times I've prayed you would come home before you went overseas…"

"Mom, the way the war is going I may not even go; quit worrying," I replied trying to reassure her. "Say, I noticed the lower orchard hasn't been pruned. Isn't it getting a little late?" I inquired, changing the subject.

"Your father is having real problems this year, Jack. The pruners are all in the service or working in defense plants. He is trying to do all the orchards by himself." Mom sadly shook her head, and continued, "And just when it looked like there would be a decent price for pears."

I knew dad alone couldn't do it all in time. I also knew if the trees weren't pruned the fruit wouldn't size up, and there would be a lot of limb breakage. I was just starting to prune the year before I went into the Navy. I had contracted the picking of both dad's and granddad's orchards my last year when pickers were hard to find, and I hired fellow high school students. Now the ones that knew how to prune were also in the service. Well, I knew what I'd be doing this leave.

The dinner was great. Mom remembered my favorite dishes and I think they were all there—even fried green tomatoes. I wondered aloud,

"Where did you get green tomatoes this late in the season?"

Grandmother admitted, "I've been protecting a late plant with a tarp just in case you got home."

The reunion picked up again after dinner and before I realized it, it was time for my grandparents to retire to their portion of the large ranch house. I'd already told granddad I planned to start pruning his lower orchard the next day, and he said he'd go with me. I suspected he wanted to be sure I hadn't forgotten how. I noticed a smile of relief cross dad's face when he heard my plans. He had been pruning granddad's orchards first and now he would be able to start on his own. I figured I should be able to at least finish up my grandfather's in the ten days I'd have at home.

That was pretty well how my leave went. I would get an early start, prune until lunchtime, return to the house for lunch and an hour's rest, then prune until dusk. I was surprised at how fast it went, and the stamina I'd developed. All my running must have helped.

Sunday, grandmother wouldn't allow any work on her place, so I took her and mom to church. I got a kick out of the way this tiny woman proudly held onto my arm as we entered the church. She normally walked by herself, just fine.

In the afternoon, I got the Model A out of the barn and Missy and I took a run up to the airport. I hadn't been back since my friend sold his Taylor Cub and enlisted.

The Placerville airport is perched on top of a flat mountain, which was part of our ranch. I could remember dad and granddad smoothing it with a mule drawn scraper to keep it usable, and then leasing it to the city of Placerville during the depression.

Missy and I walked around the deserted hangers until a jackrabbit distracted Missy. I was just as glad; the empty hangers were getting to me as the metal siding creaked in the afternoon sun. I walked over to the edge and looked down on the ranch. Even though the fruit trees were bare, the large orchards were impressive. When I remembered two men did all this with only a team of mules, I felt proud of my dad and granddad.

It was my last night at home, and mom had a special dinner. My granddad was feeling pleased about the completion of his orchards, and I had also gotten in one day's work on dad's.

He believed now he had time to finish the rest by himself. The strain seemed to be leaving dad's face, and he was beginning to look more the way I remember him. It seemed as if these ten days had brought our family a little closer together. I knew with granddad's health it couldn't always remain like this, and I savored the moment.

I told everyone goodbye then, and early in the morning Dad drove me to the other side of Placerville. We look into each other's eyes for a moment before I get out of the car. The look said it all—pride in each other, and love. Dad's last words were, "Be careful, son!"

NINE

When I returned from leave I went for a hike, and checked out the rest of Kearney Mesa Naval Air Station. In an area off by itself were a line shack and my kind of airplanes.

There were three Piper Cubs, including the one with the double seat in the rear. There was a N3N, the open cockpit bi-plane, which looked like it belonged in World War One, a SNJ, two-place advance trainer with the big radial engine, and last a SNB, twin-tail, twin-engine, Beechcraft.

I stopped by the line shack and shot the breeze with Mario, one of the seamen on duty. I asked Mario about the manpower allocation.

Mario said, "There are two seamen, with a second class petty officer in charge."

"Are there any vacancies?"

"Yeah, there is supposed to be a third class petty officer".

That was enough for me. I made tracks to the administration building and located the yeoman in charge of permanent base personnel.

"Hi, I'm Jack Barnes. I was just told there is a vacancy on the Cub line for a third class. I'd like to throw my name into the hat."

"I don't know; let me check," the yeoman replied as he began rifling through a stack of papers.

"Yeah, there is a third class slot, but the job description calls for light plane maintenance experience. I don't think the Navy has a light plane school. That's probably why the slot is vacant."

This yeoman impressed me as a straight arrow, so instead of money, my approach was different.

"Hey, I was second in command of all light aircraft maintenance at the Placerville Airport!"

I didn't mention the one airplane there was a Taylor Cub, on which I had once helped with an oil and plug change.

"The Jacksonville aircraft mechanic school we just finished had a whole section devoted to repair of fabric-covered airframe members."

"All right," the yeoman answered, "Fill in this application with your experience and check back tomorrow. It will have to be approved by both the Base Commander, and the Squadron Commander you are assigned to. I doubt if he will want to part with any of his flight engineers."

Fortune smiled! The Base Commander liked to fly the three-seat Piper, and had been concerned about maintenance. The Squadron Commander had more flight engineers than airplanes. He also may have heard of my distaste for the monster bomber; I hadn't been discreet about my feelings.

The swap was made, and I was out of those miserable Navy B24s. We had just been placed on additional fifty-percent flight pay status, and issued a leather flight jacket with fur collar. It was a real prestige item, and was only issued to flight officers and enlisted flight engineers. My name in gold, on a leather label, was sewn onto the breast. I conveniently forgot to return it, or to report I was no longer on official flight pay.

I was at the flight line early the next morning. The second class came straggling in an hour later. He was overjoyed to have me because he didn't know much about light aircraft, and had been living in fear of a serious accident. The two seamen were better mechanics than he was, and neither had been to school.

The second class took muster, announced I was in charge of maintenance, and disappeared. I got Mario to the side, and asked how bad things really were. It was a relief to find base shops were doing the major overhauls, and we were only responsible for pre-flights, post-flights and periodic maintenance. Mario admitted most of the periodic maintenance had just been checking the right box on the forms.

I checked the aircraft logs, and found the three heavier aircraft had low time since overhaul. This was a relief; they should be in good shape. The three Cubs were a different story. They got heavy use, and were overdue for some tender care. I checked the three-seat Piper, didn't like what I saw, pulled it off the active list, and gave it a quick pre-flight. When I did the run-up, I found a serious rpm drop on the magneto check.

I shut it down, pulled the plugs and found one fouled. I also ran a quick compression check, and fortunately all four cylinders were within the correct range. Mario worked with me and we went through the engine, prop, accessories, cockpit, controls, wheels and control surfaces. We ended up with a new prop— the old one was about to shed a tip— two new tires, new plugs and a re-trimmed rudder. There had been squawks from the last three flights. The Plexiglas windshield was so badly crazed from the sun we replaced it. The remaining seaman was kept busy just chasing parts. We ended up with a wash and polish. I let the seamen know the other two Cubs were due for the same treatment.

In the morning pre-flight of the SNJ, the engine sounded good, the instruments checked out, and nothing appeared wrong on the visual. I didn't have to worry about this one.

I was beginning to meet the pilots that flew the light planes, and they were a mixed bag. Roger Sanders was a likeable, twenty-two year old Lieutenant Junior Grade, who was a B24 co-pilot. He also had the added duty of flying one of the Cubs over to the large, North Island Air Station for the afternoon mail.

Fred Robinson was a happy-go-lucky Lieutenant Junior Grade who was assigned as Base Utility Pilot. He now had the everyday job of flying a Cub over a deserted airstrip, where a row of B24 turrets had been set up and plugged into a portable generator. The squadron aerial gunners had to put in hours tracking a plane making attack passes at the turrets. Lieutenant Robinson was the attacker. He was also bored with the job.

I met the Base Commander when he came for the larger Cub. I knew this was the one he flew to North Island several times a week, and it did affect my choice of which one to work on first. He seemed pleased at the improved appearance of the Cub, and said so. I mentioned the trim change on the rudder, and requested he check it in flight. He was a quiet, middle-aged man, with penetrating, steel-gray eyes. I knew I was going to like him.

The next day I pre-flighted the twin engine Beechcraft, and it was quite an experience to have two large engines going at the same time. It was a relief to find it in excellent condition. We finished the last Cub with more replacement parts and I began to relax a little. I knew the condition of five of the six, and tomorrow morning I planned on checking out the N3N bi-plane.

The Commander got back with the large Cub, and there were no squawks on the post-flight form. He signed it and complimented me on the trim. It was set exactly where he liked it.

The morning when I pulled the pre-flight on the N3N, with the wind whipping past my head in the open cockpit, I felt like a World War I ace ready to take on the Red Baron. The plane was in mint condition. I shut the engine down and as I climbed out of the plane, I noticed an older, Chief Petty Officer, standing there with an angry expression on his face.

As my feet touched the ground he growled, "Who authorized you to run up the N3N, sailor?"

Uh-oh! "No one, really, Chief. It's scheduled to fly today. The second class was gone and someone had to pre-flight it. I'm Jack Barnes, the new third class."

His voice sounded like thunder. "Yeah, well, I'm West, the lead chief, and I've been looking for you."

The chief pulled out a list and said, "I just got this list of all the new parts you've requisitioned in one week, and it amounts to more than we used all last year. What are you doing, running a business on the side?"

My new personality started to stir, but I still managed to say confidently, "Chief, would you like to follow me?"

Over behind the line shack was a pile of scrapped tires, props, windshields and miscellaneous engine parts. I picked up a tire, worn through two cords and let him have a good look, followed by a prop with a cracked tip, and another with the metal overlay about to fly off.

"Chief, I think it's a miracle you haven't lost one of the Cubs by now, and the one the Commander flies was the worst of the lot."

I could tell that shook him, and he muttered, "I didn't realize it was this bad. I heard you were some hotshot, light plane mechanic from northern California, and maybe it wasn't bull after all. The second leaves for sea duty the first of the month, and that's probably why he has been so slack."

Sensing he was backing water; I gave this conversation my best shot. "Chief, I want that second class slot, and I want Mario for my third class assistant."

The chief started back-pedaling, "That would have to be authorized by the Commander." He kept right on going before any more ideas surfaced.

Now that maintenance was caught up, flight time was next on my list. Lt. Robinson was leaving to attack the turrets. He definitely welcomed company, and in a few minutes we were circling the turrets to give them time to fire up the generator.

They waved an okay, and Lt. Robinson put on an attack, which would have done a Japanese Zero proud. I make a mental note to double-check any plane he flew. A half hour later we were waved off while the gunners changed in the turrets, and Lt. Robinson asked if I would like to try it. Would I!

I stayed close in so we could see when they signaled, and got in a figure eight, and a coordinated two minute turn. Upon completing this maneuver, they waved below, and Lt. Robinson pointed down. I peeled off on one wing, thought Japanese, and thoroughly strafed the turrets. Robinson must have been satisfied, because he let me have the whole half hour. He took the next one and I got one more. We were now low on gas so Lt. Robinson headed for home. After we landed I let him know how much I'd enjoyed it. He said, "Any time, Jack, and call me Fred when we're alone."

The next day was Saturday, and my weekend was free. I'd been so wrapped up in the flight line; I really hadn't had time to consider other diversions. It was time for Ravel, the undercover agent from Paris, to reappear.

When Cleo heard my French accent on the phone, she got all excited. "Cleo, ma cheer, I 'ave just arrived to train others for le special mission. I 'ave been desolate ever since I was weesked away on le submarine before I could tell you au revoir. Weal you be free tomorrow evening?"

"I have a date, Ravel, but I'll break it," Cleo breathlessly replied.

"Meet me at le Paris Club, ma petite. I weal try to be there at nine. Remember, not a word of these to anyone," I said in my most dramatic voice.

"Oh yes, Ravel! See you then. Goodbye."

Entering the Paris Club this evening, I flashed my reserve ID card showing my age was twenty-one, and strode on in. I looked around, spotted Cleo in a secluded booth, and slid in beside her.

Cleo looked me straight in the eye and said, "Beat it, sailor! I'm waiting for … Oh, Ravel! What are you doing in a sailor suit?"

Trying to look unshaken by her harsh words, I quickly replied, "Ah, ma chere, wearing zees uniform is one of le sacrifices for le safety of le mission."

Cleo accepted this, and I ordered a round of drinks. The music started and we drifted to the dance floor. I remembered her reaction to French phrases of endearment, so whispered them softly in her lovely ear as we danced. The response could be felt throughout the length of her seductively slim body.

She must have cast herself in the role of Mata Hari, because she kept checking over my shoulder to see if we were under surveillance. We retreated to the safety of our secluded booth, and were sitting much closer.

"Did you receive my message from across le sea?" I asked.

"Yes, and I burned it immediately. I felt sad that I wasn't able to thank Le Bon Chet for saving your life."

"Oh, what happened?"

"We were in the apartment after an evening out. I was prepared to do my very best, and slipped into a negligee. When I offered to help Le Bon Chet with his uniform, his face went white, and he ran out the door."

Cleo's lower lip was trembling; she felt she had failed her first assignment.

"Ma chere, eet wasn't your fault. Ween Le Bon Chet was a prisoner, before ees escape; the sadistic mistress of a guard did terrible theengs to eem. Apparently ee hasn't recovered yet."

Now I knew why Chet never answered my letter.

We had another round and danced again. I whispered more French endearments.

Cleo whispered back, "We are under surveillance by two men at that ringside table."

We turned so I was facing the table and she was right. They were staring at us, or to be more exact, at the rear of Cleo. She was wearing a sheath dress and her involuntary reactions had fascinated the two at the table.

"You are correct, Cleo, let us leave before theere is an international incident."

We caught a taxi to her studio apartment. The apartment was small, with only a living room, a kitchen alcove, and a bathroom. Luckily her roommate was out, and soon we were in each other's arms. Cleo agreed to model the negligee Chet seemed to find so disturbing. No question about it, this sheer creation did cause a reaction.

I slipped out of my jumper and while she was hanging it up, I removed my trousers. We had just returned to each other's arms, when we heard someone approaching out front. Damn!

Cleo quickly pulled a handle, and a Murphy bed descended from the wall. I slipped into it and she slid under the cover before the roommate entered.

Linda, a stunning, petite blond, seemed a little surprised to find a houseguest. When she discovered I was Ravel from Paris, all reservations vanished. Apparently Cleo hadn't been as secretive as instructed. Linda became an enchanting hostess. She noticed I didn't have a pillow and got me one, then hung up the rest of my uniform. I could see Cleo wasn't too happy about all this service, but she really didn't want to get up in the sheer negligee.

Linda retired to the bathroom, slipped into a shorty nightgown, and returned to the combination living room-bedroom. It was obvious the nightie didn't have a backup!

"I'm sorry we are such poor hostesses, Ravel," said Linda, as she sat on Cleo's side of the bed, "can you think of a more satisfactory arrangement?"

I was pretty sure Linda had that French trio thing in mind, and I knew for a maiden flight as a lover, it would be beyond my capabilities. Monte hadn't covered this scenario in his basic instructions! I sadly acknowledged I couldn't think of anything better either and Linda joined Cleo on her side of the double bed. I bid them both good night with a, "Bon soir, mes petites."

Like Chet, I realized I wasn't ready for the big time. I knew for the rest of my life—this would rank at the very top of my missed opportunities list!

TEN

The girls got up first, and while I scraped my face with a dull, borrowed razor, they fixed breakfast. After coffee we were all in a good mood, and the girls wanted to know my plans for the day. I had thought to hitchhike to Tijuana, and play the horses at Caliente.

I told them, "I 'ave an assignment across the border, and must meet my contact."

Cleo, who now envisioned herself as a part time secret agent, stated, "Linda has a car."

"The mission could be dangerous, but eef you are brave enough to participate, all allied nations will have the...how you say...*remerciement*? Ah, yes...thankfulness for your help."

They felt brave and dangerous.

We hopped into Linda's older Chevrolet, and were off for the border. I drove through the border checkpoint, and just followed the traffic to Caliente. It seemed most of San Diego were there for the races.

The first race was about to start; we got good seats and I placed a girl on each side. I whispered that while I was looking for my contact, it would be their duty to report any surveillance from enemy agents. This gave them lots to do, as the sight of two stunning blonds sitting with only one sailor drew the attention of every single man in the area.

I told the girls as a cover, I was going to the pari-mutual window and place a bet. On my way back I recognized Mario, the dark haired, handsome, seaman from the flight line.

"Mario. What are you up to?"

Mario seemed a little reluctant to reply

"I'm here to meet my uncle from Italy, who is a handler at the track."

I did some quick thinking.

"I have an extra blond back at the seats. Would you be interested in joining the two girls and I?"

His dark eyes flashed and I knew the answer.

I confided, "The girls think I am Ravel Deveraux, a secret agent from Paris— that I am here on a secret mission to meet my contact, who now will become you—one of the leaders of the Italian, anti-war underground."

Mario has a stunned look on his face. My last words to him were, "Speak with an Italian accent, and if you are asked a hard question— answer in Italian!"

We arrived back at the seats, I introduced Mario; he took one look at Linda with her beautiful blond hair cascading over one shoulder, and fell into the adjoining seat.

There was a roar from the crowd as the first race began. We rooted for our choices, but unfortunately none won. I was beginning to get thirsty, so I ordered beer for us all. Mexican beer had an exceptional flavor, and was the favorite drink at the races. I noticed Mario and Linda seemed to be getting on well, and I was pleased to hear the Italian accent coming through. We all chose a horse for the next race; however, none of us had enough confidence to bet. The second race ended with our horses losing again.

The first beer tasted so good we had a second, and I noticed Mario was gaining confidence. Every now and then, after a question from Linda, he rattled off a string of Italian. In a few minutes he muttered mysteriously that he must meet his associate at the paddock, and when he returned he hoped to have good news.

The third race had finished before Mario returned and I noticed Linda had been watching for him. Instead of sitting down, he knelt before us and drew our heads in close.

He confided, "My associates have arranged a winner, just for us. In the next race Golden Girl will win, because her name reminds me of Linda."

I couldn't believe it—the student was out-shining the master! The girls were properly impressed. I got Mario off to the side, "Are you out of your mind?"

He assured me, "Golden Girl will be the winner. Bet everything you have on her. It's a rigged race my uncle let me in on, and the name Golden Girl was a lucky coincidence."

We pooled all the money the four of us had, and bet it on Golden Girl.

The odds were down to six-to-one by post time and we all held our breath as the race began. Golden Girl led all the way, and I believe if she had fallen down, all the other horses would have fallen right behind her. This was my kind of race. I could tell by Linda's expression as she looked at Mario, he had made some big points.

We happily collected our winnings, had another beer, watched one more race, and decided to go to the bullfights, which were held in a circular coliseum closer to Tijuana. We got tickets for the shady side and were seated before it began.

I had never been to a bullfight before and was really enjoying the pageantry at the beginning. First, the trumpets blew, and then the matadors and the picadors and some people on padded horses came marching out. The crowd cheered madly, and we all had another cool beer.

After the parading was all over, I began to enjoy it less. The bull came charging out and every time the picadors stuck darts in his shoulder the crowd yelled, "Ole!" This went on for quite a while and finally, when there was a stream of blood coming from the darts, the picadors departed and the matador came strutting out.

By this time we all needed another cerveza. Apparently the matador was not very good, because he had trouble getting the bull to follow his cape. About then we switched our allegiance to the bull, and every time he came out ahead, we yelled "Ole!" This brought some dirty looks from the Mexicans sitting around us. We quieted down, had another beer, and then the bull got in a lucky hook with his horn, and dumped the matador on his backside. We couldn't restrain ourselves. A loud "Ole!" was shouted, and it looked as if we are going to have to fight our way out of there.

I pointed out, "Obviously the bull ring has been infiltrated by Nazi sympathizers. I need to send out le report."

I really wanted to get out of there before the matador started butchering the bull with the sword he had just pulled.

We noticed we were feeling no pain as we headed back to Tijuana, and I suspected Mexican beer had quite a kick. By then it was suppertime so we headed for the Foreign Club, the best in the city.

Because of rationing, this was one of the few places one could still get a thick, juicy, steak dinner on the West Coast. I had heard about it ever since arriving in San Diego, and had planned for this to be the *piece de resistance* of the evening.

After attending the bloody bullfight, we were so grossed out and suspicious of the meat source, we ordered seafood. We washed this down with some more of that good cerveza and soon the Mexican orchestra fired up.

It was pretty wild stuff at first, but by the time we had finished dinner, the music slowed down enough to dance. Soon, Cleo was in my arms, and I couldn't resist whispering a few French endearments just to check—her motor was definitely running!

I noticed Mario and Linda were getting pretty well wrapped up in each other's arms. I suspected Golden Girl made a bigger impression than Mario realized.

After the dance, Mario and I returned the girls to the table and made a detour to the door marked "Hombre." As we started to return, we could see two powerfully built Mexicans in zoot suits had moved in on the girls, and were sitting in our seats at the back of the table. They had brought their beer with them, and their eyes were devouring our two blond beauties.

I knew we were in serious trouble; those fellas packed switchblades, and this was their country. I grabbed Mario's arm before he could charge over to do battle.

"Hold it, Mario—I have an idea."

Just then the girls glanced our way with an uncomfortable expression. When I was sure I had Cleo's full attention, I mouthed the words, "enemy agents," and motioned first to her and then to the door. The second time she got it, and nodded her head.

I handed the car keys to Mario, and asked him to bring the car to the entrance with the motor running. He started for the door, and I saw Cleo whisper something in Linda's ear. In a moment the two girls rose—the two Mexicans remained seated at the back of the table, with suspicious expressions. Cleo leaned over the table as if to say something. When the Mexicans leaned forward to look down her dress, she gripped the edge of the table and lifted! There was the sound of broken crockery as the juicy remains of our dinner, condiments, and drinks, slid into the Mexican's laps and continued on to the floor. The zoot suits would never be the same again.

A string of angry, Spanish oaths filled the air, as the Mexicans struggled to get free of the overturned table and resulting mess. The girls ran quickly to the front door, which I was holding open. As I slammed the door behind us, the girls were already scrambling into the car. Mario had the engine racing and dug out as I landed on Cleo's lap. We looked back and could see angry Mexicans spilling from the cantina.

Cleo was exuberantly proud of her heroic deed. She felt at last she had met the enemy, and conquered. There could be no doubt how seriously she took her secret agent duties.

We were almost to the border before I remembered—we never paid for the dinner.

Ah, well, "C'est la guerre!"

ELEVEN

It was Monday and I was on the flight line when the Commander checked out his favorite Cub. He had a heavyset, full Lieutenant with him, and I noticed that, as usual, the Commander was using the taxiway as a runway. Rank does have its privileges!

I didn't believe he took into consideration all the extra weight in the back seat, because he was barely airborne, when he had to make a sharp bank to avoid intercepting the active runway.

He made the turn, but as he dropped the port wing, it hit a tall, thin, metal pole supporting a radio antenna. The pole collapsed; the Cub was turned another ninety degrees, and was headed back my way with the nose up, engine wide open, and hanging on the prop.

He was so low he couldn't drop the nose to pick up more flying speed; I expected a crash any second. He drifted my way and I was looking for a hole to dive into, then he drifted toward the tower and I could see frantic activity in the glass cupola. The next time he drifted over the taxiway, he chopped the power and came down hard. I was ready to write the landing gear off, and hoped he hadn't damaged the new prop.

The Commander taxied back to the line and parked in the correct place. I didn't say a word, just handed him the post-flight form. Under squawks he wrote, in a perfectly legible hand, "Check port wing for possible damage."

Possible damage! I could see a dent in the leading edge big enough to throw a football through. He and the Lieutenant, who was about three shades paler, started to walk off, when the Commander returned and asked, "Will this be a base shop, or flight line repair, Jack?"

I had no idea he knew my first name.

"Base shop, Sir."

"I would prefer you do it here."

"Yes, Sir," I answered, "If the main spar isn't damaged, I can."

I knew why he didn't want it going to base shops. An accident report would have to be filled out, an investigative team from North Island Headquarters would arrive, and there would be some embarrassing questions asked about using taxiways as runways.

I waited until they were out of sight, and then checked the landing gear. I was more worried about it than the wing. It was a relief to find no visible evidence of damage. Mario showed up, and I explained to him our job on the wing.

We removed the damaged portion of the leading edge, discovered the forward portion of a rib was crushed—fortunately no spar damage. It was fairly simple to replace the damaged portion of the rib with aluminum fabricated at the sheet metal shop. We reformed the leading edge, finished with a matching paint job, and there was no evidence of the repair. After checking the mount bolts and wing alignment, I was convinced we had been very lucky indeed.

The following day we completed the job and after Fred was through attacking the turrets, I prevailed upon him to give the repair job a flight test. After Fred got through with it, any plane still together was solid.

When he returned, I thanked Fred, and he then mentioned his Ford was not running well. I got the message, and suggested he pick up a tune-up kit at an auto supply, bring the car out behind the line shack, and I'd see to it. I didn't know how he found out I had four years of high school auto mechanics.

Fred arrived the next morning with his car and the kit, parked behind the shack, and was off to attack turrets. Before he returned, I had the new points, plugs and condenser installed and adjusted, and the timing reset. The engine sounded fine. I noticed the gas tank was empty, so I parked the eighty-octane fuel truck alongside the shack with the rear hose near the Ford. When Fred returned he listened to the engine, checked the gas gauge, and drove happily away.

The Commander arrived, prepared to fly one of the other Cubs. He was pleasantly surprised to find his favorite back in service. He looked it all over, and couldn't find where the dent in the wing had been. As he commented on this, I told him, "That Mario is one good fabricator."

The next afternoon Mario and I were called in to take our promotion tests. While we were there, I asked to have transcripts of my Navy schools sent to Placerville High, in hopes this would make up for the two months I was short for graduation.

In the afternoon Lt. Sanders invited me to make the mail run with him and let me fly both ways, with him making the landings. As we were putting the plane away, he mentioned his car sure needed a tune-up, and suggested I call him Roger in the future. I suspected he and Fred had been talking, but I told him to get a kit and I'll be happy to do it.

The next morning, he brought the car over, and I was impressed. It was a 1939 Ford convertible with rumble seat, in mint condition. While I had the plugs out, I ran a compression check and each cylinder checked out perfectly. I completed the tune-up, saw his gas gauge also read empty, and filled it up with Cub gas. It was ready to go when he returned from North Island.

Roger gave me big thanks, and mentioned he wanted the engine running well, so it would be easy to sell when he left with his squadron. I had forgotten he was due to ship out soon, and I inquired what price he might ask for the convertible. He thought it was worth eight hundred, and I did too. I told him he has just sold the car; I would have the cash the day he was ready to give possession. I had banked six hundred from Oklahoma's ill-gotten gains, and added one hundred and fifty from the fixed Caliente race. With what I had loose in my pocket, and with another payday, I could make it. Some yeoman had slipped up, and I was still drawing the fifty percent additional flight pay. I turned in the required four hours monthly flight time with my fingers crossed.

Friday started out great, with the lead chief coming out to the line with the approved promotions. I was now officially a second class petty officer in charge of the flight line, and Mario was my third class assistant.

I talked to Roger when he made the mail run, and we agreed to transfer the car the next day.

Mario asked, "Do you have anything planned with Cleo for the week end?"

I knew he would like to see Linda, and was a little reluctant to go alone. I had thought about Cleo, but with her apartment so small and busy, and knowing I'd have the new car, I planned on driving to the ballroom in Southgate at Los Angeles. I had been hearing great stories of the name bands who played there, and the lovely women who attended. Also there was a hospitality house close by with free lodging and breakfast.

I explained all this to Mario, and suggested we go there this weekend and then call in the middle of the week and make dates for next weekend with Cleo and Linda. Mario reluctantly started to agree, and then decided to call Linda instead. He really was hung up on that cute blond.

I forgot to withdraw the six hundred from the station bank before it closed, so when I saw Roger the next morning I gave him one hundred and my bank book to hold until Monday, when we would transfer the title. He handed me the keys, what gas ration tickets he had left, and mentioned he would leave the car insured until I could get my own. The gas tank was still full, and I was on my way.

There is a very satisfying feeling in being just nineteen years old, and behind the wheel of your own convertible, on the way to the big city for intrigue and adventure. I had smuggled my leather flight jacket out, and although it was non-regulation, I put it on and felt even more daring.

The Ford purred along like it was brand new. I was leaving San Diego, when I noticed the highway lined with servicemen headed for Los Angeles. It was quite obvious some of them might never get a ride. I started to pull over to pick up four sailors—when I saw they were each holding out a hand with five fingers pointed up. I wasn't sure if I should take this as a five-fold insult, but decided to stop anyway.

There was a mad dash for the car, the rumble seat was popped open, two sailors jammed in there, and two in the front with me. When five-dollar bills came floating my way, I realized those five fingers meant they were offering five dollars each for a ride. I was aghast I had been so dumb!

BY YOUR LEAVE, SIR

As we drove on, one of the passengers in front explained every serviceman in San Diego was trying to get to Los Angeles for the weekend. To hear him describe it, L.A. was the Promised Land. There were beautiful, lonely women, friendly civilians, and very few servicemen. The problem was the inadequate bus system. The only way to make it was hitchhiking, and there were more riders than cars. They wanted to know when I would be coming back, and I agreed to stop at a certain restaurant located at the city's edge, Sunday evening.

So far, my information seemed to be reasonably accurate. When I arrived at Southgate I dropped the hitchhikers off, rides were easy here, and located the hospitality house. It was a large residence in a commercial area, scheduled for demolition in the future. One of the L.A. service clubs operated it for servicemen with free bunks, showers, and a kitchen stocked with breakfast material. It was on a first come, first served basis, so I checked in.

It was a warm afternoon, so I put the top down and went exploring. First I located the Southgate Ballroom, so I'd be able to find it in the evening, and saw from the poster outside Lionel Hampton was playing. I knew for sure then, this would be one exciting evening. The weather was so exceptional it was difficult to realize it was already winter. I cruised along the coast checking out beaches, and was amazed there were still sunbathers. When I reached Venice, I parked and walked out on the pier.

The sun was setting, the pink glow reflected in the water, and many of the people were already leaving. The view was so beautiful; I had dinner there at a table overlooking the ocean, with a glass of wine. The sound of the waves gently breaking on shore provided a perfect background for the meal. Watching the sunset fade, and thinking of the evening's possibilities, I could feel the excitement building.

The parking lot at the dance was already filling when I arrived. I got a seat at the bar where I could watch the new arrivals, and was pleased to see there were at least two girls to every guy. Hamp was just finishing a jump piece, and he sounded a lot better in person than over the radio.

I sipped my beer, and watched the dancers as Hamp slowed down on the next song. One tall, slim, blond beauty, had caught my eye, and I couldn't believe it when her partner deserted her, right in the middle of the dance floor. She looked so bewildered I quickly made my way to her side, slid my arm around her and continued the dance.

She looked to see who had her, and said in a shaky voice, "I suppose you are going to ask, will I or won't I?"

"Will you or won't you, what?"

"Go to bed with you, that's what the other sailor asked, and when I said no, he dumped me right here on the floor."

Her lower lip was trembling, and her beautiful green eyes were starting to puddle up. I knew I had to distract her quickly, or I was going to have an emotional partner on my hands. My new personality rose to the occasion.

"You are perfectly safe with me. I'm a Buddhist Monk trainee, and of course we must renounce that sort of behavior."

After an astonished pause, "What's a monk trainee doing at a dance?"

"This is my novitiate night to discover all the things I'm renouncing. Would you place your left arm around my neck, please?"

To my surprise she complied, and this brought us into my favorite cheek-to-cheek position. Even with her recent trauma, she followed well.

"Oh, I don't know if I have the strength!"

"The strength for what?" she asked in a frightened voice.

"The strength to renounce anything as delightful as this. There is only one way to find out. Would you lift your face to mine, please?"

As she complied, I lowered my lips to hers in an intimate kiss. The music was ending, and as I raised my head I exclaimed. "My dear, your attraction is stronger than my vows—you have set me free—thank you—thank you!"

I dropped her off at the side of the dance floor, and returned to my beer at the bar.

A short while later, I was again on the dance floor. This particular one was tall and slim, and as I held her close, my eyes were closed. The beer had produced a pleasant glow, and I was off in another world. Unfortunately she wanted to talk.

"What do you do in the Navy?" It took a few seconds to shift gears.

"I'm an investigative reporter for the Stars and Stripes," I replied.

"I thought that was an Army publication," my dancing partner countered suspiciously.

"It is," I unabashedly admitted, "I'm the Navy correspondent."

"Can you tell me what you are reporting on right now?" she asked, still a little skeptical.

"Well, right now I'm conducting an intimate survey among young ladies that has created a lot of reader interest."

"What kind of an intimate survey?"

"I must warn you it really is intimate; I don't want you getting angry."

"I won't get angry," she promised, "please tell me."

"Well, it's really a one question survey, and the question is—should a young, eligible, serviceman, about to go overseas, whom you have just met and like, confess his attraction to you and plead that you return with him to his hotel—would you consider it?"

"Gee, that's a tough question," she paused, giving the matter serious thought. "I think under the right circumstances, I might."

"Thank you, my dear. The readers will be greatly encouraged by your brave answer." Oh, by the way, may I have the last dance?" With an affirmative response, I returned to the bar.

As I sat there I was aghast at my behavior. So far it hadn't been like me at all. I wondered if the warning the head doctor at the hospital gave me, about personality changes following a severe head blow—could really have been true. I decided to prove I could behave if I wanted to. I'd just mentally rearranged my future, when my past caught up. I felt a pair of soft arms around my neck and a gently chastising voice in my ear.

"When the princess kissed the frog and transformed it into a prince, the prince stayed with the princess, why haven't you been more faithful?"

It was the lovely blond with the trembling lower lip. "Please forgive me?" I said, as I took her hand and guided her to the stool beside me. "My new found freedom went to my head."

I introduced myself and found out her name was Niki Marshall, she was here with a girl friend, and until she met me, was feeling completely rejected. As we talked, I could see she was a natural blond with fair skin that positively glowed. Her large, emerald green eyes were looking at me now, and I realized I could be very fortunate indeed.

The orchestra was just starting a ballad and I asked, "Would you rather join me in a drink or a dance?"

"A dance, thank you," she replied and soon we blended together on the dance floor. She remembered my favorite position and her arm encircled my neck. We were content to let our bodies carry the conversation and it was an interesting one. I was truly sorry when the music ended.

She saw her friend, together with a marine, and we drifted over. The girls made the introductions and when it became apparent the band was on their last break, we wound our way to a table at the bar. The girls had soft drinks, the marine and I beer. The conversation was friendly and relaxed. I excused myself and headed for the restroom and shortly thereafter the marine arrived.

He wanted to know if Niki and I had any plans after the dance. It was obvious he and Mary wanted to leave together in Mary's car and of course this would leave Niki stranded. He appeared greatly relieved to find I had a car and would do my best to cooperate. The music began and after Niki and I returned to the dance floor, I casually suggested,

"Niki, I would like to take you home after the dance."

"I would like that too, Jack, but I came with Mary and I can't leave her alone."

"I believe we can work it out." I said.

I know it was about closing time so when the dance ended, I excused myself and searched for the girl who answered yes to the survey. I located her, and asked for a rain check on the last dance. She appeared disappointed, and I got the impression she was all prepared for another yes answer.

Oh well, I didn't have a hotel room anyway!

I returned to Niki's group and I could see the two girls with their heads together. They were both smiling so I gathered everyone was going to be pleased with the arrangement. Hamp began his last piece. Niki and I went back to where we left off and, as the dance ended she let me know it would be all right to leave together, providing there was no misunderstanding about what was going to happen on the way home.

She did seem impressed with the convertible, but she didn't slide over in the seat when we got under way; she just sat stiffly on her side. I suggested stopping for something to eat and found out she wasn't hungry. I guessed Niki wasn't going to be comfortable until she was safely in her own house. She directed me to where she lived and before long we pulled up in front of a modest home. When we parked she seemed to relax.

"Forgive me for being so jumpy, Jack, but after what happened earlier at the dance, I didn't know if I could really trust anyone."

"I didn't realize it was so traumatic, Niki. I probably shouldn't have pulled that corny bit about the monk trainee."

"I'm glad you did, it was so outrageous it got my mind off what happened earlier."

I found out this was the first time she has been to the Southgate Ballroom, and it was definitely the last time without an escort. I decided she had enough emotional upset for one evening so I remained on my good behavior, and walked her up to her front door. I also decided if her emotional state was this fragile, I was going to pick one next time made of sterner stuff. I gave her a quick kiss, thanked her for the dances, and headed back to the Ford.

I slid in, rolled the window down and reached for the starter when suddenly her head was beside mine at the open window.

"I'm not going to see you again, am I, Jack?" her voice echoed, sounding kind of choked up.

"I wouldn't say that, Niki, I'll be back again, and we probably will both be at the dance some time."

"Jack, I like you very much. I know you are disappointed in me, and I don't want you leaving feeling this way. Can I please get back in for a minute?"

I noticed those big green eyes were starting to puddle up, so I reached over to open the passenger door. Instead of sitting beside me she turned the other way, and slide right into my arms. Her lips were just below mine, and as I lowered my head they met in a warm inviting embrace. She was lying partially in my arms, and partially across the front seat. The twisting position caused the sheath dress to ride up much higher than the designer intended, and this exciting view, plus the activity of her mouth, should have caused all kinds of reactions. I suspected her behavior was more atonement than real desire, and I reluctantly disengaged, turning her so she was sitting beside me.

"Don't I please you at all, Jack?" came through muffled sobs.

"You please me very much, Niki. But next time I want it to be because we both want to take it further, not because you are feeling upset over something that happened before I met you."

"Oh, Jack, when will I see you again?"

"Well, I have to get back to San Diego tomorrow."

"What time do you leave?"

"Oh, late afternoon."

"Jack," Niki pleaded, "please stop by for dinner. We usually eat about one."

"All right," I agreed, "I'll see you then."

She gave me a quick kiss and slipped out her side of the car. I fired up the Ford, waved goodbye, and returned to the hospitality house.

I slept in, and it was nearly noon before I was up and dressed. The coffee pot was on and after a hot cup it was time to head for Niki's.

I was feeling relaxed and happy with the world as I pulled into the driveway, and rang the doorbell. It was a good thing, because when the door opened, I was in for a shock. There stood a tall, lovely, green-eyed blond, with that clear glowing skin— only she seemed more mature, with ripe curves, and a full, sensual, lower lip. Surely something was different!

I was frantically trying to remember how many beers I had last night, when she said, "You must be Jack. Won't you come in?"

This gives me a clue, ah-ha, an older sister. I was just inside when Niki appeared from the kitchen wearing an apron, and introduced me to Jill— her mother! They both laughed as they watched me struggle to handle this. Apparently it was not the first time their striking resemblance has caused confusion. Niki gave me a hug.

"I have a little more to do in the kitchen, Jack; make yourself at home." Mrs. Marshall added, "Come have a chair in the living room."

I was seated in obviously a man's leather easy chair with a matching footstool. Mrs. Marshall joined me in the facing rocker, and by looking closely, the only possible clues to her age were faint little crow's feet at the corners of her eyes. On the piano was a picture of a very attractive couple, obviously Mrs. Marshall and a tall, good-looking man.

"Is that Niki's father?" I asked.

"Yes, that's Steven. He was killed in an auto accident just a year ago."

"I'm sorry, Mrs. Marshall; Niki never told me."

"It's all right, Jack, I've learned to accept it, and please call me Jill. I feel more comfortable that way."

I remembered Niki's emotional ups and downs last night, and asked? "How has Niki taken the loss of her father?"

"Not at all well, they were very close, and she just hasn't been able to accept it. As a matter of fact, last night was the first time she has gone out since it happened."

"I'm sorry it didn't turn out all that well."

"Jack, I'm going to speak frankly," Jill continued, "Niki told me what happened last night at the dance, and I'm very thankful you were there. If you hadn't been, I think she would have gone right back into her shell. I know you exhibited some mature discretion later, and I am very much in your debt."

Apparently Niki had told all. I was ready to change the subject, so I asked, "Do you and Niki both work, or is she still in school?"

"We both work; I'm a bookkeeper at an insurance company, and after the accident I got Niki a job there as a typist. It meant no college because it takes both salaries to make ends meet now in wartime."

I suspected Steven had been careless about life insurance. Niki came in without the apron and a slight flush to her face from the kitchen heat.

"Dinner is served," she announced. The dining room table was set for three, and I noticed what appears to be a rack of lamb together with the carving set placed at the head of the table.

"Would you sit there?" Jill asked, and the two ladies took seats on each side.

"You carve, Jack," Niki says, "and I'll fill your plate."

"Sounds fair," I remarked, "especially if this is what I think it is."

I believed that was a safe statement in case it turned out to be something other than lamb. I did the carving; it was lamb, while Niki passed the plates. I was really glad I skipped breakfast because this was a feast. I shuddered to think how many ration tickets it consumed. The dinner was delicious; I complimented the ladies and especially Niki, who was obviously a superb cook. Instead of dessert, Jill brought a bottle of Crème de Menthe and filled the small liquor glasses on the table. The mint flavor was a fitting finale to a perfect dinner and I told them so.

"It's good to have a man at the table again," Jill responded, "That chair has been vacant too long."

I noticed they both were gazing at me with shining eyes and I had a momentary feeling of apprehension.

"When will you be able to come back again?" Niki asked.

"I'm not really sure, perhaps in two or three weeks."

"You know Christmas weekend is only two weeks away," Jill reminded me. "Do you have any plans?"

"I can't believe Christmas is so soon. It feels like summer—I haven't even thought about Christmas yet."

"Think about it." Niki pleaded, "And spend it with us. Last Christmas was terribly lonely."

"Well, I wouldn't want to put you out. Maybe I can come for dinner and then get a bunk at the hospitality house."

"Jack, the hospitality house will be full Christmas weekend," Jill firmly announced, "please stay here. Besides, our sofa is softer than those bunks."

"All right, I will. I've been kind of dreading Christmas by myself. Thank you."

I announced that if I was going to meet the sailors who were waiting for a return ride to San Diego I would have to leave. We three walked to the front door and I thanked them again for a wonderful afternoon, then I slipped my arm around Niki and gave her a warm goodbye kiss. Somehow Jill had gotten under the other arm and I was involved in another warm farewell kiss. This was all I needed—another pair of blondes!

TWELVE

It was my first day in charge. The responsibility for taking the roll and turning in the morning report was now mine. Everything seemed under control, so Mario and I had a chance to talk.

"What happened with Linda and Cleo?" I wanted to know.

"No problem, I told them you were off on another secret mission and Linda and I went out Saturday night. Sunday we all went to the races at Tijuana."

"I told them I had to meet my contact," Mario explained. "I saw my uncle and found out next week there should be a special race."

"Hey, that's great. Let's try to be there… Anything else happen?"

"Yeah," Mario reluctantly admitted. "We ran into your friends, Mike and Sammy."

"Uh-oh. Did they let the cat out of the bag?"

"No. I got them off to the side and gave them a quick rundown on the situation. They picked it up fast and before long I heard them telling Cleo they were your commanders in the secret, American, undercover unit."

"Blast," I muttered. "I suppose she believed them?"

"I'm afraid so," Mario acknowledged, "I heard her whisper she was a part-time agent herself."

I was almost afraid to ask what happened next. "Well, go on, what happened?"

"Cleo invited them to join us. We drank a lot of beer and had dinner at the Continental. We thought it might be safer than the Foreign Club."

Mario smiled in contemplation.

"What about Cleo?" I anxiously demanded.

"Ha, she had a ball. She took turns dancing with Mike and Sammy, and on the way back the three of them seemed to have a good time in the back seat of the car."

"How good a time?"

"Hey! I was busy up front with Linda. I couldn't keep score!"

There was something about that phrase I really didn't care for.

"How was it left with the girls?" I asked.

"Oh, they both are going home next weekend for Christmas but will be back for New Year's. We all are invited to a New Year's party."

"All?"

"Yes," Mario admitted, "she invited Mike and Sammy too!"

I suspected Cleo now envisioned herself as the femme fatale of all secret agents. It was time to bring up the big guns before my former classmates aced me out!

I was glad Roger showed up about then to take the mail run, so I could get my mind on something else.

Roger asked, "How did you and the Ford get along, Jack?"

"Roger, it ran like a top and the girls loved it. I'm completely spoiled already. If you're free after the mail run, let's go to the bank and complete the deal."

I drew out the seven hundred and gave it to Roger. He signed over the title and we went to the insurance agent, where we cancelled Roger's and put it in my name. I dropped Roger off at BOQ and was feeling on top of the world.

It was a promising Sunday morning as Mario and I started for Tijuana and the races at Caliente. We were both excited about the possibilities of the fixed race. I couldn't believe in this day and age that races could be manipulated.

I asked Mario about this and he replied, "Jack, that uncle of mine is one mean paesano. He has muscle from the Old Country and when he says something, I don't ask questions. If he says a certain horse is going to win today, it's going to win!"

I could tell Mario didn't want to talk about it, so we changed the subject.

We arrived at Caliente before the first race, and while Mario was consulting with his uncle, I sat where I could watch the incoming crowd and enjoy a cool cerveza. I was on my second when my attention was drawn to two Navy nurses in their officer uniforms. The one with the exciting figure and short hair looked familiar. I mentally backtracked until I reached my stay, nearly two years ago, at the naval hospital in San Diego. This was the young, attractive nurse who had distracted my ping-pong games.

I gathered up my beer and flight jacket, and plopped down next to the one I admired.

"Hi," I began, "weren't you at the San Diego Naval Hospital about two years ago?"

"Still am," she replied, "Did I know you?"

"Unfortunately not, I was too shy and just admired you from afar."

I could tell that struck a responsive note, so I introduced myself. She said her name was Jan and introduced her friend, Sandra.

"I have a friend who is at the paddock getting a list of the winners," I volunteered, "he should be back soon."

This got their attention.

"How does he manage to do that?" Jan asked.

I knew telling the truth could jeopardize Mario, so I replied, "Don't ask me how, but Mario has a way of communicating with horses. He's finding out now which ones are sure they will win!"

Suddenly it became very quiet. The beer vendor came by and I asked if they would join me in a cool one. They just nodded their heads and as I was placing the order I saw Mario. I added one more to the order and called, "Over here, Mario."

He saw us and approached very cautiously. I suspected Mario was remembering a couple of weeks ago, when he became a secret agent here.

In making the introductions, I said, "Mario, I'd like you to meet Jan and Sandra. Girls, this is Mario."

I handed the girls their beer, slid another across to Mario and kept one myself. Mario took the seat next to Sandra and turned facing our way.

"Did you get the information you went after, Mario?" I asked.

He looked surprised I would bring it up with company, and just nodded.

"That's all right, Mario. I told the girls what you were doing in the paddock."

He looked shocked, and the girls, watching his face became even more interested.

"You know, Mario, I have the feeling they really don't believe you can communicate with horses."

Relief crossed Mario's face as he at last figured out what I had done.

"Well, Jack, they weren't as confident as usual, but one little filly in the seventh race guaranteed she was going to win."

"Save your money for the seventh race, girls," I advised.

Jan couldn't believe this conversation was taking place. "You mean we are going to bet on this horse because she told Mario she was going to win?"

"Have you ever known a horse to lie?" I asked with a straight face.

Sandra was checking the seventh race on the program. "They are all fillies in that race Mario, which one were you talking to?"

"Sandra, you are as bad as they are," Jan interrupted.

"She made me promise not to tell until three minutes before post time," Mario acknowledged. "She was worried about a rapid change in the odds."

"I can't believe this is really happening!" sputtered Jan.

The first race was over and we had been so engrossed, no one had picked a winner. The race ended and it was time for a cool one.

"Isn't anyone going to bet on this next race?" Jan wanted to know.

"Not me," I replied, "I'm saving my money for Mario's friend in the seventh."

"Me too," chimed in both the others.

The friendly banter continued through the next several races, punctuated occasionally by another cerveza. The seventh race was now coming up and Mario and I began to count the money in our wallets.

"You two are really serious," commented Jan in amazement.

"Of course, horses never lie," I replied as I handed Mario my total wallet contents of seventy-five dollars. He added the fifty he had and then turned to Sandra. She opened her purse and contributed her total assets of thirty dollars. We all looked at Jan.

"You're crazy, all of you; we won't have enough for a cup of coffee! Oh, all right," protesting, she dug forty dollars from her purse.

Mario took the money and headed for the pari-mutual window.

I needed to make a trip to the restroom and as I left I couldn't resist saying, "Thanks a lot, girls, it's been nice," and quickly departed.

My conscience got to bothering me, and I didn't delay my return. Just as I suspected, they were standing there, looking desperately in the direction I had departed. When they saw me they quickly sat down, and tried to pretend they weren't alarmed.

When I sat next to Jan, she put an arm around mine, and accused, "Jack, that was sadistic!"

"I'm sorry, Jan. I couldn't resist it. Just to prove I'm sorry, after the races I'll buy you the best steak dinner at the Foreign Club."

"What about me, Jack?" Sandra broke in, "you frightened me, too."

"I'm sorry, Sandra, of course you're invited."

"Don't get all excited, Sandra," Jan interrupted, "after this next race, Jack won't be able to buy either of us a taco."

It was post time and we anxiously awaited Mario's return to find out the horse's name. He returned with a hand full of win tickets on a filly named Fancy Lady. We quickly checked the odds on the track board and saw she was five to one to win.

The horses were in the gate and then they were off! Fancy Lady got a poor start and was fourth in the first turn. She was third on the backstretch and had to go wide on the turn to the home stretch. She was gaining on the outside as they approached the finish.

All four of us are jumping up and down screaming, "Go, Fancy Lady! Go!" She passed the leader by a head as they crossed the finish and we were ecstatic.

Jan threw her arms around my waist and kept shouting, "She did it! She did it! She didn't lie!"

After we calmed down and seated, Mario went to collect the winnings. We were busy dividing the loot.

I stuck twenty-five in my wallet for the evening and put the rest in a money belt under my jersey. I didn't want to lose this bundle.

Jan told Mario about my dirty trick, and as penance I was buying dinner for everyone. Mario brightened up and I was too happy to complain. We drifted toward the exit and because we were late leaving, it took a long time to reach the Ford.

It was a long straight stretch from Caliente to Tijuana where we would turn off. The bumper-to-bumper traffic was backed up for the border crossing beyond. The opposite lane of the highway was clear; everyone was leaving, none arriving.

The temptation was too much! I pulled into the empty lane and made a run for Tijuana. I knew a lot of stalled drivers were going to be perturbed to see us go sailing by, but hey, that's life!

I was just getting wound up when, "Uh-oh," I saw a Mexican police car in the center of the stalled line. There was no way to pull back in, so I floorboard it and hoped to get lost in Tijuana.

I made a wild turn into town and could see the red lights flashing back on the highway. It looked promising until we came to a massive traffic jam. I desperately looked for an alley, a side street, anything. It was too late, the police car blocked my retreat and the driver was about to get out.

I watched in the rear-view mirror as the young officer emerged from the car. First the highly polished black boots come into view, then sharply creased brown trousers, a wide black Sam Browne belt, supported a holstered, chrome plated Colt 45, a brown shirt with starched creases and all this topped by an officer's hat, stretched so tight it has formed a bow. I could tell he was savoring the moment. He leisurely adjusted the holstered pistol, and stroked his mustache as he strode forward.

I had rolled the window down and because he was short, he barely leaned over to survey the car's occupants.

"Your keys, Senor," he demanded, as he held out his hand.

I wasn't about to part with the Ford, and replied, "You can't take my car—I'm a United States citizen!"

This was the wrong thing to say! A fist came through the window and caught me flush on the nose. I was stunned, and blinded for a moment by tears. My nose was pouring blood, and I was incensed. I grabbed the door handle, and started to open the door.

Jan, who had a better view than I, grabbed my arm and pulled me back, screaming, "No, Jack, it's not worth it."

I soon saw why. He had his chrome 45 out with the hammer back, and by the expectant look in his sadistic, brown eyes, he wanted to use it.

"The keys, Senor," he snarled this time.

I handed him the keys.

"Now, Senor, get out with your hands behind your head."

I complied; he opened the back door of the squad car, motioned me in and slammed the door behind me. The next thing I knew, I was in the drunk tank of the Tijuana jail.

The clang of the slamming cell door echoed off the dismal gray walls. Two of the dirty wooden benches were occupied by reclining Mexicans, either asleep, passed out, or dead.

Just beyond, on a third bench, another inmate was sitting, holding his head in his hands and being sick on the floor. He didn't even glance my way as I found an empty bench, and assumed the same position.

My nose had stopped bleeding, but was throbbing so badly I was sure it was broken. My lower face felt like it was covered with dried blood. I didn't even look down at my uniform. The only positive thoughts I could muster were the damage to my nose had affected my sense of smell so much, the odors in the filthy, drunk tank weren't reaching me—this and the fact they hadn't found my money belt. My wallet was removed at the admitting office.

I couldn't help thinking this was the second jail I'd been thrown into, in addition to being a prisoner-at-large. At my present rate, I'd be a habitual criminal before I was twenty-one.

I didn't know when I'd get out, and was reconciled to at least the night here on this hard bench. I wondered what happened to Mario, and the nurses, and the Ford. I know they had to be across the border by midnight, and suspected they might have already left. I thought about Jan, believed she saved my life, and wondered if I'd ever see her again. After what happened, she probably would be long gone and never want to see me again. I sure wouldn't blame her.

I heard the footsteps of the jailor approaching, and as the cell door was unlocked, he motioned for me to follow him.

He escorted me to the admitting office, where there was quite a group assembled, including a fat, angry, Chief of Police, a subdued, young arresting officer, the American Consul and Jan. She took one look at my bloody face, and started in on the Police Chief, with repeated finger pointing right in the miserable arresting officer's face. The Consul just stood there looking uncomfortable. The Police Chief gave the guilty officer a big blast in Spanish and he slunk out.

The Chief turned to me and said, "You are charged with reckless driving and resisting arrest. How do you plead?"

I looked at Jan and the Consul. They both nodded, so I said, "Guilty."

He stated, "The fine is one hundred seventy-five peso, already received. Case closed."

He handed me my empty wallet and the car keys. Jan, the Consul and I quickly departed.

Sandra and Mario were waiting outside, and we all walked to the Consulate. I was pleased to see Mario wearing my flight jacket, as I had visualized it disappearing from an unlocked car. Jan got me seated in a big overstuffed chair at the consulate, and sitting on the arm, started on my face with a cold, damp cloth. After removing the blood, she gently manipulated my nose, and decided it might not be broken. She rummaged around in her purse, and came up with two pills she had me swallow.

While I was doing this, Jan rinsed out the cloth, and started on the stains on my uniform. I decided there was a definite advantage in having your own private nurse. It was difficult to believe we met only a few hours ago.

I was feeling much better, and asked if the others had eaten. I found they had been so busy getting me out of jail, no one had thought about food.

"I promised dinner and dinner we shall have," I announced.

As soon as Jan put away the basin and equipment, we were off. We picked up the Ford, and drove to the Foreign Club, where we got a good table at ringside. I hoped they didn't remember Mario's and my last visit.

I ordered the best steak dinners for everyone, and a round of cerveza. While we are waiting for the steaks, I got the rest of me cleaned up in the washroom. After returning to the table and consuming a much-needed beer, I felt better.

As we were drinking, Mario told me what happened after I was hauled away.

"We pushed the car to a parking spot, closed it up, and located the American Consulate. The American Consul didn't seem very concerned, and said it would be taken care of in tomorrow's traffic court. He told us to go on back across the border."

"You should have seen Jan," Mario continued "She demanded something be done about police brutality, menacing with a pistol, and that you be released immediately for medical attention. The Consul still said nothing could be done until tomorrow. Jan asked his name, wrote it down on a pad, and told him she was calling the Commandant of the Twelfth Naval District, whom she knew personally, with a full report of the situation. Then she was calling the State Department and reporting him for dereliction of duty. That did it. He got on the phone to the Chief of Police at his home, and convinced the Chief to come back to the jail. You know the rest."

Jan hadn't said anything during all this. I looked at her and said, "Until I can think of a better way to show my thanks, thank you from the bottom of my heart, Jan."

She smiled, and I think we were both glad the steaks arrived then.

Dinner was about finished when the floor show started and Jan slid her chair over next to mine so she could see better. The lights were dimmed for the show, and a little later I leaned over and whispered in her ear, "Jan, do you really know the Commandant of the Twelfth Naval District personally?" Her only response was a wicked smile.

After the show, we decided to go shopping. Next week was Christmas, and we weren't short of money after the big win at the track. The girls picked up presents for their friends, Mario was shopping for several, and I picked up four bottles of Chanel Number Five, and had them gift wrapped. I added a large bottle of French champagne. As we strolled on down the main street we came to an open-air photo shop that had a stuffed donkey pulling a cart. Mario and Sandra climbed on the donkey, and Jan and I the cart. We traded hats and had the photographer take four pictures. I wondered how big my nose would appear.

The pictures came out well and it was time to return to the car. The girls had come by bus, so they were happy to have a ride back to the naval hospital. It was too cold for the rumble seat so we fit four in front, with

Sandra on Mario's lap. When we arrived at the nurse's quarters, Mario and Sandra got out first, and wandered over to a secluded area.

I turned to Jan and said, "Thanks for being there, Jan; I don't know what would have happened without you. At the best I'd still be in jail and at the worst, shot! How can I ever make it up?"

She gently pulled my head down, and gave me a careful kiss so our noses didn't collide.

"Call me some time," she said, and opened the door. I got out my side and walked her to the entrance. I slipped a bottle of perfume into her hand, and whispered, "Merry Christmas, Jan."

A few seconds later, Mario was back in the car, and we waved to the nurses as we drove off.

THIRTEEN

One morning, I saw the SNJ was scheduled, so after the paper work, I pulled the pre-flight myself. John, our new man, stood fireguard. Soon afterwards, Fred showed up, and headed for the SNJ instead of the Cub.

"Fred," I called, "Are you lost?"

"Hi, Jack, No, from today on the gunners get the deluxe attack with the SNJ—it's the closest to the Zero we have. Want to come along?"

"You bet! I've never been up in one."

My admiration for Fred's flying ability increased mightily. He pulled so many G's on several pullouts, I started to black out. Fred was having so much fun I knew it would be days, maybe weeks, before I ever got my hands on the controls of this one. I couldn't help feeling sad about the end of the Cub flights.

I managed to get a few hours sleep, before the commotion in the barracks became too loud. I had to wait in line for a shower; seemed everyone was going somewhere for Christmas. I was ready to leave for Southgate, when I realized Jan had been on my mind. I called the nurse's quarters and in a moment she was on the phone.

"Hi, Jan."

"Hi, Jack," she recognized my voice.

"Has my name crossed your thoughts this morning?"

"Why?"

"Well, I was leaving for Los Angeles, and suddenly here I am in a phone booth calling you. Merry Christmas, Jan."

"Merry Christmas, Jack, and yes, I was thinking of you. Could you stop by for a few minutes on your way?"

"I'll be by in twenty-five minutes. See you then."

"I'll be watching."

In exactly twenty-five minutes I pulled up in front of the nurse's quarters, and looked hopefully for Jan. The only movement I saw was a lovely young thing in a frock that did nice things for her figure. I had never seen Jan out of uniform, so this delightful vision was almost to the car before it registered. She was Jan! I quickly opened the door and she slipped inside. I was sure my eyes must have revealed my approval, because she came over into my arms. I just held her for a moment and detected a faintly familiar fragrance.

"Might that be Channel?" I asked

"I thought the least I could do would be to let you enjoy a sample."

"You know it's not fair to look and smell so desirable, just as I'm leaving."

"I did it deliberately, Jack—suffer all the way to Los Angeles."

"Jan, if people weren't waiting for me to arrive at a Christmas dinner, I'd stay right here."

She turned, and gave me a lingering kiss.

"Thanks, Jack. You make me feel better. I have a present for you, and then you'd better go."

She handed me a flat, gift-wrapped package. I quickly opened it, and found an extra slim, leather wallet, with my name engraved in gold. This was the hard to find size, which fit in the skimpy pocket of a Navy uniform.

"It's perfect, Jan; I'm throwing away my bulky one today. Thank you so much."

She gave me one more quick kiss, and slipped out of the car. I noticed her eyes glistening before she quickly turned, and hurried back inside.

Jan was still on my mind as I started to leave the city. I noticed the highway was lined with servicemen, desperately trying to get a ride. Some were even holding up ten fingers. I know four bodies were the most I could get into the car, so I waited until I came to a group of exactly that many. I wouldn't want to be the fifth person in this Christmas Day situation.

They started to pay but I was still feeling so good about Jan, I waved them off and said, "It's Christmas." I noticed the two in the rumble seat had found my poncho, and were using it over their heads as a windbreaker. The ones in front were concerned about getting back tomorrow evening. They said it was even more difficult than going. I told them I would stop at this restaurant not earlier than five o'clock. If they didn't have a ride they could wait until I arrived, and to save out five dollars. The return trip was business as usual.

I dropped the sailors off in Southgate, and continued on to Niki's and Jill's. As I passed the Ballroom, I saw that Stan Kenton was playing tonight for a special Christmas dance.

The girls were out on the porch as I came up the walk, and I got a very affectionate greeting from them both. I was amazed again at their striking resemblance.

As we came into the house I could see the dining room table was set, and I smelled the aroma of baking turkey stuffed with a spicy dressing. There was a small tree in the living room with decorations, colored lights, and several presents underneath. The house was warm and cheery, and I knew this was going to be a good day.

Jill came in with hot Tom and Jerrys. We all took one, and wished each other a Merry Christmas. Niki said it would be another hour before the turkey was done, and now would be a good time to open the presents. I remembered the champagne I brought, excused myself, and went for it and the two wrapped bottles of perfume in the car. I asked Niki to put the champagne into the refrigerator to chill. When no one was looking, I slipped the two small presents under the tree.

I was seated in the big easy chair, and Niki did the honors with the presents. Jill sat on the arm of the chair with her arm resting on my shoulder.

The girls had each given the other peignoirs. Jill's was black and Niki's blue. There were two presents for me—a silk lounging robe and bedroom slippers. Niki found the perfume and both were appreciative. I let the girls know how much I liked the robe and slippers, and stated that after dinner I was going to model them.

Niki went to check the turkey; Jill mixed some more Tom and Jerrys, and by the time they were finished the turkey was done. It wasn't a large bird and I carved right at the table. The meat was moist and tender and the dressing excellent. As soon as we had all been served, Jill brought the champagne and filled the glasses. It was a relaxed meal and a happy one. After dinner the combination of lack of sleep, champagne, and a full stomach, was getting to me.

I told them, "I really have to stretch out for a few minutes."

I slipped off my shoes, then the jumper and stretched out on the sofa. I closed my eyes and was just drifting off when I heard the girls giggling. They were sitting on the floor with the sofa as a backrest and our heads close together. They each had a glass of champagne and didn't seem at all sleepy. I drifted off again and then was partially awakened by the pressure of soft full lips on mine. It was nice but I refused to release my grip on this pleasant nap. Soon the lips were removed and I slipped deeper into sleep. Again there were lips on mine and I felt my hold on sleep in danger. These lips were moist and determined and I could feel an involuntary reaction. Just before I woke enough to open my eyes, those lips also withdrew. When my eyes did finally open, they both acted like giggling schoolgirls caught in a prank. I was feeling better and I knew I might have to give up on more sleep.

I tried to think of something they both might like to do, when I remembered the Christmas dance.

On an impulse I asked, "Jill, how long has it been since you have been out dancing?" I could see her eyes light up.

"Much too long, Jack"

"Girls, there is a special Christmas dance at the Ballroom, with Stan Kenton. If I were to show up with both of you, I'd be the envy of every serviceman there. Would you like to go?"

I could tell the idea had instant appeal. They both said yes and then tried to decide what to wear. They were discussing this on their way to get ready. I closed my eyes and returned to my disrupted nap. It was a good one this time, until two lovely ladies all dressed up for a night out awakened me.

"Jack, please wake up," Niki implored. "It's after nine o'clock."

"Give me a couple minutes," I replied, and headed for the bathroom. A face full of cold water wiped away the last traces of sleep and I was ready.

As we drove to the dance I laid down a few ground rules. They could dance with whomever they pleased, and so could I. If either of them was given a bad time they were to call me immediately. Whenever they were ready to leave, so was I.

They both agreed this sounded fair, and when we entered the ballroom it did give my ego a boost to arrive with two beautiful women. However, I quickly discovered keeping them was another matter.

A sailor approached from one side; a marine from the other, each hoping the one he asked was the extra. In a moment I was standing there by myself, as both Niki and Jill waved goodbye.

I watched them for a few minutes, and when I saw all was well, I gave the rest of the dance my attention. It was quickly apparent there were a lot more fellas here than last time. That was all right. I had a pretty good edge!

I was still a little concerned about Niki, remembering her unhappiness the last time. I had no idea how Jill would handle this so I decided to wait before I got involved elsewhere. The dance was over soon, and I noticed both girls' partners were sticking close. Everyone looked happy so I felt safe in going exploring.

The music started before I could find one exciting enough to pursue. Both Niki and Jill were back on the floor so I found a seat at the bar. I did notice an attractive young lady in the adjoining seat, and we both turned, watching the dance floor. The music ended, and soon Stan began a ballad I really enjoyed. I saw Niki and Jill were still on the floor, so I relaxed with my beer.

"What's the matter, sailor, don't you dance?" came from the gal sitting next to me.

I didn't care for her tone of voice, so replied, "This is the first dance I've been too."

"You're really serious," she said incredulously, "I thought all sailors could dance."

"My case is a little different; I came into the Navy directly from Father

Flanagan's Boy's Town. I never even talked to a girl until recently, and that was to order a hamburger."

"I can't believe it!" she exclaimed, "What are you doing here at a dance?"

"Some sailors from the base dropped me here, and said to hitch-hike back. Is dancing hard to learn?"

"Sailor, we are about to find out."

Taking my hand, she led me toward the dance floor. As I stood at the edge, she placed my hand on her waist and took my other in hers.

"Now just relax and let your body sway to the music, the rest will come later."

We got a pretty good sway going, and soon I noticed we were much closer. I took a few deep breaths, and she asked, "What's the matter, sailor?"

"Nothing, except, well, being this close to a girl is affecting my breathing."

"Don't let it bother you sailor, girls aren't all that much different."

Soon we were even closer. Fortunately, she was reasonably tall, and it was amazing how quickly I was learning to dance. The music ended, and she said, "Sailor, I'm proud of you; you're doing exceptionally well."

"I wish holding you close didn't make me so nervous. They never told me about this at Boy's Town."

"All you need is confidence, as soon as you get accustomed to it, you'll relax and enjoy dancing. I'll show you on the next one."

The music began, and I was glad it was another easy one. This time we ended up in my favorite cheek-to-cheek position, with her arm around my neck. It was surprising how rapidly my dancing was improving.

"See," she exclaimed happily, "all you needed was self-confidence."

"You're wonderful," I answered, "You've changed my whole life. How can I ever thank you?"

"I may think of something," she murmured.

When the dance ended, we returned to the bar hand in hand. I quickly checked for Jill and Niki, and finally saw them standing together with their backs to me. I suspected they might be searching for me, so I thanked my instructress again for my new confidence, and told her I was now going out to try my wings. I received the impression she really didn't think I was ready to fly yet, and I know she was watching as I headed for my blondes. I came up behind them, and slipped an arm around each waist.

"Jack, we were looking for you; where have you been?" queried Niki.

"Over at the bar feeling sorry for myself, while you two neglected me."

"Don't believe him, Niki. I saw Jack on the floor, and he sure didn't look neglected!" Jill exclaimed.

To change the subject, I asked if they would like something to drink while the band was on break. Soon we were at a table, some distance from my former tutor.

I didn't need to ask if they were enjoying themselves. The heightened color of their beautiful skin and their sparkling eyes was response enough. The waitress brought our drinks, and Niki asked, "Jack, when are you and I going to get a dance?"

"Just as soon as you are free. I've been patiently waiting."

"You've never danced with me," Jill chimed in.

"Be patient, Jill, everything comes to she who waits."

The band began again with some good music, and I quickly took Niki's hand as I saw a marine headed our way. As we reached the floor, I noticed he had Jill in tow.

Niki was much more relaxed than last time. She came right into my favorite position.

I asked, "Niki, what happened to the unhappy girl, I met here a couple weeks ago?"

"I'm not sure, I think having you and Jill here has made the difference. I'm having a wonderful time, and I'm not worried at all."

Just to prove it, she turned her face up and gave me a quick kiss.

When the music ended we returned to the table, and in a moment the marine delivered Jill. The next one was a fast jitterbug, and I wasn't unhappy when a sailor asks Niki. Jill and I slid our chairs closer together to watch. Niki and the sailor were very good, and I could tell Jill was pleased to see Niki enjoying herself.

"Jack, the idea of coming to this dance was a stroke of genius. It's just what Niki and I needed. It's been a long time since I have felt carefree and happy, and just look at Niki. You're good for us, Jack"

"You're good for me, Jill. This is going to be a Christmas to remember."

The fast one ended, and when Stan got going on a romantic ballad, I reached for Jill, and told her the moment had arrived. She must have been watching Niki and I dance, because she came right into my favorite position. This was where any similarity between dancing with Jill and Niki ended. Dancing with Jill was a sensual, standing, seduction. She followed my every move like we were wearing the same skin. I was conscious of the pressure of two firm breasts, and by shifting a little; she had my leg between hers. A little experimentation soon developed an erotic dance variation to take full advantage of this unique position. We didn't attempt to talk, it was all body language, and it should have been censored! It was a good thing the dance ended when it did.

We reached the table, and I needed a cold beer. The first glass helped bring my blood pressure back down, and Jill was finishing her cocktail.

"Jack, I'm sorry, that wasn't fair. I didn't know I could still get carried away."

"Don't apologize, Jill. It was the most sensational dance of my life. You may have changed my dance style completely."

The music began again, and Jill was off with one of her former partners. Niki was still with hers so I went to the bar for another beer. I found a seat and noticed my instructress was no longer there. When this dance ended, she was returned by a marine, and seemed surprised to see me.

"Well, sailor, I thought you were still out on the floor, making love to all the blondes."

"Not me! All I've been doing is what you told me to—gaining confidence."

"At the rate you've been going you should have your share by now. What did you tell those two blondes?"

"Only what I told you; that this is my first time with girls. They did mention they were willing to help further my education."

"I'll bet, come on, sailor, this is my training program."

She then proceeded to demonstrate, there was more to dancing than just dancing. I still had a head of steam from the dance with Jill, so the demonstration was definitely an erotic success. She looked a little flustered as we returned to the bar.

It was getting near the end of the dance, and I started looking for Niki and Jill. My instructress saw this; I never did get her name, and asked, "Are you looking for those two blondes?"

"Yes," I answered, "I was supposed to meet them before the dance ended."

"Why?"

"I'm not really sure; they said they had something in mind, something about furthering my education and showing me what I have been missing. Oh, there they are now!" I said, and thanked her again as I left.

It was the last dance, and I got to Niki ahead of a soldier.

"Jack, I thought you had deserted me."

"Never, Niki, you have been hard to catch."

She came in close and said, "Jack, this has been a wonderful evening. I don't know when I've had such a good time. I hope you did, too."

"It's been interesting," I replied. "Have you seen Jill?"

We watched as we danced, and soon I saw Jill dancing with a tall marine. We relaxed and enjoyed the rest of the dance. As we wandered toward the exit we could see Jill in deep conversation with the marine. It was obvious he was asking her to come with him. I didn't know what she might want to do, so we paused briefly as we passed. Jill saw us, and I heard her tell the marine good night. Then she took my other arm. The marine just shook his head, as I departed with a lovely blonde on each arm. We were just going down the outside steps, when I saw my instructress standing where we would have to walk by.

The girls and I had our arms intertwined by now, and as we passed, she scowled at the blondes and said, "You should be ashamed of yourselves."

I kept them going, and as soon as we are out of hearing, Jill asked, "What was that all about?"

"Obviously a case of mistaken identity," I replied, "unless you girls have been misbehaving."

Jill had a suspicious look on her face, but didn't say any more.

The girls chattered all the way home about the dance and it was pleasant to drive, listening to their happy voices. I wished I could pigeonhole my relationship to these two lovely women. Right now it seemed to be a mixture of father, husband, and maybe lover. There was a word for that which I didn't care for. I reluctantly decided there could be all kinds of unfortunate repercussions unless that last category was held in abeyance. What this threesome needed was a strong father figure!

We arrived back at the house, and I could still smell the turkey. Niki read my mind, and was soon fixing cold turkey sandwiches with cranberry sauce. While she did this, Jill fixed my bed on the sofa, and got some good music on the radio. There was enough cold champagne left for a glass each, which went great with the turkey.

Jill remembered that I had promised to model the dressing robe. While they were finishing in the kitchen, I went to the living room, slipped out of my uniform and into the robe and slippers. After being in a uniform so long the smooth silk felt good.

The girls came out, reclined on my sofa bed, and watched as I put on a little show, like one of those New York models. I got a round of applause, and told them it was their turn. They accept the challenge, retired to their bedrooms, and in a short time returned in their peignoirs.

Niki went first, and her lovely slim body was exceptionally graceful as she whirled and turned. The blue peignoir did things for her blonde hair, and it was a delightful combination. When she finished Jill and I applauded, and she sat beside me to watch Jill.

Jill's presentation was something else. The combination of black peignoir, blond hair, and superb ripe figure, were breathtaking just standing still. When she went into the model moves, it was even more exciting.

The radio music shifted to a racy beat, and Jill couldn't resist. She went into a burlesque routine that could cause heart failure. At the end she had the outer portion removed, and was swinging it in time to the music, a la Gypsy Rose Lee. Niki and I were enthusiastically applauding, as she collapsed beside me on the sofa. I told them now I knew how a Turkish sultan felt, with his troupe of dancing girls.

It was a relaxed happy feeling, and it was also three in the morning.

Niki yawned, "I don't know about you two, but I'm tired and sleepy." She turned, gave me a good night kiss, and murmured, "good night all," as she retreated to her bedroom.

"Jack, I must go too; help me up, please," Jill asked.

I struggled up from the low sofa, took Jill's hands, and pulled her to a standing position. She came into my arms for a good night kiss, and then as it changed, brought her arms around my neck. Mine went around her waist and pulled her close. There wasn't much to the inner portion of the peignoir, and anywhere I put my hands seemed to be only Jill. They had just naturally started drifting downward, when I heard Niki's door start to open, and Jill and I stepped apart. Niki muttered something about, "You two still up?" and continued on to the bathroom.

I think in a way Jill and I were relieved. She whispered, "Saved by the bell," and scooted for her bedroom. I shed my robe and slippers, stretched out on the sofa in just my shorts, and tried to get my breathing under control. Niki staggered back to her bedroom, and finally I drifted off to sleep.

It was late the next morning before we got going. When I found they had hot-cake flour, I volunteered to cook breakfast. Niki got the coffee brewing and soon I was turning out hot cakes and fried eggs. This was one meal I enjoyed cooking. We sat lazily over the second cup of coffee deciding what to do next. The girls knew in a few hours I would have to leave, and when they found I had never been to Hollywood, we went on a tour.

We drove down Hollywood Boulevard, stopped at Grauman's Chinese Theater to view the star's footprints in the cement, passed several studios, and then drove to the residential area where many stars lived. Niki had been there before, and acted as a guide. She put on a spiel for each star, and seemed to have the latest information. We ended up at the Hollywood Bowl, and it was then time to return.

I thanked the girls for the great Christmas, and decided to leave my Christmas gifts there—they insisted I stay with them whenever I returned. When I kissed them goodbye, this time it was just a warm, friendly one from Jill.

I still wasn't sure how my relationship with these two lovely women was going to turn out, and what was even worse—I was beginning to feel a sense of responsibility for the outcome.

FOURTEEN

Wednesday evening, I called Cleo and was happy to hear her answer the phone.

"Cherie."

"Ravel?"

"Oui, ma chere."

"Oh Ravel, it's good to hear your voice. I've missed you."

"Me also, Cleo"

"Ravel, you won't believe this, but I met two of your commanders at Caliente, when I was there with Mario and Linda. I knew you'd be glad I invited them to our New Year's Eve party."

"Eet was big of you, Cleo."

"You will be here, won't you Ravel? Remember, New Year's Eve is just two more days."

"I wouldn't miss eet, ma chere. I have something very special for you from, 'Le Grand Charles'."

"Oh Ravel!"

"Cleo, shall I meet you at the apartment or the hotel?"

"Please come by the apartment, and Linda asked if you would bring Mario?"

"What time?"

"Eight would be just fine."

"Bonsoir, ma petite. I weal see you then."

"Bonsoir, Ravel."

The next morning, I reminded Mario we were to be at the apartment at eight on Friday, and in the afternoon I went shopping.

I stopped at an exclusive uniform shop, and went to the department where there were cases of medals from all countries. In the French section I located one about the size of a fifty-cent piece, in the shape of a cross. There were intricate designs on all four arms in gold, and two French words in the center, which I couldn't decipher. It was suspended from a narrow, tri-colored sash and was impressive.

The clerk didn't know what the medal was for, but he believed it had something to do with the French Foreign Legion. I ordered the medal, and a black, satin lined case, with a blank, gold, inscription strip inside. I had to wait for the special inscription. I thought the inscriber was regarding me rather intently as I quickly departed.

Friday Mike and Sammy came out to the flight line, and smugly let me know Cleo had invited them to a New Year's Eve party that night, in the ballroom of one of San Diego's finest hotels. I appeared properly impressed, and didn't mention I had a room reservation there for Mr. and Mrs. Jack Barnes. I believe one of the reasons for our rather strained friendship, other than the convertible and Cleo, was they hadn't received their second stripe yet.

Mario and I met that evening and drove to the girls' apartment. Cleo seemed delighted to see me, and I noticed she was wearing her new cocktail dress. Mario and Linda had obviously progressed considerably since I last saw them together. The girls had mixed drinks ready and a beer for me. I was a little curious about tonight's party. Cleo explained the company she worked for gave all the employees, mostly office girls, two tickets to this party. Everything was included: dinner, drinks, favors, and noisemakers. They did it every year to help keep their employees happy. Some of the girls were those who attended the bash with the Free French, that memorable first night. Two girls agreed to be the dates of Mike and Sammy when Cleo mentioned they were in the same operation. The French really made an impression.

When it was time to leave, Mario and Linda took Linda's car, and we met at the hotel.

Mike and Sammy were waiting in the lobby, and appeared chagrined, to see Cleo and I together. I knew exactly what erotic fantasies they had conjured up for after the party.

Cleo explained that her two friends would be arriving soon with their tickets. These were two of the girls from that long ago French evening, and both recognized me. I got a couple of hugs, and then Cleo made the introductions. They were both pretty girls with outgoing personalities, and soon Mike and Sammy were looking more cheerful.

We all strolled into the rapidly filling ballroom, where Cleo searched for and found a long table with her company's name. Our group filled one complete end. A friendly cocktail waitress, with a very short skirt and good legs, took our drink order and we were busy trying on and exchanging party hats. The first round appeared, the orchestra started up, and the party was off and rolling. There were menus already at each setting and the selection was turkey, ham or beef. Cleo and I chose beef with a glass of good Cabernet wine as a complement.

With our order in, we headed for the dance floor. It had been a while since we had been close and I had been looking forward to this. Cleo remembered my favorite position and I murmured a few French endearments to be sure her motor was running. It was! Yes, this was going to be the evening I had been waiting for!

At the next break I excused myself, and hurriedly got the medal and my shaving kit from the car. I picked up my room key at the desk, and deposited those items in the room.

Dinner was just being served as I returned and it tasted even better with the Cabernet. Cleo and I were feeling very French so we switched to champagne in between dances. I noticed Mike and Sammy were getting on well with their dates. There was no question about Mario and Linda. This reminded me I hadn't clued Mario in on my plans. I got him aside and explained unless something went very wrong, the apartment would be his tonight. Mario's dark eyes flashed and I know he got the message.

It was approaching midnight, and as Cleo and I were dancing in a very intimate embrace she whispered in my ear, "Ravel?"

"Oui, ma Petite."

"You said something about, 'Le Grand Charles', and a presentation.

"I have not forgotten. My instructions are to make the presentation immediately after midnight, and een complete secrecy. 'Le Grand Charles', does not want to compromise your covair."

"Oh, Ravel!"

"Remember, cheri, right after midnight, you and I sleep out the side door to the lobby."

Just as the dance ended the orchestra broke into Auld Lang Syne, and our embrace turned into a passionate kiss. While the celebration was going on, Cleo and I slipped out the side door, and proceeded through the lobby to the elevator. My room was near the top and as we entered, I left the lights off and pulled open the drapes of the large, picture window. The lights of the city partially illuminated the spacious room, and we stood there for a moment admiring the view. I turned on the tiny lamp on the dresser, and reached for the small, gift-wrapped bottle of Chanel perfume.

"Ma chere, I am desolate to be late with your Christmas present."

I handed her the gift. She quickly opened the wrapping, and was delighted that it was French perfume.

"Now, ma chere, on direct orders of 'Le Grand Charles', I am to make the presentation."

I reached for the medal case on the dresser and started to open it. Cleo was so excited she could hardly wait for the lid to be lifted. As she saw the medal, resting on the black satin, over the folded French tri-color sash, and the inscription in French on bright metal below, she was beside herself.

I translated the inscription, "To Cleo, For Meritorious Service" and just below it was signed, 'Le Grand Charles'.

"Ravel, 'Le Grand Charles', is that really Charles De Gaulle?"

"Oui, ma chere. You see, thees is the Meritorious Service Medal, and is to be presented only to heroes of La Belle France. Because of thees he must use hees other name. 'Le Grand Charles', has made this special presentation because of your heroic action een Mexico"

"Oh, Ravel,"

I continued, "Because of thees he requests you wear the medal only next to your heart, nevar where hees enemies might see eet."

I removed the medal from the case, unfolded the attached tri-color sash and started to slip it over her head.

"Oh no!" I exclaimed.

"Ravel, what's the matter?"

"Ah, Cheri, I was about to commit the big indiscretion. This medal ees to be worn only next to your warm, bare skin."

Cleo turned her back and leaned her head forward to expose the zipper for me. As she slipped out of the dress, I was happy to see that beneath was mostly Cleo. Her journey to the closet in high heels, silk hose and garter belt was inspiring.

Cleo returned to the large oval mirror in the center of the low dressing table, and I stood behind her with the medal. We both watched in the mirror as I slipped the sash over her head. The medal complimented her golden suntan, however, there was one discordant note; it overlapped her black, lace bra.

"Cheri, we have the problem."

"I know."

"Shall I?"

"Please do."

I unsnapped the bra and watched as she removed it. The medal was now nestled between perky, conical breasts, and Cleo was turning this way and that in admiration. This, combined with the remaining high heels, silk hose and garter belt, made me fear it was going to be all over before it hardly got started. Cleo came prepared for secret agent action—unhindered by panties.

"Cleo, eef you would put on a little of the Chanel, I will feel like I am back in Paree."

As Cleo placed drops of perfume in appropriate places I slipped out of my clothes. It took several torrid kisses to get Cleo's mind off the medal, and to an area that desperately needed her attention. I murmured French endearments, and remembering Monte's crash course, I took special pains not to disgrace the French with my first effort as a lover. This was fortunate, because at the crucial moment Cleo realized there was a lot of me, and became a little concerned.

"Ah, Cheri, a secret agent must be prepared for anything that comes up. I know you can do eet."

When Cleo discovered she had unplumbed depths, she relaxed and let her passionate nature have full reign.

Daylight was creeping through the window before I realized somewhere along the line I had overdone it. Cleo was insatiable!

I staggered to the bathroom and pulled on my clothes.

"Ravel, where are you going?"

"I have a meeting I must keep. Eet breaks my heart to leave you but duty calls. You were sensational. I will call you for the next mission."

I made it to the elevator—a mere shell of my former self!

I thought longingly of my bunk and sleep as I drove toward the air station. I remembered driving under the camouflage netting at Consolidated Aircraft, and woke with one wheel in the gutter and the other on the sidewalk—mowing down young palm trees. I watched in a detached sort of way, as the second went down, the third, the forth. Oh-oh, there came the pedestrian, traffic signal light. The Ford took the light with the right front fender, the light came apart in sections, with a bright arc as the wiring shorted out. The top portion with the lights crashed through the canvas roof of the convertible, and landed in the seat beside me.

This stopped the car, and I just sat there, dazedly staring at my new passenger. We hardly had time to get acquainted before a San Diego Police car pulled up beside me.

The two officers walked around the car, checking the damage, then looked back at the four downed palm trees, and the remains of the traffic signal.

"What happened sailor—go to sleep?"

My mind finally shifted into gear. "GO TO SLEEP! Didn't you catch the black sedan that forced me off the road?"

The officers looked at each other, then each way on the deserted street.

"What black sedan?"

By then I was out of the Ford, and looking at the damage. I felt sick. The palm trees had wiped out the bumper, grill, radiator and fan, the traffic light had finished the right fender and top.

"The one who forced me off the road and caused all this damage," I replied. "If you let him get away, who is going to pay for all this?" I waved at the damage to the front of the Ford. They were looking at the palm trees and traffic light, as if they were wondering who was going to pay for them.

One officer was writing this all down in a black notebook; the other was calling for a wrecker on his radio. When the wrecker arrived I told the driver to take it to the Ford garage. I removed my shaving kit, and talked the officers into driving me to the bus station.

Their last words were, "You will be hearing from the city!"

FIFTEEN

Monday began as usual at the flight line. With the completion of the turret training program, Fred was now flying the twin engine SNB on a morning shuttle to Long Beach. He was transporting new electronic parts, which were being installed in all the B-24s.

As I watched his take-off, I wasn't too happy to see it was carrier-style. When Fred reached flying speed, instead of pulling up, he retracted the wheels. This brought props dangerously close to the runway and if he miscalculated, he was going to hit two props and possibly crash the airplane.

Suddenly I heard over the loudspeaker, "Jack Barnes report to the tower on the double!"

It was repeated about every thirty seconds and I knew I had trouble. I dashed madly up the tower stairs and into the glass cupola. The two traffic controllers were anxiously awaiting my arrival.

"What's the problem?" were my first words.

"The SNB has an emergency," replied one controller. "The pilot asked specifically for you."

My first thought was that Fred got one or both prop tips on his take-off. Fred's voice came over the radio wanting to know if I was there yet.

The controller handed me the mike and I acknowledged.

"This is Jack, Lieutenant. What's the problem?"

"I'm having a little trouble with the landing gear. It's stuck part way up. It won't go up or down."

Well at least the props were still okay. "Lieutenant, are you flying alone?"

"No, I have Lieutenant Hanson flying co-pilot."

I had an idea. "On the deck, just aft of your seats, is a hinged door labeled 'Emergency Gear Handle.' Have Lieutenant Hanson try to crank it down manually."

"Roger, Jack, will get back to you," Fred said as he went off the air.

I returned the mike to the controller, and he continued on with his other arrivals and departures. Soon Fred was back on the radio.

"Jack, we tried manually and it won't budge."

"Okay, Lieutenant, let's try one more thing. Have Lieutenant Hanson take a strain manually in the down position. When he is ready, you pull out of a dive and hit the down, electric gear switch. Maybe the three together will break it loose."

"Wilco, Jack"

While this was taking place, the glass—enclosed tower had been filling. The Base Commander and Fire Marshal were both there, as well as several officers I didn't know.

Fred called back, "We tried them all at once, Jack, and still no change."

"Okay, Lieutenant. I need a low, slow fly-by. Hold it just a minute."

I suddenly realized I was a little low in rank to be taking over control of the tower. I turned to the officers congregated behind me and held out the mike, "Would someone else like to take over?"

No response, so I turned to the Base Commander.

"With your permission, Sir, I am going to ask Lieutenant Robinson to make a very close fly-by. I need to look into the nacelles to see what's wrong."

"Permission granted, Jack."

I turned to the controller and suggested he suspend operations until this phase was over. I didn't want Fred running into anyone. He seemed relieved at the suggestion and closed the field.

"Hello, Lieutenant, we are ready for the fly-by. I am going to use the binoculars, so come by about one hundred feet out on a gentle port bank. This should give me the right angle."

"Wilco, Jack, I'm approaching now."

Fred came by at the prescribed angle but the binoculars were so powerful I couldn't keep them focused on the inside of the wheel nacelle.

"Hello, Lieutenant."

"Roger, Jack"

"The binoculars won't work. This next one needs to be as close as you can put it without getting the tower. Same angle."

I turned to the officers, "Knowing Lieutenant Robinson, this one is going to be in our laps. There is still time to leave the tower."

There was considerable foot shuffling but no one wanted to go first. It was then too late. Fred brought it in so close I could almost reach out and touch the gear and in that brief instant I saw what was wrong.

After the tower quit rocking, I called Fred, "I found the trouble, Lieutenant. The torque tube on the port gear is bent and the sliding collar is hung up at the bend. I'll bet the starboard is also."

With all the brass behind me, I didn't want to accuse Fred of starting to retract the gear too soon after commencing his carrier style take-off. The weight of the plane on the partially retracted gear is what would have caused the damage. I knew this was the only possible explanation, and I suspected Fred knew all along what he had done.

"Lieutenant, I believe if you land very carefully, the gear will stay where it is. I'm trying to figure a way to save the props. Any elevation of the nose will make a big difference."

"Roger, Jack. Will do my best."

"Lieutenant, I'm turning you over to the controller now, good luck."

I suspected if the landing gear wasn't so fragile, Fred would have shut off the engines and brought it in dead stick, with the props positioned out of the way. He liked doing weird things like that.

The controller and the fire marshal conferred over where to place the fire trucks and crash wagon. Then Fred called in, saying he was making a pass. I asked the controller to request he shut off the engines immediately upon touchdown and not to use the brakes; just leave it sit and we would tow it in. I asked the other controller to have a tug with a tow bar, stand by. I didn't want to tie up the main runway any longer than necessary.

Fred made the first pass, experimenting with landing in a nose high position. The SNB lands normally on the main gear with the tail high in the air and the nose down. Not only did he have to land nose high to clear the props, but also he couldn't bounce without collapsing the gear. It wasn't going to be easy. Fred wasn't satisfied with his first pass. I watched with the binoculars and the second pass looked better. He still wasn't satisfied.

The third pass I could tell, Fred was coming in. I focused the binoculars on the starboard prop. As Fred flared out and gently touched the main gear, I didn't see any sparks. He immediately chopped the engines which brought the tail down even more, and let it coast to the side of the runway. I heaved a sigh of relief, and turned to leave the tower.

The Base Commander was standing by the stairs. "Well done, Jack, my congratulations."

"Thank you, Sir. I'm glad Lieutenant Robinson was doing the flying."

"So am I, Jack. Oh, by the way, if you should find out how that torque tube got bent, I'd like to know."

"Yes, Sir," I replied, and beat a hasty retreat.

By the time I got to the line shack, Fred and his co-pilot were arriving by jeep.

"Did you save the props, Fred?" I anxiously asked.

"Never touched them, Jack. How did you like that last fly-by?"

"I liked it fine. I'm not too sure about the Commander."

Fred didn't look very happy hearing this news. "You mean he was in the tower?"

"Sure was, along with half the brass on the base."

"Uh-oh."

"By the way, Fred, the Commander wants a report on the
Bent torque tubes."

"Damn! Do the best you can, Jack. It won't happen again."

"I will. That was a great landing."

The SNB was now being towed to the line by the tow tug, and I showed the driver where to park it. I had to check the prop tips myself to be satisfied. Any time a moving prop hits something solid, it puts an internal strain on the engine. This meant removing the engine, tearing it completely apart, and magnifluxing all moving parts for cracks. It was a major and time-consuming job.

I wasn't about to crawl under the wheel nacelles until Mario, John and Eddie had jacks underneath and raised the plane into flying position. This completed, I quickly check the nacelles and it was as I had seen from the tower. Both tubes were bent, however; there was no other sign of damage.

The Lead Chief showed up and wanted to know if we could repair it here, or should it go to base shops. The Commander had called him, and wanted it back in service as quickly as possible. I thought it odd that the chief was asking me. This was his responsibility.

"You get two new torque tubes, Chief, and we'll have them installed in one day," I optimistically declared.

The Chief believed me, and located the tubes at the Naval Air Station on North Island. Fred would pick them up in the SNJ early tomorrow morning.

I got Mario aside, and explained he and Eddie would take one gear, and John and I the other. We crawled into the nacelle and I showed Mario exactly what would need to be done to get the old tubes out. It was not going to be easy, because of the way the sliding collar was jammed over the bend. After my rash promise to the chief, we spent the rest of the day removing bent tubes.

Early next morning, Fred arrived with the new torque tubes, and my crew got busy installing them. When we finished, I moved to the cockpit, retracting and lowering the gear. We gave it one final check, then lowered the jacks and placed the plane back on active status.

Tuesday, the first thing I did was to check my insurance policy. I was aghast to find Roger had only the car covered—no liability and property damage. I knew I should have checked when we transferred the policy. The car had a fifty-dollar deductible policy so I called the Ford garage and told them to fix it. The price they quoted was almost as much as I had paid for the car! They let me know it would take several weeks to get the parts and probably a month in total. I told them to get started as soon as the insurance company gave the ok. I would sign papers as soon as I got to town. I was trying to visualize how much four young palm trees and a traffic light might cost and the total was frightening.

Early in the afternoon the lead Chief came by and said I was to report to the legal office at fifteen hundred hours, and to bring any insurance papers I had. I didn't like the sound of that.

I reported promptly, the legal officer, a former Philadelphia lawyer, showed me the letter and bill from the City of San Diego. They had placed a value of three hundred fifty dollars each on the palm trees, and five hundred on the traffic light. With a few other incidentals it came to over two thousand dollars.

The legal officer appeared sympathetic and asked me to give him all the facts. I was careful to pick a safe beginning point, and explained what really happened, including my improbable story about the black sedan. The subject of insurance came up and I could tell he wasn't pleased with my lack of coverage.

When all the facts have been divulged he stood there massaging his chin and said, "Jack, you have trouble."

Great! I wish he would tell me something I didn't know.

"However, that black sedan may help."

"Oh?'

"It all depends if there are witnesses," he continued. "If the city can't prove negligence on your part, I believe we can stall indefinitely. Maybe even beat it."

I begin to feel better.

"However..."

"Uh-oh."

"I definitely recommend your immediate transfer somewhere else, preferably overseas."

Ouch! Just when I had all my ducks in a row—Jan, Cleo, the convertible and Caliente.

"Let me call the Commander and get his thoughts," he continued.

I sat there, listened to one side of the phone conversation, and the portion I heard didn't sound good. Finally he hung up and said, "The Commander would like you to meet with him in his office right away."

I thanked the legal officer for his help, and headed for the Commander's office.

"Come in, Jack," greeted me as soon as I entered the outer room.

The Commander waved me to a chair. He had a handful of official looking Navy documents, and was just finishing reading the last one.

"Jack, I'm sorry about this. I'm sincerely going to miss you on the flight line."

My heart sank.

"You have done an exceptional job, and I am placing a letter of commendation in your record."

"Thank you, Sir," I meekly replied.

"I have been going over these special requests, and there is one that should fit the bill."

"Which one is that, Sir?"

"This one here and he removed the one at the top." A new seaplane tender has just come off the ways and is being outfitted at San Pedro. They need an Aviation Machinist Mate with automotive engine experience."

"Automotive engine experience?" I replied like I never heard those words before.

"You know, Jack, like those car engines you work on behind the line shack."

"Oh. Yes, Sir." I didn't know he knew about that.

"I'm notifying them of your immediate availability. I would suggest you wind up any personal matters promptly. Your orders will be cut for Friday."

"Thank you, Sir."

"Jack, do you have any recommendations for the flight line?"

"Yes, Sir, I do. Mario is fully qualified to take charge of the line. I recommend him highly. Seaman Eddie Hodges is developing into an excellent mechanic, and would be the logical choice for the next third class slot."

"Thank you, Jack, I'll mention that to the Lead Chief. Good luck on your next assignment."

"Thank you for your help, Sir. I do appreciate it." With that I threw a snappy salute and departed.

In the morning I broke the news to the flight line, let Mario and Eddie know my recommendations, and informed Mario until he received further word, the flight line was his.

I caught the bus to town, signed the necessary papers for the Ford repairs and tied up my other loose ends in San Diego.

When I got back to the base I made arrangements at the bank for my savings account to remain there, and to make future deposits by mail.

That evening I called Cleo and told her I was off on an important assignment and would call as soon as I returned.

I felt badly that Jan and I would not have the opportunity to get better acquainted. I called and told her so, explaining most of what happened, and thanked her again for saving my life. I then felt I had done all that could be done, and the next morning I was on the bus to San Pedro.

SIXTEEN

I had orders to report to Warrant Officer Simmons, in charge of the gasoline detail on the seaplane tender. I located the shipyard at San Pedro, then the ship, and last the dock shack where the gasoline detail had its office. Warrant Officer Simmons was behind the desk, so I introduced myself and handed over my orders.

"Oh, you're the aircraft mechanic with automotive experience. I didn't know they were sending a kid. Check your gear in at the barracks and report back here."

This was not starting out well at all. Warrant Simmons reminded me of the banty rooster Mexican cop that punched my nose. He looked different; middle thirties, thinning hair, slim, with broken facial blood vessels indicative of a heavy drinker, but his attitude was the same. I bit my tongue and didn't reply.

Simmons waved his hand in the general direction of a group of buildings, and went back to his paper work. I made some inquiries, located the right barracks, and found the gasoline detail bunked at one end of the lower deck. They were listening to a radio, reading and sleeping, in that order.

I introduced myself, "Hi, I'm Jack Barnes, the new aircraft mech from Dago."

This stirred a little interest in the two who were awake. The one with the radio turned it down and said, "Hi, I'm Steve, this is Will," the one with the book waved, "and our sleeping member is Ted."

Ted woke up and Steve ran through the introductions again.

I liked Steve right away. He appeared to be a couple of years older than me, medium height, built like a wrestler, and with a friendly, outgoing personality. I instinctively recognized a kindred spirit.

Will was about the same age, wore glasses, and judging by the title of the book he was poring over, was the studious type.

Ted reminded me of Slim, down in Florida. A tall, skinny, southern boy with that drawl I had learned to like. We were all second class, Aviation Machinist Mates.

"Doesn't look like the duty is too tough here," I commented.

"We have liberty every night." Steve moaned. "Unfortunately we are all broke. You wouldn't have any extra?" he asked hopefully.

"Sorry, I'm in the same boat," I cautiously replied.

I remembered I was to report back to the Warrant, so I asked, "How are you getting along with Warrant Simmons?"

"No problem—once you get him figured out. Just listen to his sea stories about what a great lover he is, and you'll get along fine. If you laugh or even smile, you're in trouble."

"Thanks, Steve. I'd better report back there now."

I headed back to the shack, where Simmons had finished his paper work, and was reading a girlie magazine. He leaned back in the swivel chair and asked, "Well, Kid, did you find the barracks?"

I really hated being called *Kid*. "No problem, Sir."

"Forget the 'Sir'. Just call me Warrant. The engineering officer wants to see you aboard ship," and he waved his arm in that direction.

I located the ship, which viewed in profile was an impressive sight—larger than I expected. The aft half looked like an aircraft carrier, with a massive crane mounted on the aft starboard quarter. Forward of the flight deck was an enclosed hanger—large enough to receive a twin engine, flying boat. Forward she looked like an attack transport, mounting five-inch guns.

The gangway was easy to locate and I went aboard. Where the gangway ended, at the forward part of the flight deck, there was activity everywhere. Electrical cables draped over the side and snaked down each ladder to the lower decks. There, in the eerie glow of arc welding, workmen scurried about. I got the distinct feeling this was a rush job.

I finally located a Lieutenant wearing fatigues, and asked for the engineering officer.

"Oh, Lieutenant Canby, last I saw of him he was down the aft manhole on the flight deck."

I figured that out, and went looking for a manhole cover in the up position at the rear of the flight deck. I located it and peered down. About fifty feet below, at the bottom of the ladder was an officer in fatigues checking lines and valves against an unfolded diagram. I watched for a while and when it began to look as if he might come up, I decided to wait.

Soon, a pleasantly rugged face beneath a soiled officer's hat appeared beside the hatch where I was sitting. I scrambled to my feet and as he straightened out, I saw he was even taller than me. He had those lines beside his eyes that men get when they look into the sun a lot. I threw a salute and said, "Jack Barnes reporting, Sir."

"Barnes, oh, you're the aircraft mechanic with automotive experience."

"Yes, Sir."

"Good, I've been wanting to go over some equipment with you. Let's do it now."

Great, I had been wondering why they needed an automotive mechanic on a seaplane tender. I followed where he led.

We wound our way over the electrical cables and hoses strung across the flight deck, and into the hangar area. The massive doors were open and the interior seemed to go on forever. There was a partial deck above the hangar deck much like a mezzanine in a department store.

Lieutenant Canby led the way up a ladder to a cubicle about ten feet by five feet, along the edge of a catwalk. Here was the answer to the mystery.

It was an ordinary, four-cylinder, automotive engine; however, the exhaust was hooked up to more plumbing than I could believe.

"What did you say your first name was, Barnes?"

"Everyone calls me Jack, Sir."

"Okay, Jack, the gasoline detail's job is to handle, store, and disperse several hundred thousand gallons of aviation fuel and oil. Your specific job is to keep the voids surrounding the fuel tanks fire and explosion proof. This little machine here does it all. You run the exhaust through all these filters and pump it into the voids that surround the fuel tanks. It then has no oxygen and if there should be a fuel leak there won't be an explosion. You will have a complete set of replacement parts for the engine, and once we take on aircraft fuel, it damn well better be kept running until we're recalled or sunk."

All of a sudden the war was getting a lot closer.

"Yes, Sir."

"Jack, I'm sending you to a special school in Seattle that is just starting on this equipment. You will leave in a week. Before you leave, I want you to learn intimately, every tank, pipe, valve, and void in this system."

"Yes, Sir." One thing I could say for this man, he knew what he wanted, and he didn't stutter.

"Here is one set of prints," he handed me the ones he had been checking out. "Now would be a good time to get started."

"Yes, Sir."

I took the prints and got out of sight to study them.

I quickly discovered the aviation fuel storage and handling system on the USS Pine Island were extensive and complicated. When the inert gas system was added, it became chaotic. To familiarize myself with this system in a few days meant up at daylight and working till the evening meal. I thought of the remainder of the detail lying on their bunks, and wondered how I got so lucky.

Occasionally I ran into Lieutenant Canby, and if he had time, he was friendly. I was beginning to realize the responsibility he was carrying to get this ship ready for commissioning and overseas duty.

I had the fuel system pretty well memorized near the end of the allotted time. A few nights before departure for Seattle, I decided to have a beer at a little bar near the shipyard. It was late before I got cleaned up and arrived. The bar was fairly quiet, the jukebox turned down low. I slid into an empty seat at the bar. In the dim light I noticed the person sitting to my right was an officer, but I didn't think any more about it.

I ordered my beer and just got it poured when the officer said, "Good evening, Jack."

I recognized the voice and replied, "Good evening, Lieutenant."

"When we're off the ship, Jack, you can call me Dan."

I glanced over and saw Dan was nursing a highball and reading a letter. This wasn't the same brisk officer I had been working with all week. Dan was really low, and I instinctively felt the letter was the cause.

I finished my beer. He was still rereading the one page so I ordered for both of us.

Dan came out of his gloom long enough to say, "Thanks, Jack," and then sank back in.

I was beginning to get worried. This was the one man that controlled all the machinery on the U.S.S. Pine Island, and knew what it is supposed to do. The thought of him cracking up just as we left for overseas—I didn't want to think about it.

We finished this last one and Dan ordered another round. Before he could escape back into the mental miasma that letter produced, I asked, "Anything I can do to help?"

"I didn't realize it was that obvious, Jack. Thanks."

He paused and then indicated the well-worn letter. "I just found out from my brother that my only daughter married last week. I'd always envisioned being there to give her away, and I didn't even get an invitation."

I could tell he was completely crushed. Once the dike of self-control was broached, it all came pouring out.

Dan had been an officer in the Merchant Marine before the war. It caused a real strain on his marriage so he gave up the sea, and started a marine engineering business in Bremerton, Washington. Unfortunately, it was too late to save the marriage. His wife divorced him, married her lover, and the daughter went with her. About then Pearl Harbor was bombed and Dan returned to the sea—in the Navy this time.

"What happened to your engineering business in Bremerton?"

"It's going full bore. I took my older brother in as a partner, and we have more government contracts than we can handle. I'm trying to get there for a week before we ship out."

I knew if Dan had really wanted to, he could have gotten a national defense deferral. This suggested how badly he had been burned emotionally. Dan perked up when he got talking about the business.

When his daughter was mentioned, he sank back into gloom. I decided a change of subject was in order, and besides, maybe he could help.

"Dan, I have run into a situation I don't know how to handle, and I sure could use some advice."

"I'll try, but right now I'm not making any promises."

"I don't know if there is a solution to this one, but here it is," I continued. "About a month ago at the Ballroom in Southgate I met this lovely young girl about eighteen. She was having emotional difficulties, and when I took her home she invited me to dinner the next day. She and her mother live alone and look like sisters instead of mother and daughter. When you see the two together it's startling."

I took a sip of my beer, and noticing I had Dan's attention, continued.

"Anyway, the next day I arrived, the dinner was great, we got along beautifully. I did find out the husband and father was killed in an automobile accident about a year ago, and the two hadn't completely recovered. They insisted I spend Christmas with them, and I had a great visit."

I paused, and Dan commented with irony in his voice, "Doesn't sound to me like your problem is too serious."

"I'm getting to that," I told him. "I have a feeling, subconsciously; they are placing me in the role of the missing husband and father. I'm placed at the head of the table, and expected to carve the roast. In the living room I'm seated in the husband's lounge chair, and they perch on the arms. It's spooky, Dan. I think the world of these two people, but I'm too young to play the role of a father or husband. I'd like to see them Sunday before I leave for Seattle, but I'm halfway afraid to call."

Dan nodded his head. He was beginning to understand my dilemma.

That was when I made my pitch. "Dan, I know if I call, I'll be invited over for Sunday dinner. What I'd really like to know is what would happen with an older man present? Could I possibly prevail on you to come, if the invitation is offered?"

I knew it was cheeky to invite your engineering officer on a double date, but I needed help!

Dan hesitated, "All right, Jack, but only if I am specifically invited."

Friday I called the girls and they were overjoyed I now was stationed practically in their backyard. As I had anticipated, I was invited to

Sunday dinner. When I mentioned Dan and how badly he felt about his daughter's marriage, they said by all means to invite him.

I passed the word to Dan and Sunday afternoon we were headed for Southgate in Dan's car. I took my hat off and slid down in the seat. I didn't want to get Dan in trouble for fraternizing with an enlisted man. He was a lot more like his old self and I felt better. As we got out of the car, I noticed he picked up a bottle of wine off the back seat.

As usual both girls came to the front porch as we came up the walk. I enjoyed watching Dan's expression as he first saw them together. They looked especially lovely, and it was obvious they had taken extra care with their appearance. I got a kiss from Niki and one from Jill, on the cheek this time, and made the introductions.

The girls were cheerful, and Dan blended right in. He dropped the wine off in the kitchen and we ended up in the living room. I deliberately went in last and just as I hoped, Dan was seated in the big chair. The girls had to hear my sad story of what happened in San Diego, and why I was now at San Pedro. I also broke the news that I was to be in Seattle the next ten days. This seemed to upset Niki.

Jill and Dan got to talking about raising girls. When it was time to check on dinner, I went to the kitchen with Niki. The roast smelled mighty fine.

Niki said, "It won't be long now, Jack. You know I'm going to miss you when you leave for Seattle."

With that she put her arms around my waist and gave me a lingering kiss. I was happy to return it and it got pretty interesting before we returned to the living room.

I saw Jill had a picture album out and was resting on the arm of the chair showing Dan some of Niki's pictures. Soon Niki was on the other arm trying to cover up some early ones that were a little short on clothes. This was one time I didn't mind being excluded. The three look blissfully happy and I suspected Dan was catching up on family life.

When the album was finished, Niki scooted for the kitchen and in a few minutes announced, "Dinner is served."

I was overjoyed to see Dan placed at the head of the table, and inherit the carving job. I got to sit by Niki and relax. Jill thanked Dan for the wine and served. I saw it was a Rosé, which was a good hedge on Dan's part. He had no idea what the entrée might be. The dinner was exceptional as usual. I wondered how long Niki had been doing the cooking.

After dinner, Niki cleared off the table and announced a girl friend gave her a Monopoly game for Christmas and she hadn't had an opportunity to use it yet. She got a little kidding but went right on setting it up. Because of our attitude, she elected herself as banker. It was a good close game, and it took several hours to complete. I was surprised Dan won. I used to be an excellent Monopoly player.

Dan noticed the piano and asked if either played. We discovered from Niki that Jill at one time sang professionally. Jill let us know Niki had inherited her voice. Dan asked the girls for a sample and Jill slipped over to the piano bench. She fooled around with some Gershwin, and then slid into *I'm in the Mood for Love* in a husky contralto.

I wondered if the song choice was an accident. I felt goose bumps on my arms; this lady was an accomplished vocalist. She ran through it once and then Niki joined her on the verse. Niki's voice was the next range higher and when they harmonized, listening was pure pleasure. Jill invited us to join in and I was really sorry I couldn't carry a tune. Dan had a pleasant baritone and it blended nicely. They were having so much fun time slipped by.

Finally, they ran out of songs. Dan glanced at his watch, and we were thanking them both for a grand day. As we left, I gave Niki a goodbye kiss and I noticed Jill gave Dan a quick hug. We were invited to return soon and Dan and I were on our way. I knew things appeared to go well with Dan, but I wasn't prepared for the emotional thanks he gave me for inviting him. He said it was the greatest day he had in years. I told him I was the one that felt obligated. I could already see an improvement in Niki. I let him know I soon had hopes of being accepted as just a boy friend, with no Freudian hang-ups.

When we get back to the ship, it was back to an officer—enlisted man relationship. He wished me well at the school, and added that he was going to check on how I did!

SEVENTEEN

I reported to the gasoline detail shack early the next morning, and was surprised to find the whole crew there with packed seabags. This included Simmons and a new Chief Petty Officer—an older, heavyset man named McGuire.

I discovered there were several phases to the school. I was going to *Inert Gas*. The rest were going to *Fuel Handling and Fire Fighting*.

We caught the Pullman passenger train to Seattle, with a four-hour layover in Portland. At Portland, Simmons and the chief headed for a bar, while we four went exploring.

The train was about to pull out when we discovered the Warrant and Chief were missing. None of us would have been too concerned, except the Warrant had the tickets and orders. The train was due to leave in twelve minutes.

We scattered through the skid row bars and Steve located the two with just minutes to spare. They were both drunk and protesting as we hurried them toward the train. The conductor was just starting to give the go-ahead signal, when he saw us coming and held the train. If this was indicative of our leaders' usual behavior, we were in trouble.

What was even worse, Simmons pounded my ear most of the way to Seattle, telling me what a great lover he was and the connections he had in Seattle. He seemed to have singled me out and keep saying, "When we get to Seattle, Kid, I'm going to show you how it's done."

When we did arrive in Seattle, I discovered the school was on an island out in Puget Sound. It was a half-hour ferry ride just to get there. The island was beautiful, with tall evergreens, summer homes, and a small Navy station.

Our classes started the next day and I knew right away I wouldn't have any trouble. Dan had practically given me the whole course aboard ship. They had an exceptional fire-fighting course with realistic fuel fires, with the students learning to control them quickly. I talked the inert gas instructor into letting me take the two most important days of fire fighting.

We had liberty from noon Saturday, until midnight Sunday. The first Saturday afternoon we were all on the ferry, headed for Seattle. Simmons started in on the wonders of the *Passion Pit*, the Navy term for a lounge in the basement of one of Seattle's older hotels. The way Simmons told it, he knew all the eager ladies personally and he was going to fix us all up. I could see the others were intrigued, but the thought of being called *Kid* all night was more than I could take. I invented a friend I wanted to look up and Simmons took this as a personal affront.

"We'll think about you tonight, Kid, when we are shacked up with beautiful broads and you are taking the ferry back alone."

I agree that it would be entirely my fault and disappeared as soon as the ferry docked. I missed the company of my three friends, but Simmons was just too much.

Seattle was an exciting city that needed exploring. I felt even better when I passed a ballroom and saw there was a name band playing that night. I located a restaurant overlooking the city, and enjoyed a leisurely dinner with a glass of wine.

It was getting close to nine, and I had learned from experience that it paid to be early at a dance. I checked in, and got a seat at the lounge where I could watch the entrance.

The ballroom was filling with servicemen, couples, and a few single women, but none to generate any real enthusiasm. The dance was going well by then, and I was rechecking the 'maybes' when I saw her. She had come in by herself, and stepped back into a secluded nook where she could watch without being easily seen. Even at this distance it was obvious this was one lovely lady; tall, slim, expensively dressed with the word 'class' coming easily to mind.

I watched for a moment and I could tell she was enjoying the music. I also could tell she was not going to stay. This called for immediate action! I got there as quickly as possible without knocking people down.

Just as she started toward the exit I asked, "Do you really want to leave this music without one dance?"

She looked startled. "How did you know I was leaving?"

"I've been watching you and trying to get up enough nerve to ask you to dance. When I saw you start to leave I knew it was now or never. Let's finish this one."

I held out my hand, she hesitated and then reluctantly joined me.

"I really shouldn't," she said as her body was picking up the rhythm. "I just stopped to watch for a minute."

It quickly became apparent we danced well together. I began to relax and enjoy the remainder of the dance.

When it ended she said, "Now I really must go."

She hadn't started for the door yet, so I asked, "Do you mind my asking why you can't stay longer?"

"No, I suppose that's a fair question. I'm married, my husband is overseas, and I have the blues tonight. I decided to stop in for a few minutes of this music, nothing more."

The band began a ballad I really enjoy, and I could tell she did also. "Could we possibly dance this one before you disappear?"

She hesitated, and then returned to my arms.

"Let me at least introduce myself. I'm Jack Barnes, hello."

"Hello, I'm Anita Cochran. What are you doing here in Seattle by yourself?"

"I'm not really by myself. There are six of us here from San Pedro attending a special school. The others went somewhere else tonight. I was in a dancing mood."

"Oh, where did the others go?"

"I'm not really sure. The Warrant in charge of our detail described it in glowing details as the answer to every sailor's dream. I believe he called it the Passion Pit."

"Is it a lounge in the basement of a hotel?"

"That's it."

"Well, he didn't miss it far," Anita, continued. "That's where some of the lonely wives go for R and R. I'm surprised you're not with them."

"Right now I'm very happy where I am, thank you," I replied, and felt her move a little closer.

The dance ended and the conversation continued without her immediate departure being mentioned. I found out her husband was the Executive Officer on a submarine out of Pearl and had been gone for three months.

The music began again, and she came into my arms without my asking. I slid through several variations and she stayed right with me.

"Anita, I'm glad you decided to stay a little longer. You're making my evening."

"Jack, I want one thing understood right now. If I do stay longer, it's for the music and dancing. I'm not looking for a pickup and I am going home alone!"

"Hey, if I had more than dancing on my mind I'd be with the others. Let's relax and enjoy the music."

After this dance the band took a break, and she agreed to join me for a drink. As she sat across the small table, I had an opportunity to really get a good look at this statuesque beauty. I would have guessed that she was in her late twenties—one-way or the other. As she turned, her profile reminded me of a movie star. She was wearing a cocktail dress and when she crossed her legs; her skirt rode high on shapely thighs. I tried not to stare.

We got to talking about what there was to see in the Seattle area as I had the next day off. She suggested a visit to Victoria on Vancouver Island, one of her favorite places. I believe we were both surprised how quickly and easily we were becoming friends.

The band began again and soon we returned to the floor. As she came into my arms I asked, "Anita, would you feel uncomfortable about slipping your arm around my neck? I seem to dance better this way."

She hesitated, and then murmured, "I guess not, Jack."

That of course brought her into my favorite position and I was delightfully happy the rest of the evening. I somehow got the feeling she was enjoying it too.

By the time the dance ended, she had agreed to be my guide to Victoria and we were to meet at the ferry depot in the morning. As we left the dance I walked her to her car and saw that she was safely inside. I told her good night and started to walk toward the ferry.

"Jack?"

"Yes Anita?"

"Where are you going now?"

"To the ferry."

"Would you like a ride?"

"If it won't make you nervous, I wouldn't mind."

She opened the other door and as I slid in I noticed it was a Ford much like mine. We started toward the dock and when we arrived it looked very quiet. I got out and read the schedule. The last ferry was at 0200 and the next one was 0600. It is now a little after 0200. I walked back to the car and thanked Anita for the ride.

"When is the next ferry, Jack?"

"It'll be a couple hours."

"What time?"

"0600."

"Come on, get back in. I have a guest room at home. It's foolish for you to sit here all night. I'd like you to be my guest, if you absolutely promise not to take advantage of the situation."

"Anita, you're most thoughtful. You do have my word."

Soon we pulled into the driveway of an attractive, newer home. The double garage door opened easily and I noticed a nearly new Buick in one side as Anita parked the Ford in the other. She unlocked the back door of the house and turned on the lights. It was obvious this was a lovely, three-bedroom home, expensively furnished.

While I was admiring she called from the kitchen, "Would you like a sandwich, Jack?"

"Sounds good."

Soon I was munching a cold beef sandwich with a glass of milk. Anita settled for just a slice of the beef.

When we finished Anita showed me the guest room and asked if there was anything I needed. I knew she meant pajamas so my reluctant reply was, "No thanks." I said good night and slipped into bed, where it did take a while to get to sleep.

In the morning there was a tap on the door. When I answered Anita announced, "Breakfast in twenty minutes." I found shaving gear and a new toothbrush laid out in the bathroom.

Breakfast was served in a sunny, glassed-in room off the kitchen with a view of the harbor. The table was already set for two. I hardly recognized Anita. Her amber hair was combed out shoulder length, and she was wearing a sweater, skirt and walking shoes. She sparkled and looked about nineteen.

"What happened to the sophisticated lady I came with?" I inquired.

"She had to leave. You'll just have to make do with the one that's left."

"I don't believe I'm going to mind that at all."

Anita popped the first waffle out of the iron and onto my plate. I hadn't had waffles since joining the Navy, so it was a treat. When I had it buttered she added fried eggs on top.

As we walked toward the garage she wanted to know if I would mind driving the Buick. The battery needed charging and she was only familiar with the Ford. The Buick had gotten dusty so when I got it backed out, I gave it a quick going over with the garden hose. It was a pleasure to be behind the wheel of such a fine automobile and I was doing a little fantasizing on the leisurely drive to the Victoria Ferry Building.

On our way we passed the school ferry dock, and as I glanced ahead, I could see Simmons and the chief standing there. It was obvious they had just come from the school—which meant they must have struck out at the Passion Pit.

"Anita, up ahead is the Warrant who considers himself such a great lover and insists that he is going to show me what it is all about. It would give me great personal satisfaction to give them a ride with a beautiful girl sitting beside me."

"By all means do it," she agreed. "This should be interesting."

I pulled the Buick up to the dock and stopped. The Warrant and chief couldn't see who was driving from their position so Anita called, "Would you like a ride?"

They got all excited as they climbed in back, and then realized the driver was a sailor. I turned and asked, "Where would you like to be dropped off?"

Simmons was so dumbfounded it took a minute for him to come up with an answer. He finally mentioned a waterfront restaurant in a choked voice and I pulled out. Anita' became very affectionate and snuggled up close. I knew she was doing it deliberately and I tried to keep a straight face.

Finally Simmons couldn't take it any longer. "I didn't know you knew anyone in Seattle, Jack"

"Sure you do, Warrant. As we left the ferry yesterday I said I was going to look up a friend."

"I'll bet Jack never added, a warm, personal friend."Anita chuckled and snuggled up even closer.

"What are you two planning on doing today?" the Warrant asked. I suspected he had hopes of coming along and cutting me out.

"Whatever Jack wants to," Anita replied.

"I'll think of something, Warrant," I added.

As we arrived at the restaurant, I pulled over to the curb. I could tell Simmons was reluctant to leave and he had run out of excuses to stay. Finally he decided to be big about it and announced, "If you're late getting back, I'll cover for you."

They got out and Anita and I continued on to the Victoria Ferry. All of a sudden it hit me—Simmons hadn't called me Kid, once. I let Anita know she had made my day and she said she enjoyed doing it. I parked the car and we caught the ferry to Victoria.

The weather was so inviting we spent most of the trip on an upper promenade deck enjoying the scenery. Anita made an excellent guide when we arrived and I got the deluxe tour of Victoria.

This was a unique city with a British flavor. It had everything from horse drawn carriages to flowerpots hanging from the street lamps. We had a late lunch at the massive, historical Empress Hotel and it took us back to another time and era. In a way it reminded me of St. Augustine, and I was thoroughly enchanted. The sun was setting as we finished and it was time to catch our ferry back to Seattle.

The air was cooling so we found seats inside the cabin and drifted into a friendly conversation. I found out her husband had been on a mission for several weeks and was due back at Pearl tomorrow. With the difference in time it would probably be late tomorrow before he could call. I know she was anxious.

"Anita, I'm curious. With security so tight, how can you keep track of his submarine?"

"Wives' grapevine. One of the officer's wives is in Honolulu and she keeps the others posted."

I hoped the wrong person didn't plug into that grapevine.

"What are you going to do next weekend, Jack?"

"Probably go out with the fellas. I'm going overseas with them soon, and I don't want to create problems before we leave. Thanks to you, the Warrant may pick someone else to train as a lover."

"I'm going to miss you."

"I'm going to miss you Anita. You've made my visit to Seattle."

Our ferry docked; I fired up the Buick, drove to the school ferry and parked. This ferry was just pulling in so I knew I only have a few minutes before it departed.

"Are you sure you won't have any problem with the Buick?" I knew she had never driven it.

"I'm sure, Jack. It has the same shift as my Ford. I need to start driving it to keep the battery charged."

"Well, goodbye, Anita. I hope your Commander gets home soon."

"Thanks, Jack, Good luck."

I made a run for the ferry and waved goodbye as the ferry pulled out. She waved and slowly drove away.

The rest of the crew was already on base. Simmons and the chief had their own quarters so I got a chance to compare notes with my three friends.

"How did the Passion Pit turn out?" I inquired.

"Not bad," said Steve, "but I'm glad we had reservations at the hotel. The ladies were friendly but weren't dragging us home for the night."

"What happened with the Warrant and chief?"

"No one knows. They left with two gals and I guess it didn't work out," Steve replied. "They sure don't want to talk about it."

The three wanted to know how my weekend went and I leveled with them. When I got to the part about picking up the Warrant and chief I saw some big grins. They agreed not to divulge to Simmons that my big romance wasn't what it seemed to be.

We finished the school the next week and it was pretty tame except for the fire fighting. I almost got singed before I had my blaze under control.

We had one more weekend in Seattle and were scheduled to depart the following Monday.

Late Saturday afternoon, we were on the ferry ready to make the most of this last liberty. The chief wasn't feeling well so didn't come. I wasn't going to be satisfied until I viewed the Passion Pit. The rest agreed it was still probably the most promising.

Simmons wanted to know where I was going with Anita and I replied, "Warrant, you have described the Passion Pit in such glowing terms I have decided to come with you."

He shook his head like I wasn't too bright, but couldn't really say anything.

The ferry docked, the crowd dispersed, and our group was left standing, waiting for a bus. Simmons was the first to spot the Buick parked across the street.

"Jack, isn't that your girl friend over there in the Buick? I thought you were coming with us?"

I looked, and sure enough it was Anita. "Be back in a minute fellas," I muttered as I crossed the street.

"Hi, Anita, I wasn't expecting you today."

She looked lovely, and fragile. "I didn't expect to be here, Jack, but I have the blues so bad I can't stand being alone. I thought you might like a ride somewhere."

"Hey, what's the problem?"

"Hal's submarine is overdue."

"Uh-oh! Anita, we are on our way to dinner, and then probably the 'Pit'. Would you like to come along?"

"Would the others mind?"

"Are you kidding? A beautiful girl with a car—slide over and I'll drive." I made a U turn and wheeled the Buick up to where the others were standing.

"All aboard," I called out the window.

When they were all in, I noticed Simmons was sitting next to Anita. I introduced Anita to the three in back and announced she was coming with us. This pleased everyone, especially Simmons.

We debated about dinner, finally settling for Italian, and Anita directed us toward a good restaurant. We got a big table with a circular booth, located in a secluded corner. The place had atmosphere with lighted candles and Italian music. The waiter brought baskets of French bread and a big bottle of red wine with the menus. We got to nipping on the wine while we were waiting for the orders to be filled, and I could tell this evening was going to work out. Each of the fellas was competing for Anita's attention and this was just what she needed.

The savory Italian dishes arrived, along with another bottle of wine. The food was served family style so we all got some of each dish. By the time dessert arrived, it was such a happy group we were beginning to sing along with the Italian tenor—in Italian.

Just before we left, Steve remembered hotel reservations and prepared to make a phone call. Even Simmons added his name. I started to, but as I glanced at Anita I saw her shake her head.

We loaded up the Buick and headed for the 'Pit'. Everyone else had been there before but I wasn't too sure what to expect. It turned out to be a cozy lounge in the basement of one of Seattle's older hotels. The five-piece combo sounded good and we soon had two tables pushed together for our group. Ours was the only group so far. As I watched the door I saw most of the patrons arrive singly and many were attractive women. It was obvious that this was the meeting place for the singles, and I could guess how the name originated.

The combo started a good one and I quickly asked Anita to dance. I somehow felt I wasn't going to get many dances tonight.

"I'm grateful you asked me to come, Jack; I'm feeling much better and I like your friends."

"I'm glad, Anita. Better keep your eye on Simmons—he will probably make a pass."

"I will, Jack, if you don't get a better offer, the guest room is yours tonight."

"That sounds fair," I replied and then enjoyed the rest of the dance with this lovely lady.

As I suspected, that was the last I saw of her for a while. Everyone at the table wanted a dance, and this freed me to do a little exploring.

The first one I asked was attractive, friendly and—married. I came back to the table after the dance, finished my drink, and watched Anita and Will do well on a fast one. Steve beat me to Anita on the next dance, so I tried the singles again. Another married one! I tried several others and I was beginning to doubt that there was an unmarried woman here tonight. When I returned to the table, Simmons was dancing with Anita and I could see he was really in there pitching. I make a point of being available when the music started again and Anita quickly came into my arms.

"Welcome back, Jack. I didn't know if you would make it."

"You have spoiled me, Anita. The others are just pale imitations. Besides, I didn't want you flitting away with Simmons."

"Not very likely, although he did make it sound inviting."

Steve, Will and Ted had been concentrating more now on the singles. It appeared that their prospects were promising. It was getting near closing time, and Simmons had been so busy pursuing Anita, he didn't have a standby.

I kept Anita on the floor until the finish of the last dance, during which we accidentally let our bodies become too friendly. None of our group seemed to need further transportation so we said goodnight and returned to the Buick. I drove to the school dock, parked, and saw the last ferry was still there.

Anita seemed surprised and disappointed. "Aren't you coming home with me, Jack?"

I hesitated, "Anita I'm afraid our defenses are down tonight. How would we feel if Hal called at an inopportune moment?"

"Good point—thanks, Jack; I'm glad one of us is thinking."

"Goodbye, Anita. I'm sure the phone call will be coming soon."

I would have liked to kiss her goodbye but I was afraid this might start something we couldn't stop.

EIGHTEEN

It was Wednesday when we arrived back in San Pedro. I stowed my gear and headed for the ship. Everything looked much the same as before. I didn't know why I expected miraculous changes in two weeks.

"How did the school turn out?" Dan asked.

Easy, the only part you hadn't covered here was engine overhaul. I even managed a couple days of fire fighting. How's the ship progressing?"

"Commissioning has been moved up three weeks. The ship we are to replace in the South Pacific took a kamikaze mid-ship, and is barely limping home. We're needed out there now."

Wow! The war was really getting close.

"Dan, have you had a chance to talk to the girls since I've been gone?"

"As a matter of fact, I've been over there both weekends. I'm becoming very attached to that family."

"Hey, I'm glad; I feel the same way."

"Niki said to tell you she expects a call as soon as you get back."

"I'll do it this evening. Dan, if you won't need me Saturday, I should go to San Diego to pick up my car. The garage sent a letter saying it's ready and they are closed on Sundays."

"I guess we can spare you. I would like to see you here Monday morning."

"Will do, Dan. Thanks."

I called Niki in the evening and she seemed overjoyed to hear my voice.

"Jack, when did you get back?"

"Just a few hours ago. Hey, you sound great."

"I'm feeling great and I've missed you. When will I see you?"

"That's been bothering me. I have to pick up my car in San Diego Saturday. By the time I tell my friends goodbye, I doubt if I'll be back in time to see you."

"If you're free tomorrow night, Jack, why don't I drive over and meet you at the main gate?"

"That would work—how about seven o'clock?"

"I'll be there Jack, good night."

Thursday, I caught up on my loose ends, and at seven Niki was waiting outside the main gate. She indicated the driver's side and slid on over. I no sooner had the door closed when there were two arms around my neck and I was receiving an exciting welcome home. She was even lovelier than I remembered, and her beautiful clear skin had a rosy flush.

I noticed the guard at the gate seemed to be enjoying our reunion, so I headed down the highway. A few miles further on, I found a parking spot overlooking the ocean and pulled in. I adjusted the radio to soft music and Niki snuggled up close.

She had to have a report on my trip and I only left a few things out. I asked how she and Jill have been.

"Oh, Jack, it's been a good two weeks. Dan has been over both weekends. We both really think the world of him. I haven't felt this fine in—well, a long time. I know he is good for my mother. Thanks for bringing him."

"Hey, I think you two are the ones that are good for him. Now, enough about Dan. Let's concentrate on Niki and Jack"

I had a hint that evening of what this lovely young lady would have been like without the emotional trauma she had been through. It was encouraging, and I was happy for her as I drove back to the main gate. She had to be at work Saturday morning and I was leaving for San Diego.

It was easy to get a ride to San Diego on Saturday. It was the other way that was difficult.

I headed for the garage first and was pleased at how well the repairs came out. With a complete new paint job and new top, it looked like it just came off the assembly line.

I paid the fifty-dollar deductible, fired up the Ford and drove to the hotel where I spent New Year's Eve. I reserved a room and then made a run for my former base. I wanted to get out of town in the event the City of San Diego had a warrant out for my arrest over the palm trees and traffic light. I didn't know how well the legal officer was succeeding with his stalling tactics.

There was time to drive to the line shack and say hello to the crew. Mario was especially glad to see me, and couldn't believe how well the Ford came out. He was in charge of the flight line with Eddie as assistant, and another new seaman.

Mario kept admiring the Ford. "How soon you going overseas, Jack?"

"About a month."

"What are you going to do with the Ford when you go?"

"Sell it to you, Mario, if you've been lucky at the races."

"I've got four hundred in the bank and I can dig up fifty per month. How much are you asking?"

"Eight hundred, just what I paid, plus fifty for the new paint and top"

"If you'll take the four hundred now and the rest on payments, you've got a deal."

"All right Mario, we'll set it up at the bank —but I keep the car for the next month. You'll have to come to San Pedro after it."

I asked about Cleo and found the situation was still the same at the apartment. When I returned to the hotel I parked in an area not visible from the street. I stretched out on the bed and as I reached for the phone, I debated over calling Jan or Cleo. I would have liked to have a date with Jan before I left, but I had been feeling amorous ever since the near miss with Anita, and Cleo was marvelously constructed and motivated.

Jan was an unknown factor in the bedroom and deserved better than what I had in mind for a first date.

"Cleo, ma chere, "

"Ravel, where are you?"

"Right here in San Diego. I would be to see you already but I 'ave the big problem; could you help?"

"Certainly Ravel, anything."

"Cleo, enemy agents have found out I have the secret documents with me and I am followed. I need help in shaking away."

"What can I do?"

"Can you be dressed as if you were going out? At ten I weal park in front and blink my lights twice. You get in quick and fast we leave."

"I'll be waiting," her voice tensed with excitement.

All indications were that it would be a long night. Remembering the last time Cleo and I were together; I curled up on the bed and caught a nap. It was after four when I woke and I headed for a downtown stationery store. I knew secret agent props turned Cleo on, so I bought a manila envelope, four pages of heavy bond paper, and red sealing wax.

When I returned to the car, I folded the sheets of paper, slipped them into the envelope and melted a gob of the wax over the flap. While it was still soft I impressed my class ring into the wax. When I was finished it looked and felt very official. I slipped the envelope into the glove compartment.

At ten o'clock I blinked the lights twice, and in a moment Cleo was slinking toward the car in her best secret agent stride. I opened the door on her side.

As soon as she slid in I anxiously said, "Cleo, ma chere, watch behind for any pursuers."

She turned around and intently watched out the rear window. The view from my side distracted my driving. Fortunately we were not pursued at the moment. I heaved a sigh of relief and muttered, "Maybe I lost them."

"Ravel, what is happening?"

"I'm sorry to involve you een anything so dangerous. Enemy agents have discovered I have the vital, secret documents I must deliver; they are trying to intercept them."

I drove to the hotel and parked.

"Cleo, reach eento the glove compartment and see if the envelope there will fit your purse."

Cleo removed the envelope very carefully.

"I will have to fold it to make it fit."

"That's all right; do eet."

She got the envelope inside the purse and as we entered the lobby, I could hear the combo playing in the lounge. An intriguing thought crossed my mind.

"Cleo, let's sleep eento the lounge, find a seat where we can watch the entrance and see if we are followed."

I could see the excitement building in her expressive face. I located a secluded booth with a view of the entrance and ordered champagne.

"Remember, ma chere, the documents are een your purse."

Cleo sat there with her eyes glued on the entrance and a death grip on her small purse. It took more champagne before she began to relax. The orchestra started a romantic ballad, and I remembered the intriguing thought that prompted our detour.

"Come, my petite, let's dance thees one."

She came into my arms and we hadn't forgotten how to dance together. She held the purse tightly in one hand and it was time for the grand experiment.

"*Cleo, ma chere, je t'adore,*" I whispered in her ear.

It still worked; the rotating pelvic movement began, and subsided. I noticed the leader of the trio also seemed entranced.

As the tempo of the music changed, I slid into the erotic leg position I had learned from Jill. I could feel Cleo hesitate, and then continue with renewed interest. We explored the possibilities and all kinds of wild things were happening. Then for the coup-de-grace, I whispered French endearments into her ear while all the rest was at full intensity. The involuntary reaction began; the results were unbelievable. If Cleo was a pinball machine her eyes would read tilt, and smoke would be coming out her ears. I couldn't even describe my reactions. The music came to an end and I quickly led Cleo to the elevator. I didn't want this mood to dissipate; she had become so distracted she even forgot to watch for secret agents.

The minute we were inside the room, Cleo came into my arms. The kiss hardly got going good, before she turned for me to reach the zipper at the back of her dress. As the dress slipped off I noticed the Meritorious Service Medal nestled between her breasts, suspended from a gold chain. By morning, there could be no doubt, she truly deserved the gold star on the medal!

Cleo must have awakened first and resumed her secret agent duties. I opened my eyes and saw a nude Cleo, on her hands and knees, peeping down the hallway through the keyhole. It was quite a sight! I'd just made up my mind to see if she needed help when she must have remembered her purse and its contents. She scrambled to her feet and located the purse on the dresser. I watch her open the purse and remove the envelope. As she unfolded it I saw the seal had cracked and the flap was open. Cleo was holding it in such a way the four blank pages drifted to the floor.

Uh-oh! I knew I was in trouble. My usually fertile brain seemed drugged by last night's wild activities. Cleo picked up the papers, glanced at them, and then looked more closely. She turned a suspicious eye toward the bed, saw I was awake and accused, "Ravel, these papers are blank!"

We stared into each other's eyes for what seemed an eternity.

What a disillusioning betrayal, and what an embarrassing way to lose such a passionate bedmate. I felt chagrined and ashamed. To break the impasse, I started to get out of bed. The brief moment I was out of range of those accusing eyes my old self kicked in. I knew the best defense in an untenable situation—offense!

"Cleo, I hope you haven't mixed them up."

"But Ravel, these pages are blank."

"I know. That ees why they cannot be mixed. They are to four secret agents in invisible ink—we don't want one agent getting another's secret orders."

"Of course," Cleo heaved a sigh of relief and carefully replaced the papers in the envelope. I also breathed a sigh, and hoped Cleo hadn't noticed the sudden disappearance of my French accent!

We showered together, and with Cleo wanting to make amends for her momentary suspicion, and me being a morning person—she happily spent time on her knees!

We had a leisurely breakfast in the hotel dining room, and decided we had escaped the enemy agents. As I drove Cleo back to her apartment, I told her that all France was in her debt and I would call her when she was needed for another mission. Cleo almost swaggered as she walked to her door and waved goodbye.

With this traumatic morning following such an active night, I returned to the hotel, hung a *Do Not Disturb* sign on the door, and crawled back into bed.

NINETEEN

Monday, I reported to Dan and he asked, "Did you get your car, Jack?"

"Sure did, and have it pre-sold. My replacement in San Diego is taking it when we ship out. Is it true you're taking a leave soon?"

"That's right. I'll be on my way to Bremerton by train. It starts Saturday and I report back the week after Monday. "

"You haven't heard from Jill and Niki, have you?"

"Yes, I took them both to dinner and a show Saturday night and had dinner there Sunday. Niki wants to see you."

"You know, I'm going to miss them while we're gone."

"Jack, I've been having the same thoughts. I'd like to ask Jill to come to Bremerton with me but I don't like leaving Niki alone—she is still emotionally fragile. Niki is becoming more like a daughter to me all the time. Jack, would you mind if I asked them both?"

"Do it Dan, right now Niki needs a father more than she needs a boyfriend. I hope they can get away without losing their jobs."

We spent the rest of the morning checking out the now completed inert gas system, and found an error caused by hurried workmanship. Dan assigned the repair responsibility to me, and hurried on to more pressing problems.

The next morning, I saw Dan briefly. He reported that Jill would know today if she and Niki could get away. Dan called her at noon and the answer was affirmative. I called Niki early in the evening and she answered the phone.

"Niki?"

"Jack!" she happily exclaimed, "Where are you?"

"At the dock. I waited until I was sure you would be home."

"Have you eaten, yet?"

"No," I replied hopefully.

"I'm just putting a casserole in the oven. Can you come over?"

"I'm on my way now. Bye."

I quickly cleaned up and headed for Southgate. I knew how that girl could cook.

Jill came to the door when I rang. "Jack, where have you been?" she asked as she gave me a big hug. "We've missed you."

Niki came out of the kitchen with an apron still on and I got an enthusiastic hug and kiss. It felt good to be so obviously welcome. The table was set and Niki slipped the casserole out of the oven, a crisp salad from the refrigerator and dinner was ready. I didn't know what was under the melted cheese but I began to feel ashamed when I went back for thirds.

Knowing how close those two were, I suspected Niki had already been told about Dan's and my suggestion.

"Would you like to go?" I asked Niki. I could tell from her pleased expression the answer was yes.

"I'll miss you, Jack, I wish you were coming."

"I do too, but unfortunately I've already had my leave this year. I know you will be back before the ship leaves because Dan has to be aboard."

A week and a half later, after Dan and the girls had returned from their train trip, I noticed smoke coming from the ship's stack. The boilers had been fired up, which meant we were going somewhere soon on our shakedown cruise.

I was awakened by the words, "*Now hear this. Prepare to get underway,*" over the PA. A tingle of excitement coursed through my body. I headed for an early breakfast, and found a good location to watch the departure. My specific duty was the inert gas machine, so I could relax and watch the bosun mates earn their pay.

The line handlers were busy as each line was cast off on order. The gangway had already been secured. I felt the throb of the twin screws through the deck, and we were underway.

We worked our way slowly out of the harbor to the open sea where our speed increased. When the curved bow cut through a lazy swell, it produced a burst of spray. The deck picked up the undulating rhythm and it required more attention to move about.

The PA speakers seemed to be emitting a steady stream of bosun's whistles, announcements and orders. I heard the gasoline detail mentioned and reported to the hangar deck.

One of my duties assigned by Dan was a fire fighting detail for gasoline fires. I was also assigned a battle station on one, of a row of twenty-millimeter machine guns mid-ship on the starboard side. Should we have a bombing attack while anchored, I was to operate the smoke generator mounted on the stern of the fuel barge.

Dan passed the assignments on to the Warrant, and then took the four of us with gun assignments to our battle stations.

I was pleased to see the twenty-millimeter was not much different from the fifty calibers I was familiar with. It was a pedestal-mounted gun taking a shell about three times the size of the fifty calibers. Fortunately, it used the same ring sight.

Dan ran through the loading sequence, and fired a few rounds. We each had a chance to do the same, and I could tell I was going to be comfortable with this gun.

It was time to return to Warrant Simmons and fire fighting instructions. We had all been to school, so it was just a matter of familiarizing ourselves with the equipment locations.

Chief McGuire took me to the flight deck where the fuel barge was secured and explained the operation of the smoke generator. This put out a dense, black, oily, smoke, which would completely hide the ship as we slowly circled. Hopefully, enemy bombers wouldn't waste their bombs if they were unable to see the ship.

The rest of the day, we were kept busy with drills. We no sooner secured from general quarters than we were fighting a simulated fire in the hangar. The fire supposedly got out of control, and we were into an abandon ship drill. With all the aviation fuel we would have aboard, we would be a big floating bomb.

That evening we went into a darken ship routine. This meant all portholes were dogged shut and no light visible topside. This was more than a drill since a submarine could be lurking right here.

We secured from the drills, had supper and lights went out early. I was just getting into my first dream when the klaxon horn sounded general quarters. It was a frightening experience and produced mass confusion in our dark, tight quarters.

I had no sooner made it out of my bunk and reached for my clothes, when Steve jumped from his middle bunk, and landed on my back. Steve was no lightweight. Before we could get off the deck, Ted landed on us from his top bunk. I was on the bottom and sure hoped this was a drill and not the real thing.

We finally got unscrambled and made it to our battle stations. It was a drill. Everyone did so poorly we had two more during the night. We ended up sleeping fully dressed.

I had a little discussion with my two upper bunkmates, and we worked out a better way to depart. It took a lot of strong coffee the next day to stay awake. Fortunately, that night there was only one general quarter.

The next day was gunnery practice. We dropped off a raft, which had a large canvas sail. The ship continued on, and when we were well away, commenced firing.

The first time a five-inch gun went off, I nearly fell overboard. What a noise and concussion! The twin forties picked up the target and cut loose. It was too far away for the twenties, so I just watched. The ship turned back and forth so both sides got a chance to fire. When we recovered the target, we found where it had been hit twice by forty millimeter shells and was unscathed by the five-inchers. The Captain wasn't too happy about this and made a caustic remark over the PA.

I heard the drone of aircraft engines and saw a small plane making passes high above us. The PA announced this was a radio controlled target drone and to get it! The five-inch guns opened up first, and the target plane impudently continued its passes. The twin forties took up the challenge and did no better.

After a couple more passes, the controller of the drone in the other airplane, decided to really rub our nose in it and dropped the target to just above the water in a stern attack. The five-inch guns and twin forties both opened up—with the usual results. If our guns continued to miss, the controller would have to take the drone past either the port or starboard twenties. I was praying it would be starboard. Blast! It took the port side. Then, just as the port twenties opened fire, the controller pulled the drone into a sharp climb. This threw the gunners off and it appeared it would get away.

I could estimate the trajectory from my side and see the drone was going to clear the ship just forward of the radar antenna. I used the antenna for a guide, brought the 20 around as far as it would go and had the drone in my sight the second it cleared the ship. The drone had lost speed in the climb and for a moment was a perfect target. I cranked in just the right amount of lead and listened to the sweet sound of the twenty-millimeter. I got the engine first and then worked back to the radio controls. I could see big chunks of the fuselage disappear and the engine stop. The drone hung there a second and then dove into the sea and disappeared.

The ship's company let out a wild cheer. The port gunners were excitedly taking credit for the kill, and I had to bite my tongue to keep quiet.

Dan strolled by, checked my empty clip and said, "Good shooting, Jack."

"How did you know?"

"I've seen your scores at aerial gunnery school; besides, you are the only one who fired after that steep climb."

The next general quarters I glanced at the base of my twenty-millimeter and saw where some joker had painted an American star on my gun pedestal. After we secured, several of my buddies came over to kid me.

I laughed and said, "Four more and I'll be a Japanese ace!"

Thursday morning we were back at the dock amid a burst of activity. The shipyard workers scurried back aboard to complete any last minute jobs and to correct any problems that developed on the shakedown. The gasoline detail got word we would take on aviation fuel as soon as all repair activity was completed.

I wasn't too sure how this would affect my weekend liberty. I called Niki to let her know I was back, and would try to be over Sunday.

Friday, there was a steady stream of stores coming aboard. I fired up the inert gas machine so the voids would be fireproof when we took on aviation fuel. I had deliberately waited as long as possible to purge the voids due to the danger of a workman inadvertently entering one of the hatches, not realizing there was no oxygen. I now had a big warning decal and a padlock on each hatch and I carried the key.

Saturday morning, we found we would be fueling late into the night. The fueling went well for a first effort, and by midnight we were finished. The smoking lamp was lit, and all the smokers who couldn't sleep immediately lit up.

The Warrant let us know we would have liberty Sunday until midnight. This pretty well told us Monday was departure day.

I knew Mario was due here to pick up the Ford, so Sunday morning I called Niki and explained my schedule. She said Dan and I were both expected for dinner about five and to come as soon as I could.

Mario showed up early in the afternoon all excited about finally getting the car. He checked it all over, and I was glad I just had it washed.

"Mario, can you drop me off in Southgate on your way home?"

"Sure, Jack. You ready to go?"

I slid into the passenger side and Mario took off.

"Tell me, what's happening in San Diego?"

"Well, the flight line is still about the same. Eddie made Third Class, and I should have my Second class soon. Oh yes, Cleo says she is available whenever you need her services."

I noticed Mario smiled over that one.

"Are you still hitting the races at Tijuana?"

"Not really, something went wrong and my uncle is under suspension."

We were approaching Niki's house and I guided Mario to the driveway. We were finishing our conversation when I noticed Mario was losing his train of thought. Just as I suspected, Niki was coming down the walk.

I got out, and as I walked around the car, she came up and slid her arm around my waist. I introduced Mario, and then I remembered he had a thing about blondes. Mario finally got his thoughts organized and told us goodbye. We both waved as he drove off.

Niki and I slowly strolled back to the house, our arms around each other's waists. When the front door closed, she turned and came fully into my arms.

"I've missed you, Jack," she said in a husky voice.

"I've missed you, Niki," I replied, trying to make my hands behave.

"Where are Jill and Dan?"

"They left early this morning for a drive to Big Bear. I expect them back soon."

It was probably just as well. If Niki was feeling anywhere near the way I thought she was, we could be in big trouble.

The dinner already smelled great. Niki went in to finish the salad, slipped it into the refrigerator, and we returned to the living room. I avoided the sofa and picked the easy chair. Niki curled up at my feet with her head resting on my knees.

"You're leaving tomorrow, aren't you, Jack?" she asked.

"It looks like it. I wasn't sure I'd be able to get away today."

"I'm really glad you did. What time do you have to be back?"

"Midnight."

"Jack let me drive you back; we'll have that much longer."

We heard a car door slam and in a minute Dan and Jill arrived. I could tell from the expression on both their faces something momentous had occurred.

"Shall we tell them now?" Jill asked with a conspiratorial smile.

"Might as well," Dan replied.

"I can already guess," Niki excitedly announced, "you're engaged!"

I hoped Niki was correct or it was going to be embarrassing.

"No secrets in this family," Dan muttered, trying to appear upset. He gave up when Niki rushed into his arms for a big hug.

"I'm so happy, Dan. You've been my choice for a dad ever since you came that first time with Jack."

I congratulated them both, and Niki had to have a blow-by-blow account of who said what and when. She did find out the wedding was planned shortly after we returned from overseas.

Niki went to check the dinner, Jill to change, and Dan and I had a few minutes to talk.

"Are you going back to your business in Bremerton after the war?" I asked.

"Looks like it. Jill likes it there and she and my brother and his wife hit it off. I'm sure the business will support two families in peace time."

"Sounds great. I hope Niki likes it."

"She seemed to, there's a lot going on for young people. Oh, by the way, Jack, when did you leave the ship?"

"Middle of the afternoon. Why?"

"Anything unusual going on?" Dan asked.

"Not really. Oh yeah, the skipper was pacing the flight deck and kept watching the dock."

"I was afraid of that."

"Is there a problem?"

"Well, his jeep hasn't arrived. There's supposed to be a jeep for the Commanding Officer's use on shore. We have all the parts to overhaul it, but no jeep."

"He did look upset."

"Upset is too mild, Jack He's madder than hell. If the jeep isn't aboard before we pull out, we may have a rough cruise."

Niki announced dinner was ready. Jill arrived with a bottle of chilled champagne she had been saving for a special occasion. She filled the glasses, and before we began dinner I proposed a toast to the newly engaged couple.

Niki had outdone herself on this meal. She knew that Dan and I both enjoyed lamb. She also knew I was hung up on casseroles, so she had both. Dan carved the lamb. With the champagne and excitement of the engagement, it was a supercharged evening.

After dinner, Dan talked the girls into singing some of his favorite songs. I guess it was pretty obvious we were storing up memories for the days ahead. Niki took the lead on *I'll Be Seeing You*, and looked right into my eyes as she sang it. It caused a lump in my throat and I couldn't help wonder when I'd see her again.

It was getting late and I suspected Dan and Jill might like a little privacy. Niki had the same thought, so we told Jill and Dan good night. Jill gave me a big hug and told me to be careful. Dan hugged Niki and mentioned it was going to be great to have a daughter again. There were several moist eyes before we got away.

Niki asked me to drive and she snuggled up close as we headed for San Pedro. She found some music we both liked so instead of stopping at the dock, we drove to the ocean viewpoint.

Niki slipped into my arms. "How long do you think you'll be gone?"

"I hope not over a few months. Our bombers are plastering Japan right now. That's what the seaplanes from our ship will be doing, picking up the crews of bombers that had to ditch."

"Will I ever get to see you again?" she asked in a little girl voice.

"I sure hope so. I'll call when I get back."

"Please do, Jack I'm missing you already."

"Me too, Niki; you have really spoiled me."

I noticed our last kiss tasted salty. I held her in my arms for what seemed like only a short time, however, when I glanced at my watch I saw an hour had passed. It was time to report aboard.

TWENTY

"**N**ow *hear this; prepare to get underway.*"
It was a repeat of our departure a week ago, only this time we knew we weren't coming back.

We knew we were headed for the South Pacific, but the actual destination was a deep secret. The first few days we had the same drills we had on the shakedown cruise.

One morning, we awoke with Diamond Head visible in the distance and knew we were approaching Pearl Harbor. We took on a pilot at the entrance and wound our way through the crowded channel to our assigned anchorage. The harbor was all we saw, as twenty-four hours later we were headed back to sea.

The rumors had us going anywhere from the Marshall Islands to the Aleutians. The weather was ideal, and day after day we cruised toward our destination.

Friday evening was happy hour, with the hangar converted into a theater. A low stage with a curtain was assembled at one end. The wardroom chairs were brought out for the officers, with the mess hall benches lined up behind.

Stan, the photographer's mate, became the MC. Stan was an artist, as well as having been on stage. With our large crew, there was considerable talent and with Stan to guide and direct, we had some exceptional happy hours.

Stan informed the gas detail, "You are scheduled for a skit next happy hour!"

Four sailors looked at each other with horror!

None of us could sing, so we finally decided to do a parody of the Andrews sisters. There was a record player, which connected into the speaker system, and we picked a record that had lots of action. Steve looked more like a wrestler than a girl, so he was delegated to handling the music.

We got the moves down pretty good and then it was time for the costumes. The parachute rigger parted with enough silk from a surveyed parachute to make three wrap-around skirts. The top was to be a makeshift bra underneath tee shirts. We got three new swabs from the storekeeper and talked the cook out of six apples. Will and I choose medium size ones, but Ted got carried away. We devised long blond wigs from the swabs and stuffed the makeshift silk bras with apples.

Friday we were the last act. Stan started his build-up with, "And now direct from Hollywood, we bring you the world famous Andrews Sisters singing Chattanooga Choo Choo."

The curtain was drawn and the spotlight was on us. Immediately there was such a crescendo of wolf whistles Steve had to wait to start the record.

We managed to get the pantomime and the music together. It really was going well, until near the middle we begin to hear an occasional snicker. This progressed to ribald laughter. I glanced toward Ted who was in the center, and saw the reason. The oversized apples he picked were too heavy for the material holding them. With all the bouncing the bra had stretched. The lower the apples went, the louder the laughter. The audience was in hysterics by the time we finished. We got a great applause; however, I decided show business was not for me.

When we returned to our quarters, Will called me over to his bunk. "I've got something here I think you will be interested in, Jack," he said as he rummaged through a stack of magazines.

He located the one he wanted and turned to an illustrated article. The lead picture was of a light plane on skis with wolf pelts draped over the struts and prop. The article went on to describe hunting wolves from the air around Nome, Alaska. It told how the wolf packs were decimating the caribou herds. There was a fifty-dollar bounty from the government, as well as another fifty from the natives for the pelt, which they used to line the hoods of fur parkas.

The article went on to mention other ways Alaska bush pilots were making big money. I realized, here was the answer to my post-war uncertainty. I had been trying to decide what to do when I got out of the service. Adventure, flying and money had been high on my list, and this had them all.

Will let me keep the magazine and soon I knew the article by heart. The right airplane was going to be a must, and I knew it was going to be expensive. I had about one thousand dollars in the bank and the way the war was wrapping up, I'd have a limited time to get the rest. Most of my thoughts were now devoted to moneymaking schemes.

The ship continued on through the tropical seas, and we passed schools of flying fish. They were over a foot long, and as the ship approached, they used their tail to propel themselves along the surface with their fins outspread. The fins were so large they acted as wings. The fish glided above the water for surprising distances.

It became official that our next stop was Saipan in the Marshall Islands. Saipan, as well as the neighboring islands of Tinian and Rota, had recently been re-captured from the Japanese. The two with large airstrips were serving as bases for our bombers

The Skipper still had a scowl, and it seemed we were having an unusual amount of drills and musters. The next time I saw Dan I asked about the jeep. Just as I suspected, it never arrived.

A few days later we pulled into the dock at Saipan. The damaged landing craft and the denuded trees were a reminder there had been recent fighting here. The scuttlebutt was we would only be here twenty-four hours. There would be no liberty.

Warrant Simmons instructed Will and I to report to a Navy warehouse ashore and pick up two packages for our department. We were delighted for the opportunity to do a little exploring, and took a wandering route.

Most of the men we met were Army personnel, and it looked as if they had pretty well taken over the island. At the edge of a compound, on a rise, we blundered into the Army motor pool. We could see trucks, staff cars, ambulances and jeeps. Most of the jeeps appeared to have had a hard life, but at one end several looked almost new. I checked the tires of the last one and smiled when I saw they were brand new. There was no key in the ignition.

We continued on to the warehouse, picked up our supplies, and on our way back ambled past the motor pool again. There still was no one around.

Interesting!

We delivered the supplies and located Ted and Steve. Four fertile minds engaged in a logistical challenge—how to get this jeep aboard without getting caught.

We went back topside and saw that while we were gone several large wooden crates had been deposited on the dock. Steve knew the crane operator and checked to see when the crates would be hoisted aboard. Will located the painter who had taken over the cubicle intended for the jeep. He had a canvas draped over the opening and had been using it for spray painting. Ted rounded up a couple cable slings and a large tarp. Steve reported there was one more crate due on the dock, and then they all would be hoisted aboard. Dusk was approaching and it was now or never.

Steve, Will and I headed down the gangway like we were going to prepare the crates for hoisting. When this didn't draw any attention, we kept right on going. We nonchalantly strode to the motor pool and were relieved to find there was no guard.

A few minutes later a practically new jeep coasted down toward the dock with three sailors aboard. We held our breath as we passed a group of soldiers. Fortunately, we didn't draw undue attention. Just before we reached the dock, the ground leveled out and we had to push it the rest of the way.

The crane was swinging the next to the last crate aboard when we pushed the jeep up against the remaining one. Ted was there with the tarp and cables. We quickly covered the jeep, lashed the tarp tight and slung the cables underneath. The crane operator brought the big hook right overhead. In a moment the jeep was hoisted to a secluded spot on the flight deck. The crane went back to its regular work.

The hangar doors were partially open and we saw the painter give a thumb up. We quickly wheeled the tarp-covered jeep into the hangar cubicle designed for it and the painter dropped the canvas.

The next morning, when we departed Saipan, a half a dozen sailors heaved a sigh of relief. We all had been envisioning a detail of MP's shaking down the ship.

There was a lot of action taking place behind the canvas. I went through the spare parts kit, found the replacement ignition switch with key, and installed it. The painter sprayed over the Army's olive drab with Navy gray. The tubing bender devised an aluminum frame for a convertible top. The parachute loft made up the top from the heavy gray canvas used for parachute bags. The top looked so good we removed the seats and covered them with the same material. By then there must have been twenty enlisted men involved in the project.

Friday's happy hour was chosen for the presentation. The evening's entertainment began much the same as before. The officers were sitting in front with the enlisted men behind.

Near the conclusion, the MC announced it would be necessary to turn off the lights for a moment. In this interval the audience could hear the commotion we made as we pushed the jeep to the stage.

Two spotlights were turned on behind the curtain. To those not involved it was obvious something momentous was about to take place.

Stan stepped through the curtains and announced, "As many of you know, we departed from San Diego so hurriedly, we thought a very necessary item had not arrived. Imagine our surprise to find it has been here all the time. Captain Madden, we would like to present to you, the keys to your missing jeep."

With these words the curtain was drawn. There, bathed by two spotlights, was the jeep.

Even though I'd seen the finished product in the daylight, I was impressed. It glistened. The dark gray top and seats complimented the lighter gray paint. Lettered on the side was, COMMANDING OFFICER USS PINE ISLAND. It wasn't exactly regulation, but it was beautiful.

Stan was holding the keys. The Skipper got up and started forward. A third spotlight shifted to him as he accepted the keys, started to say something, changed his mind, and made a slow circle of the jeep. He climbed into the driver's seat, hesitated a moment and started the engine. There was a roar of approval, whistles, and applause from the audience. I was just happy the engine started.

The Captain just sat there, put his hands to his face for a moment, then shut off the engine and came to the mike. I suspected it had taken that long to get his emotions under control.

"Men, I'm so pleased, I'm not even going to ask the storekeepers how they could have mislaid an item this large."

This brought a round of laughter, as well as a sigh of relief from those of us involved.

"The only way I can think of to show my appreciation," the Skipper continued, "is to state that when we reach Okinawa and get the jeep ashore, a beer bust is scheduled for the enlisted men. Thank you!"

He returned to his seat with the only smile I had ever seen on his face. The applause was deafening in the tightly packed hangar. I wasn't sure if it was a slip, but this was the first official word we were going to Okinawa.

I hadn't realized how really great an artist Stan was, until one day when I glanced into the area he normally used for photographic work.

There on a low easel was the largest canvas I'd ever seen. Standing beside it was Stan with brush in hand. Pinned to the wall were pin-ups of Rita Hayworth and Betty Grable, as well as a Vargas calendar painting where the artist got completely carried away.

Stan was painting a life-sized nude using the best from all three, as well as his own ideas. I could already tell it was really going to be something. Stan worked fast and by Friday the painting was completed and framed.

That evening at the close of happy hour, the lights were dimmed and Stan stepped through the curtains at the front of the stage.

"Gentlemen, I regret to report there have been complaints to the entertainment committee over our ship having no figurehead. Your entertainment committee has researched the problem, and discovered figureheads went out with sailing ships, however, if it's a figurehead you want, it's a figurehead you get.

The curtain was slowly drawn. There, bathed in the spotlights, reposed the painting. There was a moment of stunned silence. Then there was wild applause. She was full size, leaning forward with her arms outstretched to the audience. A long scarf of sheer chiffon, lightly draped across one shoulder and her waist, only enhanced her nudity, and the two ends seemed to flutter in a breeze. She was a redhead with her long hair tossed by the wind. The legs were pure Grable and the rest seemed to be an improvement on Hayworth. She was utterly delightful.

After happy hour, most of us milled around for a closer look at the painting. The Skipper was so impressed, he authorized Stan to permanently mount the frame above the stage. I went for the tools, and while we were at it, we mounted a spotlight, which would illuminate the painting.

The hangar deck became the most popular spot on the ship.

TWENTY-ONE

One evening, we could see the outline of Okinawa beginning to rise from the horizon. The next morning, as we pulled in to tropical Chimu Wan Bay, I stayed close to the rail. The horseshoe shaped shoreline lined with palm trees and white sand reminded me of a picture from a travel bureau. I could see no evidence of the recent battle.

The ship let go her anchors, and soon we were hoisting out the boats.

The boson mate's first job was to anchor a row of floating buoys. That afternoon the squadron of PBM flying boats arrived and tied up. We were now ready to assume the duties we had been trained for. The flying boats would be standing by every morning to pick up the crews of the B29 bombers who didn't make it home.

That evening, we were in for a nasty surprise. The Skipper had been allowing the radio operator to switch Tokyo Rose into the main speakers for an hour each evening. She had been playing hit parade music and we all had found the propaganda amusing. We didn't laugh when the next song was dedicated to the crew of our recently arrived ship. The selection was *Many Brave Hearts Lie Asleep in the Deep*. She added the invincible warriors of Japan would be coming over for a visit soon!

We all looked at each other with shock. We had no idea the Japanese knew who we were or that we were even in the area.

After our poor showing during gunnery practice, the Captain decided it was better to hide the ship than risk shooting it out with Japanese Kamikazes. Word came down from the top, and the next thing I knew I was on our small barge with the three other members of the gas detail. It was my responsibility to man the smoke generator while they operated the barge, and we practiced circling the ship until we had it covered. The fumes were fierce, and we made a larger circle each time so we didn't run through our own smoke. With the generator belching great thick, oily gobs, soon our ship disappeared in a dense black plume.

There wasn't any breeze and it went well. When we thought we had it covered, we pulled back to admire our handiwork. Much to our chagrin, the radar antenna was sticking right up through the top of our smoke cloud.

There was nothing more we could do so when we advised the ship of the difficulty, we were instructed to remain in the clear as observers. Soon we could see the smoke rising from a generator on the ship. We let them know when the antenna was concealed and were ordered to secure. No one wanted to breathe that repulsive, oily smoke longer than necessary.

It was a good thing we had the practice run because later that night we received the promised visit. Our radar picked up their approach, general quarters sounded and the PA added, "*This is not a drill!*"

Our crew made a mad scramble for the gas barge. Fortunately the smoke generator fired right up. While we were making our circles, the generator on the ship was busy covering the superstructure. We pulled out of the smoke into the moonlight to report the ship was covered and stayed in the open to watch for any smoke drift, and especially to have a ringside seat for the action.

A low flying flight of kamikazes came right over the top of the smoke. One was so close I believe I could have hit it with a slingshot. Apparently none of them wanted to gamble on a miss of the ship with their one chance for eternal glory. Our gas barge was too small a target, so they kept right on going to Buckner Bay and the rest of the fleet. We waited with bated breath for the next action, but that turned out to be it. Almost an hour later we received the all clear.

When I got back aboard ship, I realized we had the best job of all. Everyone else had inflamed eyes and was coughing up black gook from the smoke.

Later we learned that, although the they did some damage, none of the kamikazes made it back to their base.

The next morning, we watched the seaplanes take off on air-sea rescue, standby missions. The seaplanes were back by early afternoon, one with a B29 crew they picked out of the sea.

We filled the gas barge with aviation fuel, and the four of us left to service the flying boats. It was only mid-afternoon when we finished, so we detoured to the dock near our anchorage and went exploring.

The native Okinawans seemed an industrious lot. Men and women both were working in the taro and sugar cane patches. The men were short, skinny, with bandy legs. The women were tiny. We got a surprise when we came to one group. About half the women were bare from the waist up. On second look, they were so flat-chested it really didn't matter.

We could see what appeared to be a crashed plane up ahead. The tide was in, and the Zero was partly awash. The gear was still retracted and the prop tips bent back. The fuselage was riddled with bullet holes. The pilot must have still been alive to get it set down on the beach. The canopy was back and the cockpit empty. I could see the instruments were still on the panel.

I didn't hesitate. I crawled into the small cockpit and started removing instruments with the screwdriver blade of my pocketknife. The others started stripping anything removable. Before we left, we had everything with any souvenir value.

We made it back to the ship in time for supper and after dark brought our booty to the crew's quarters. We were the first enlisted men to get ashore. When the word spread about what we had, there was so much interest we moved our display to the mess hall, where each lay out his wares on a separate table. The instruments with the Japanese symbols created the most excitement. I ended up selling them all for almost fifty dollars. I could see right away the souvenir business had a great potential.

There was a fair sized island in Chimu Wan Bay, and one day we explored it. I took along a thirty-caliber carbine, just in case the wrong people might inhabit it. A portion of Okinawa still had Japanese who refused to surrender.

We found several deserted palm huts, but for the present the island was completely deserted. The cove with the sparkling white sand was an ideal swimming beach. During an underwater swim, I discovered a bed of unusual shells about the size of robins' eggs. I brought several to shore and Ted remembered having seen a necklace made of these cat's eyes in a San Diego gift shop. We had a large sack full by the time we left.

We displayed them on a mess hall table that evening with a pitch about how they were sold as exotic, expensive necklaces. Most of the sailors decided they wanted to make a necklace for their girl friend and we had a going business. We got a dime each for the shells. I don't believe the necklace makers realized just how many shells it would take to finish one. Business was great until the Skipper threw the beer party for the enlisted men—on our island! Our supply of shells was discovered and there went a source of revenue.

There was an Army Base on a plateau near our dock with a pier extending into the bay for about five hundred feet. A small Army liaison plane had been landing and taking off on the pier. This was most unusual performance and I wanted to get a good look at the airplane.

One day, when we are on the beach, I saw it land and I jogged on over. The pilot was sitting on the edge of the pier beside the plane, apparently waiting for something. I said, "Hi," and walked around the plane, which looked like a big two-place Cub with lots of plexiglass. There was no indication of how it managed such exotic performance. The Warrant Officer pilot had been watching me and drifted over.

"What kind of a plane is it?" I asked the pilot.

"Stinson L-5."

"How does it get that short field performance? It looks pretty conventional."

"Come over here," he said, "and I'll show you."

The pilot climbed into the front cockpit and started turning an overhead crank. I saw the words 'droop ailerons' beneath the crank. I turned to watch the trailing edge of the wing. Both ailerons were coming down like flaps. When they were fifteen degrees down, he dropped the flaps a couple of notches and I could see most of the wing now had flaps.

"Now," he said, "combine this much lift with a one hundred ninety horsepower engine and you have performance."

"Wow!" I exclaimed. I could see it now. This was the plane for my Alaska bush pilot plans.

"Do you fly?" the pilot asked.

"Just Cubs," I replied, "and I had to bootleg that."

"I'm waiting for film to fly to Buckner Bay to trade for a new movie."

"You Army guys have all the luck. We don't have anybody to trade with so we get stuck watching the same movie over and over."

I went back to admiring his plane. He must have noticed how taken I was with it.

"You can come along if you want." He offered.

"Great, I'd like to see this beauty in action."

A jeep arrived with two cans of movie film. The pilot lifted the handle of a long luggage compartment door. He pointed out that by removing the rear seat this could become an air-ambulance with a stretcher fitted into the back. I could see more commercial possibilities.

The pilot loaded the film. I crawled into the back seat and he took the front. He fired up the engine, left the droop ailerons down, and retracted the flaps.

I was looking at the end of the pier and the water beyond. The pier looked shorter every second. He shoved the throttle to the stop, held the brakes, and then released them. We began trundling down the pier. The tail came up almost immediately. As we reached the end of the pier, the pilot popped a notch of flap and we were immediately airborne. No doubt about it, this was some airplane.

The pilot set up a climb, and then asked, "Would you like to try it?"

"Oh yes!"

It felt good right from the beginning. As soon as we were high enough to clear the hills, I leveled off and crossed the island. He pointed out Buckner Bay and the airstrip where we would land. The pilot made the landing and we traded film.

"Want to make the take-off?" he asked.

I nodded, and taxied to the end of the strip. Because the droop aileron and flap controls were in the front cockpit, I asked him to crank down the ailerons. One thing I discovered right away: there was a lot of torque from one hundred ninety horsepower. I had to stay on the right rudder to keep lined up. The strip was long enough I didn't really have to use droop ailerons and flaps, but I wanted to feel the lift. The second we were near flying speed, I asked the pilot to pop a notch of flap. I pulled back on the stick and we were climbing.

The L-5 performed like a dragonfly. I never in my life expected to make such a short take-off. I asked the pilot to retract the flaps and drop ailerons and we began to pick up speed.

The pilot let me play with it on the way back and before we landed I was sure this was the plane I wanted.

He vividly demonstrated its short field landing capabilities as we came in to the pier. The pilot got set up out over the water with droop ailerons and full flaps. It was like hanging out two barn doors. The pilot used a lot of throttle just to stay in the air. We approached at about forty-five miles per hour with the nose up, the tail down and hanging on the prop. The pilot had to look out the side to even see the pier, which looked short and narrow. The second we crossed the end; he chopped the throttle and was on the brakes. This fella could fly!

"Hey, thanks for the flight. After the war I'm flying to Alaska to hunt wolves from the air, up around Nome. There is a fifty-dollar bounty. Up till now I haven't known what kind of a plane would be best.

He said, "The L-5 would make a super-performing floatplane and do even better on skis. There should be a bunch for sale surplus, when the war is over."

I almost got the impression I might have created some post-war competition.

I waved goodbye and drifted back to the dock, my mind going ninety per. I had to raise more money fast.

I noticed the sky was developing a pointed cloud and a breeze had come up. We headed the gas barge back to the ship and made it in time for supper. In the mess hall we heard: "Now hear this, all flight crews report to the hangar deck with full gear—on the double!"

I finished supper wondering what could be going on. Instead of retiring to my quarters, I went topside to the hangar deck to find out.

The flight crews were going down the ladder to the waiting motor-whaleboats. The way they were bouncing I knew the waves were rapidly increasing. The air had an oppressive feeling and the sky a brassy glow.

The wind was steadily increasing.

I saw Dan watching and came over. "What's going on, Lieutenant?"

"Hi, Jack, we have a typhoon approaching and are flying the PBMs to the Philippines. It's going to be a bad one."

I felt the adrenalin start to pump. I'd heard about typhoons.

As the boats took the crews to their planes, I glanced across at the supply transport anchored close by. This was our recently arrived food supply. I could see they were loading a small LCVP alongside, and used this small landing craft as a shuttle for the supplies.

I could see the engines of the first PBM fire up. As I crossed over to watch, I noticed the waves were already much larger. The other plane's engines were starting now as each crew reaches their PBM. The first one started its take-off run and it obviously was having difficulties. Finally it bounced off the top of a wave and stayed airborne. The second and third made it, then the fourth and fifth. Almost at flying speed, the sixth bounced off one wave and smacked right into a big one. The hull split open and before our horrified eyes, it continued to the bottom. We didn't see anything come to the surface. The crew never had a chance.

A red rocket was fired from our bridge, and the remaining four planes taxied back to their buoys where the motor-whaleboats picked up the crews. We could see they were having a difficult time making it back to the ship. The remaining flight crews were white faced as they returned to the hangar deck.

The PA was busy spitting orders: "*Now hear this: prepare to get underway; hoist small boats aboard; double lash flying boat on the flight deck; secure for heavy weather.*"

The wind was blowing so hard I had to lean forward to stand, and I could see it was swinging us on our anchors. I glanced at the transport and could tell she was swinging also. As I watched it seemed she was definitely closer. Suddenly her prop started turning and I saw her anchor chain coming aboard. She was running for the open sea. I wondered what happened to the LCVP.

Soon our props started turning and our anchors were hoisted. We had to crab to make good our course for the entrance to the bay.

I didn't have any idea what big waves really were until we reached the open sea. They were so large that, standing on the flight deck, fifty feet above water, I was looking up at them. We were running before the waves and I discovered the most exciting place was on the ship's fantail.

A towering mountain of water approached and, as I looked up, it appeared there was no way we could avoid being over-run. At the last second, the fantail rose like an express elevator and the mountain of water passed beneath the stern. Before it continued on beneath the ship, the top of the wave came so close I could almost reach out and touch it. This action drove the bow into the wave ahead. As the wave continued on beyond the center of the ship, the fantail dropped as fast as it had risen. I felt I had to hold on or I would be left hanging in mid-air. It was more exciting than a roller coaster.

When I tired of this elevator game, I started to return to my quarters, but even before I got there, I knew I couldn't stay. Some sailors had lashed themselves in their bunks and so many had become sick; the smell was overpowering. I made a dash topside before I also contributed.

The wild wind cleared my head, but I was afraid of being blown off the deck. When I couldn't keep my eyes open, I made my way over to a circular, metal protected area for the guns called a gun tub. It looked to me like the safest place on deck, and curling up inside I went to sleep. Topside was where I remained for the next two days.

The second day, I made it as far as the mess hall. There had been no way to cook, and no customers if a meal was prepared. Instead there were sandwiches and coffee around the clock.

Later that day, the wind slackened and we headed back.

The PBM lashed to the flight deck looked like a skeleton. In places the aluminum skin has been completely blown away. The wind stress on the massive twin tail had been so great it had twisted the fuselage. Our orders were to remove the engines and instruments, and then the big hook dropped the remainder over the side.

We arrived at Okinawa the third day after the typhoon. The once busy harbor was now deserted. With binoculars, I quickly scanned the area where we left the flying boats. The PBM's were gone, as well as the mooring buoys. I swung the binoculars and searched the beach for the remains of the planes, and found nothing but pristine, white sand.

The ship let go her anchor and when Dan approached, I requested permission to swing the gas barge out and search the beach. Permission was granted.

The crane operator hoisted out the barge with Ted and Steve aboard, they brought her around to the fantail where Will and I used the rope ladder to swing aboard. I thought to myself it was a shame the supply ship arrived at the same time as the typhoon, and wasn't able to transfer our rations before both ships had to run for the open sea. Our ship was down to beans, bread and coffee. Breakfast hadn't been much, and I really hoped the supply ship survived the storm.

We cruised opposite the area where the big planes were once moored and worked our way south. So far there were no clues as to the planes whereabouts. We passed a large LCI landing craft blown way up on the beach. I wondered how they would ever get a ship that size back in the water.

"Over here, Ted," Steve called. "I see a lagoon where we can tie up the barge."

Ted coasted the barge in and soon we were combing the beach. After seeing how far the big LCI had been blown ashore, I searched all the way back to the edge of the jungle. I noticed up ahead an unusual mound of sand at the base of several trees. After a quick inspection, I called the others and we gathered around.

Ted trotted back to the barge for a shovel and we took turns digging. The shovel struck metal and with a little more digging, we realized this was an upside down LCVP landing craft. I took my turn, and managed an opening under one side. By squirming I crawled under the boat and in the faint light explored the inside. A quick search revealed no dead bodies, so I checked out the wood and cardboard cases tumbled about the interior. Several had burst open. In the dim light, I tried to read the writing on the contents: canned ham, Canadian bacon, corned beef, peaches, and fruit cocktail.

"Hey, fellas, you better come in here," I called.

Soon all four of us were examining the treasure. Steve found several large tins partially buried and discovered they were five-pound cans of cheese. Ted operated on a can of corned beef and we had a snack right there.

"Looks to me like they had just started unloading the officers' goodies when the typhoon hit," I commented.

"What a shame," Steve replied. We all had big grins on our faces.

"Let's get it aboard the barge before someone else shows up," Ted suggested.

It took two round trips before we had it all concealed in the cabin.

"Where can we hide it on the ship?" Will wondered.

"There is a locked manhole cover close to where we secure the barge and I have the key." I replied.

Early in the afternoon we returned to the ship, swung the barge aboard and made preparations for the evening. Steve knew one of the bakers and talked him out of two loaves of bread. Ted knew an electrician who had a homemade double hot plate with a grill, who would loan it for a share of whatever we might be cooking.

The electrician knew secluded place topside to plug in the grill. Soon we had ham, cheese, and Canadian bacon sandwiches grilling on the hot plate. The aroma had our mouths watering. The first grilled sandwich tasted so good, we all had another. It was a feast and we topped it off with canned peaches and fruit cocktail.

We agreed to meet again the next night and I happily returned to my bunk. It was time for lights out and usually the men in our quarters were prepared for sleep—not this night!

"What's going on?" I asked one of the sailors.

"Can't you smell it?" he retorted. "The officers are having ham, bacon and cheese and I don't know what else, while we get bread and beans."

I saw Chief McGuire returning from officer's country, and he looked angry. "What's the matter, Chief?" I asked.

"The Lieutenant had the gall to call me to his quarters and ask if the chief's mess has some hidden food," he replied. "They are all smelling bacon and ham up there in officer's country and the Skipper wants to know where it is coming from. I told him all we have is bread and beans and to check out the warrant's mess."

It suddenly dawned on me; we had been preparing our feast hidden behind the big ventilation hood. The soft rumble I heard must have been the big pump blowing our cooking aromas throughout the ship. It took almost an hour for the air to clear and the men to calm down. We quickly decided to find another location for tomorrow evening's meal.

TWENTY-TWO

We were just getting back into our old routine when a rumor flashed through the ship. Some super-bomb had been dropped on Hiroshima. Three days later what they called an atom bomb was dropped on Nagasaki. Just five days after that the PA announced Japan had unconditionally surrendered. The war was over!!

That evening, we heard shellfire coming from all over the island, especially heavy from Buckner Bay. At first, I thought it was a last ditch attack, and then I realized it was a celebration. The Army heavy artillery were pointing their guns toward the sky and letting fly. When I saw the splashes from the spent shells falling around our ship, I found a place with a roof over my head.

The next morning, we hoisted our boats aboard and got under way. The crew was divided as to whether we were going home or on to Japan. Japan won, and in a short time we were the first American ship to put into Sasebo, a ship building port on the southern island of Kyushu.

We were scheduled for liberty the next day and that night we had an indoctrination session in the hangar on how to behave in Japan. A VD film followed this. To be perfectly safe, in the morning a corpsman stood at the gangway passing out rubbers to all liberty parties. I noticed everyone took one.

We four had planned on searching for saleable souvenirs—but this rubber in our pocket was too distracting. We headed into town looking for the local house of pleasure.

This was our first friendly meeting with the Japanese and it was a surprise to see them step off the sidewalk and bow as we passed. They were very small people. The ship's doctor said it was a matter of diet and I believed it. The Japanese I went to high school with were standard size.

Locating our destination was a little embarrassing in a city where no one seemed to speak English. Finally an older man understood our sign language, and pointed us in the right direction.

We remembered the lecture and left our shoes in the entranceway. Inside in the reception area, we saw two older Japanese men and an older Mama-san.

Mama-san spoke Pidgin English.

Steve asked, "How much?"

"Eight hunner yen, but girls hear Merican too big. You go somewhere else."

This was an unexpected development. Steve turned out to have the sweet talk.

"Oh no, Mama-san, Merican very small—see," and he spread the thumb and forefinger of one hand.

Mama-san still seemed dubious. "Me hear Merican big—too big!"

We all followed Steve's lead and denied the charge.

"No, no, Mama-san. Merican very small," and we shortened the distance between our fingers.

The sailors who came in behind us picked up the refrain, and Mama-san relented. She already knew the exchange rate was three hundred yen to the dollar. She went around collecting our money and then called the girls.

Bamboo and paper doors slid open along a long hallway with doors on each side. The girls came trooping down the corridor. From a distance they were very striking with their different colored kimonos. As they drew closer I realized something was dreadfully wrong! They were young, lovely —and in miniature! I could visualize problems ahead; however, Mama-San already had my money.

I hopefully chose the largest of the group and followed her down the hallway to her room. We entered and she slid the paper and bamboo door closed behind us. The room was empty except for a colorful mat on the floor and a low chest against the wall. The walls looked as if they were made of the same fragile material as the door.

She hesitantly began to remove her kimono. Not so hesitantly, I got my uniform out of the way. As I turned to her my doubts returned. She had an attractive, petite figure with small breasts. I doubted if she weighed ninety pounds.

Suddenly I remembered the VD film and I located and handed her the rubber. I know she was nervous as she fumbled with its installation—which was producing a result that made her more nervous yet. At last she finished and reluctantly lowered herself to the mat. There was something about this nude, slim body reclining there, that no matter how hard I tried to keep from getting overexcited—I knew what was happening.

As I came toward her and started to descend, I could see her look of apprehension turn to one of fear. She tried to keep her eyes on my face, but at the last second dropped them lower. I could see those attractive almond eyes getting rounder and rounder. Her mouth opened and—"AIIEE!!"—A scream of sheer terror reverberated through the fragile walls as she rolled to one side, scrambled to her feet and ran from the room. I couldn't believe that much noise came from such a tiny girl.

This chilling scream seemed to trigger a response in the other rooms, and I could hear the voices of upset sailors.

Mama-san charged down the hall, came to a halt before the open door of my room and caught me in an embarrassing moment. Her eyes also seemed to get rounder.

"Aiiee! I knew Merican too big. Out!! All Merican out!!"

She went down the hall jabbering Japanese and opening doors. In a short time there were about a dozen sailors in the reception room getting their money back, and being instructed to never return.

Our group got together outside, and Steve asked, "Who was in the room the scream came from?

Ted and Will denied it, and I sure didn't indicate it was me. We decided the big sailor in the second group must have been the culprit.

This was my first visit to this type of an establishment and I had real reservations about any return engagements. To come this close and fail so dramatically was a traumatic experience.

When we returned to the ship, the main topic of conversation was how some S.O.B. closed the only house in Sasebo.

The ship spent two more days at Sasebo and then departed for Tokyo Bay. We anchored just off the naval base at Yokohama along with part of the fleet. Even from the ship's rail we could see the base had received cruel punishment. The hangars were shattered and collapsed. Burned airplane hulks littered the runway.

We hoisted out the gasoline barge and serviced our PBM flying boats, which had already arrived. When we finished, we continued on to the ruined base and tied up at a concrete ramp.

We started out on a souvenir search, but were distracted by the Japanese pontoon trainers in the damaged hangars. Apparently an American demolition team had already been through there with axes. It was obvious they would never fly or float again.

In the third hangar, behind a partially collapsed roof, we found a biplane trainer on floats. It reminded me of the N3N back on the Cub line in San Diego. The axe wielders had chopped on the wings; however, the rest appeared to be in fine condition. The fuselage had a big red meatball painted on both sides.

I pulled the prop through and the compression felt good on the seven-cylinder, radial engine. I checked the floats for damage and was pleased to find they appeared watertight. An idea began to form.

"Hey, fellas!"

"Yeah, Jack?" Steve replied as all three turned and walked over to the plane.

"If we took off those chopped up wings, what would we have?"

Steve saw the possibilities. "A hot hydroplane."

"Right," Ted and Will added as they also saw the potential.

We checked the wing attaching bolts and realized they were metric and our tools wouldn't fit. We shook the other hangars down and found what used to be the tool cage. This hangar had received a lot of damage and the tools were badly scattered. While rummaging around, we found not only the right sockets but also a box of leather aviator helmets with goggles. I could see the resale possibilities and brought the box back with us.

We returned to the floatplane and begin removing the wings. Fortunately, the lower pair had a stub on each side. This would furnish some lift. The top wings detached from the fuselage, leaving the center section, which contained a small fuel tank.

The four-wheel dollies under the floats allowed us to easily push the plane outside, where we stopped at the top of the slanted concrete ramp. The plane didn't look like anything I'd ever seen before. With the short stubs on the bottom, the two cockpits with small windshields and the big red meatball on each side, it looked like something out of science fiction.

We filled the fuselage tank with gas. I got into the front cockpit and tried to figure out where the mags, throttle and mixture controls were. When I thought I had it, Steve stuck the crank of the inertia starter into the side of the accessory section and started cranking. Slowly at first and then with increasing speed, Steve wound up the starter. He had it fairly screaming when he gave the thumbs up.

I engaged the starter lever. The propeller started rotating. Finally there was a puff of blue smoke from the exhaust. The engine caught and then died down. I pumped wildly on the wobble pump and it started again. This time it kept going and smoothed down to an even, fast idle.

Ted and Will attached a rope to each of the wheeled dollies. Steve climbed into the back cockpit, and I taxied to the top of the sloping ramp.

There were no brakes on the dollies. In a second we were coasting down the ramp at an accelerating speed, and we hit the water with a burst of spray. The ropes to the dollies were too short, and Ted and Will were up to their waists in water before they could slide the dollies out from under the floats.

With just the thrust from the idling engine, we were moving right out into Tokyo Bay. I looked back at Steve; he gave thumbs up and I pushed the throttle to the stop.

The plane leapt forward. Just as the floats started to climb to the surface, the prop sucked the top off a wave and dumped about five gallons of seawater over us. It blinded me and I frantically pulled the throttle back. Now I knew what those helmets and goggles were for.

Steve and I managed to force the small helmets part way over our heads. I pulled the goggles down over my eyes and tried again. The moment the floats started skimming the surface, our speed accelerated at an alarming rate. I could turn, and raise and lower the nose with the tail controls. Without ailerons I had no way to keep it level, as we occasionally got airborne off the top of a wave. It meant heading directly into the waves on both our outward and return trip.

It was a wildly exhilarating ride. When I figured I'd used up about half the gas, I pulled the throttle back and let it idle. Steve and I clambered from one cockpit to another and Steve made the return trip.

Steve brought her in close to the gas barge, and we gassed up again. This time Ted and Will made a run. When they returned, we got the dollies under the floats. By giving the engine full throttle and pushing, we maneuvered the plane back up the ramp and into the hangar.

All of us were wet, tired and happy. We hadn't had so much fun since we borrowed the jeep on Saipan.

The next day we gained confidence and ventured further out into the bay and closer to the anchored ships.

Ted and Will were on their return run, when I saw they were on a collision course with a gig from the flagship. I grabbed the binoculars and sure enough, it was the one with an Admiral's flag flying from the stern.

I raised the binoculars out to the cruiser and could see the turrets were tracking the seaplane. Any second I expected to see them fire and blow the seaplane out of the water.

"Steve, come here quick. We've got big trouble!"

Steve took the binoculars and focused on the plane. Ted now saw the Admiral's gig and changed course to clear it.

I motioned to Steve. We fired up the gas barge and headed around the point where we could get out of sight of the fleet. Steve waved to Ted to follow us. As quickly as we were out of sight, we signaled Ted to cut the engine. When the prop stopped, we pulled right up alongside.

Ted and Will scurried into the barge. They realized what they had done. I hopped over onto the nearest float and with a big ballpein hammer knocked a hole in it below the water line. I then jumped to the other one and did the same. The seaplane was already sinking as I made it back to the barge. Steve pulled the barge away and as we looked back, the nose was already down with just the tail in the air. A moment later it too disappeared.

Steve made a big circle and returned to the ship from the direction of our flying boats. As we approached our ship, we could see signal lights blinking on most of the ships in the bay. I felt a cold, clammy perspiration break out on my forehead.

As we climbed aboard I saw the Warrant watching all the activities through a pair of binoculars.

"What's going on, Warrant?"

"Haven't you heard, Jack? Some crazy kamikaze they call *Mad Meatball* tried to crash the Admiral's gig in a wingless seaplane!"

"Why do they call him Mad Meatball?"

"I guess because of the two big meatballs painted on the fuselage. He's been tearing up and down the bay for a couple days now—just waiting for the Admiral."

"Did they get him?"

"Almost... the flagship was ready to blow him out of the water, only they were afraid of hitting the Admiral. Mad Meatball, disappeared around the point where those two motor whaleboats are headed."

The Warrant handed me the binoculars. As I got them focused, I saw the boats were filled with armed marines.

"Say, Jack, where were you when all the action was taking place?"

"Out on the barge, servicing the planes. Guess we missed all the excitement."

I left and quickly located the others. I had their full attention when I explained what happened. We all had an apprehensive feeling someone had seen the gas barge and the seaplane together. Every time the PA sounded, we were sure it was for us to report to the Officer of the Day.

The ship buzzed for the next few days about the fruitless search for Mad Meatball.

TWENTY-THREE

Mail call brought a letter from Mario, who ended with the question, "Is it really true what they say about Oriental women?"

I'd been asked this question before and I still didn't know what they were talking about. As I passed the photographer's workshop I glanced in and saw Stan painting another nude. I stepped inside to admire this latest creation, and it occurred to me Stan might know the answer.

"Stan, what do they mean when they ask if it's really true about Oriental women?"

Stan chuckled, "Jack, somehow the rumor got started in the States that because their eyes have a horizontal slant, another part of their body does also."

I was stunned. "There isn't any truth to it, is there?"

"None at all—it's just a wild rumor."

An idea began to work its way to the surface.

"Stan, could you produce a picture of a nude Japanese girl, suggesting this really is the case? You know, something tasteful, and with a negative so lots of copies could be made."

A glint came to Stan's eyes.

"Jack, I can, and it would sell like hotcakes. What's in it for me?"

"You name it—with the understanding this is my exclusive."

"All right, Jack, I'll make the original for twenty-five dollars, and furnish all the copies you want for two bits each."

"You've got a deal—how long will it take?"

"I'll get started right now. This sounds more interesting than Sally here. I should have the original finished day after tomorrow. You can tell me then how many copies you want."

The second afternoon I dropped by and Stan uncovered the finished product. It was breathtaking! She was so lifelike; at first I thought it was an actual photograph. I looked closer, and I suspected a combination of Stan's artistic and photographic skills, as parts of her body looked familiar.

She was reclining on a white bear skin, with one leg drawn up enough to partially obscure her lower anatomy. There was enough revealed to strongly suggest this beautiful Japanese girl was different. Her breasts were superb; I doubt if there was a girl in Japan who could match them. Her almond eyes were demurely downcast; however, a full, sensual, lower lip belied her shy expression.

"Stan, you have really done it! This little lady is going to make us some big money. Could you make a hundred copies right away?"

Stan nodded with a pleased smile, while I dug up fifty bucks for the original and copies.

Stan got to work, and by evening delivered a hundred, post card size reproductions. I had those sold in an hour at a buck each, and never left my sleeping compartment. I rushed back to Stan and ordered five hundred for the next day.

The word had spread, and in the chow line the next morning I was already getting orders. By noon these were gone; even the officers were buying. By evening I was selling pictures that weren't fully dried.

Apparently I'd stumbled onto *the* souvenir of World War Two. The thought crossed my mind when those pictures reached home; the United States was going to be firmly convinced Japanese girls really were different!

I asked Stan how much sensitized paper he had left.

"Jack, we can run off another five hundred, and then this ship is out of the picture business."

"Well, by all means run them off. If they sell this well on our ship, they'll do just as well on the other ships here in the bay."

"Jack, that's the answer. I'll visit the photographer mates on the other ships and deal them out of their surplus paper. That way they won't be able to make a negative out of one of our pictures, and go into business for themselves."

A makeshift dock had been built at the air station ruins, and this was where all the liberty boats disembarked. Stan and I caught our liberty boat to the dock, and waited for one from another ship to arrive.

When it showed up, I started hawking pictures to the new arrivals, and Stan took the empty boat back to their ship. By the time Stan returned, I'd sold over a hundred pictures to the several boatloads that had disembarked. Stan handed me a box of paper, and I took it back to our ship while he headed for another. By evening, we had all the Navy surplus paper in Yokohama. Fortunately Stan was a sharp bargainer; because this was above and beyond our original deal, I had to pay for it.

I'd been so busy with the seaplane, and then the picture business, I hadn't made a liberty into Yokohama yet. The next day, I went ashore with the rest of the gasoline detail, and brought along a hundred pictures, just in case.

Yokohama was one of Japan's major cities. Now, it was sad to walk down streets where there wasn't a building standing. There were people half-heartedly poking through the burned rubble of what once were their homes. The city was now checker-boarded with one area untouched and another completely destroyed. Japanese homes were mostly wood and paper and the fire-bombings had been especially devastating.

We located an area where the B29's missed, and shopped for souvenirs. Each shop had much the same goods: kimonos, fans, paintings, and ivory doo-dads. The shops were filled with sailors, all looking for something different.

I casually pulled out a picture, and loudly started describing it to Steve. In a moment we had a crowd of onlookers, and soon I was doing a better business than the storekeeper. The biggest surprise was when two Japanese men came over to see what I had, got all excited and each bought one. I couldn't believe it—with the anatomical error and all.

I had a similar success in each shop I visited, until the pictures were all gone, and I had bought a fancy kimono for my sister and a beautifully embroidered robe for mother.

All day Japanese men wanting to buy American cigarettes had approached us. The going rate was fifty yen per pack, or five hundred per carton. We got them for a nickel a pack at ships' stores, but were only allowed to leave the gangway with one unopened pack. I could see a real profit potential here.

As we walked back to the dock, we passed an impressive Japanese home, with a lagoon and dock. There was a large warehouse to the side, which had been damaged.

We were abreast of the home, when an older Japanese man came out, and tried to tell us something. He didn't speak much English, we didn't speak any Japanese, and sign language wasn't working too well. Finally in despair, he turned to the house and called something. In a moment a lovely, young Japanese girl came out to act as interpreter.

I was afraid my face revealed my reaction. This was the first girl I had been attracted to since arriving in this country. She was tall for a Japanese girl, slim, and with just what might be breasts under that tight band Japanese women seemed to all wear.

She bowed gracefully, and with a friendly smile said, "Papa-san regrets he not able to speak personally. He like to be your trading representative while you here in Japan. He have many unusual items he sure you find interesting. He have need for American cigarettes and food."

The more she talked the more intrigued I became. Not only was she lovely, she projected an inner self-confidence. This girl was completely different from anyone I'd met before. Somehow, I had to get to know her better.

"Your English is very good," I complimented her, "where did you learn?"

"From a university professor here in Yokohama. I have almost four years before the university burn." I noticed an unhappy expression cross her face.

"If I locate the things your Papa-san wants, where should I bring them?"

"Right here to the house. Just call for Kumiko—that's me."

"My name is Jack, Kumiko. This is Steve, Will and Ted." She bowed, and they just naturally bowed in return.

Papa-san had been watching our conversation and when it ended he smiled and bowed. We smiled and bowed and continued on our way.

"Wow! What a chick!" Steve gulped.

"Yeah, but did you see the sharp eye Papa-san keeps on her?" reminded Ted.

We discussed the possibilities, business and otherwise, all the way to the dock.

After chow I located a cook I knew, and make a deal for two steaks. It cost me two pictures and five hundred yen. I picked up four cartons of cigarettes at ships stores, and talked Steve into running me in to the beach with the gas barge. We took Ted along as bow hook.

The barge was tied up below the fantail and when Ted got aboard; I dropped my package down to him, and then climbed down the rope ladder. Steve climbed aboard and we quietly pulled out for the beach out of sight from the gangway and the officer of the deck.

The tide was in and Steve took her into the lagoon, pulling right up to Papa-san's dock. I jumped off with my package and pushed the bow off so Steve could turn around. Anyway, I'd just as soon they were gone before Kumiko showed up.

Steve called out to ask, "How are you going to get back, Jack?"

"I'll come on the morning liberty boat," I called back.

They were almost out of the lagoon, before they realized I planned on spending the night.

I walked to the entrance of the house and Kumiko already had the door open. After all our commotion, she could have no doubt she had company. Kumiko invited me in, and I remembered to slip my shoes off first.

We stepped directly into the living area, which was dominated by a round, ceramic receptacle, a low table, and a chest with doors on each side. Cushions were scattered around the table.

Papa-san and Mama-san both bowed from the table as we entered, and Kumiko said something in Japanese. I caught the "Jack" part. They both bowed again, I bowed, and then I sat down on a cushion.

Mama-san was an older version of Kumiko and still an attractive lady.

Both she and Kumiko were wearing the plain robe Japanese women wear when they aren't all dolled up in their kimonos. I could feel warmth radiating from the large low urn, and realized this was their heating and cooking system. There was a charcoal fire inside.

Mama-san had been brewing tea, which she poured and Kumiko served. I could tell it was a regular little ceremony, so I watched Papa-san and did what he did. The tea wasn't anything I was going to get hooked on, but it was palatable.

I remembered the package and begin to open it. The steaks were wrapped separately, and I handed this package to Mama-san, with as much of a bow as I can make from a sitting position.

"Please tell Mama-san this is a present," I instructed Kumiko.

She finished speaking Japanese about the same time Mama-san reached the top steak, which was beginning to thaw. I could tell how excited she was by how round those almond eyes became. There was a lot of Japanese talk, and even Papa-san had to come over to see. They all marveled at this steak like they have never seen one before.

"Jack, this is more meat than we have seen since the war!" exclaimed Kumiko. "Mama-san is overwhelmed! She wants to know if you have eaten yet."

I told her no. I had purposely skipped supper with this in mind. Mama-san went right to work. She slid a cutting board out of the chest, and then with an incredibly sharp knife, chopped the thawing steak into small pieces. She placed these into what appeared to be a flattened version of a Chinese wok. She added a little oil and lowered it to brackets over the charcoal fire. While the meat was braising, she took the remaining steak to another room and returned with some crisp garden vegetables. She chopped and added these to the wok, a little sauce from a bottle, and stirred it all together slowly. In just a few minutes, she retrieved the wok, and scooped the contents into bowls. Everything was fine until she handed me a bowl—and chopsticks.

I knew right away I was in trouble. What was even worse, the food smelled delicious, and I was suddenly ravenously hungry.

I watched the others and made a valiant effort. I kept the bowl under the chopsticks, so as the food fell off, at least it wasn't lost. Unfortunately, by the time the sticks reached my mouth, they were empty.

Kumiko saw my difficulty and showed me a better position with my fingers. I tried again with the same results.

I was so hungry I'd about switched to fingers, when Kumiko came to the rescue. She popped a mouthful from my bowl on to her sticks and into my mouth. It was delicious. Mama-san and Papa-san got to laughing every time she made the transfer.

After dinner, Papa-san and I got down to business—with Kumiko as interpreter. I brought out the four cartons of Lucky Strikes, and Papa-san's eyes lit up. He peeled off two thousand yen, and Kumiko said that he could use all I could bring later.

This was small potatoes compared to my picture business, but being around a beautiful girl like Kumiko, more than made up for it.

She asked how I was going to get back to the ship, and when I told her I was taking the morning liberty boat, she said she would fix a sleeping mat right here.

Kumiko explained to Papa-san what was going on, and while she was getting the bedding, they bowed good night and retired. Kumiko returned with a mat, a quilt and a sandbag for a pillow. It was a pleasure to watch her fixing up the bed. When she finished I stretched out and, although I overlapped the mat by about a foot, I knew I'd be able to sleep.

I slid over a little and motioned for her to join me. She hesitated then gracefully sat on one edge of the mat. She relaxed as we got to talking, and I found out what it was like to be on the wrong side of a war.

Papa-san had been a well-to-do rice merchant before the war. They had a car, spent their vacations at a mountain inn, and she was one of the few girls taught by a professor from the university where only boys were allowed to attend.

When the war came, a bombing raid blew out one end of Papa-san's warehouse and he lost a great deal of his rice. He was just now beginning to get back in business.

Kumiko had been engaged to a university student, who was a reserve naval cadet. When the homeland was about to be invaded, he volunteered for "the divine wind," or kamikaze. It was a one-way flight for him!

Kumiko's job was to act as interpreter for Papa-san, and to help get his business back on its feet. Papa-san felt his future was tied to trade with the Americans.

By then it was getting late and she said she must leave. I rose to my feet and pulled her up. This brought her up close, and when she didn't back away, I opened my arms. She hesitated just a second then slipped inside. I'd almost forgotten how great it felt to have an attractive female body this close. Her head came right under my chin. I dropped a gentle kiss on the top of her head and this caused her to look up. I knew I shouldn't, but I was starting to home in on those inviting lips when she recognized my intent.

"Oh no, Jack, Japanese girls don't kiss!" she exclaimed, and ducked out of our embrace. "Good night, Jack," she said sadly, and left the room. I figured I'd really blown it, and had a hard time getting to sleep.

In the morning when I woke, Kumiko was already there, and had tea brewing over the charcoal fire. She poured us both a cup and joined me on the mat. Her freshly brushed hair was loose about her shoulders, and she was utterly captivating.

"Jack, I hope you not mad about last night?"

"No, Kumiko, I know we each have different customs. I just didn't know about that one of yours."

"I never kiss anyone before—even my fiancé."

I glanced at my watch and saw it was time to leave for the early morning liberty boat. I slipped my jumper on, then retrieved my shoes from the entrance, "Tell Papa-san and Mama-san goodbye, perhaps I can come back some time."

"I hope you do," she said, and dropped to her knees to tie my shoes.

That was a custom I could learn to like. When she stood up I was prepared to leave, but she came up close and slipped into my arms for just a moment.

"Please come back, Jack," she whispered, and quietly returned to the inside of the house.

I felt so good I whistled all the way to the boat dock.

When I returned to the ship, I found everyone excited about the new rotation plan. It was on a point basis, with so many points for each month of service, and so many points for each month overseas. I checked the list, and found I was about a third of the way down from the top of the going home list.

Everyone else was excited about going home, but I was worried. I knew the time to get the airplane money was very limited. I had only mailed a thousand to the bank so far and I knew I'd need at least two thousand more.

I gathered up the last printing of pictures, and spend the rest of the day on the boat landing.

That evening I got four cartons of cigarettes from ship's stores, lowered it to the gas barge, and covered them up. I was surprised they still sold them in such quantity.

When we finished with the seaplanes the following morning, I got Steve to pull into Papa-san's dock. I dropped off the cigarettes, and told Kumiko I would be back that evening.

The cigarettes must have made an impression, because I got a royal welcome when I arrived on the evening liberty boat. The coxswain of the liberty boat tried to hide his curiosity about why I was traveling in the wrong direction this time of evening.

Mama-san had gone all out on dinner, including soup, rice and the last of the steak. I did better with the chopsticks when I wasn't so nervous.

After dinner Papa-san went into another room and returned with an automatic pistol and leather holster. It had been freshly oiled and appeared to be in excellent condition.

Kumiko translated, "This is Japanese officer's pistol with full clip. Papa-san say he trade it for the cigarettes if you not need yen."

I didn't hesitate. I knew if I could get the pistol to the States it would bring big money—if I didn't keep it for myself.

"Papa-san, you have a deal. You keep the pistol here till I leave for the States."

When this was translated, the fact I trusted him seemed to make an impression.

Papa-san and Mama-san retired early. Kumiko fixed my mat and this time it was easier to get her to join me. The fact kissing was forbidden made it all the more intriguing. I tried a little psychology.

"Kumiko, I know you say Japanese girls don't kiss. American boys like to kiss very much. I have a compromise in mind."

"I don't think so, Jack"

"How can you say that, Kumiko, when you don't even know what I'm thinking?"

"You're thinking about kissing."

"That may be true, but I'm not going to ask you to do anything you don't want to. Lean back a little and I'll prove it."

Kumiko hesitated, and then slowly leaned back against my chest. I slipped my arms around her waist. She was stiff at first, but when nothing terrible happened, she relaxed and came on back into my arms. This felt mighty fine with her hair against my cheek. I nuzzled her hair until I found a bare spot on her neck. I moved my lips across this smooth skin and she started to straighten up. I moved on past and she came back. A couple more times and she stayed right there. I enlarged the working area and soon we were up to an ear lobe. I got a pretty violent reaction there, so set it aside for the time being.

By then I was getting a crick in my back and we shifted positions. I got my back against the wall for support and held her cradled in my arms. This was comfortable for both of us and brought her lovely face into range. I moved closer.

"Jack, what you doing?"

"Just bringing your pretty face closer to mine."

"You know what I say about kissing?"

"Oh yes, I know but it takes two to kiss. If you don't do anything—not kissing. Now if my lips should touch your face, be very still and you'll be safe."

While she was thinking that one over, I brushed the soft skin of her forehead with my lips. I felt her stiffen and slowly relax. I continued on to a smooth cheek and then to the soft spot just above her lovely chin. I took enough time for her to get used to the idea, then started working up. I had just reaching the forbidden area when she ducked her head and scrambled to her feet.

"Good night, Jack," she said, kind of breathless, and disappeared into her room.

When I awoke the next morning, Kumiko was waiting with a cup of hot tea.

"Good morning, Kumiko. You sure left in a hurry last night."

"Jack, I get scared. I think pretty soon we be kissing. I hope you not mad."

"No, Kumiko, you're my favorite Japanese girl."

"When will you come back?"

"I should have something soon for Papa-san. I'll come then."

I caught the early morning liberty boat back. It was the same coxswain I had coming over and he gave me a conspiratorial wink. I was glad he didn't know how slowly I was progressing.

By then, Stan had another five hundred pictures ready and the next two days I was busy at the dock selling them. The third day I remembered the food cases left over from Okinawa. We had finished the ham, cheese, bacon, peaches and fruit cocktail, but there were several cases left, I lowered these down to the barge along with a carton of cigarettes. Ships stores were no longer selling them in large lots. I remembered to get some more steaks.

We serviced the aircraft and then pulled into Papa-san's dock, where I dropped off the food and cigarettes. Kumiko happily came out to see me, and I told her I'd be back that evening.

My welcome was even warmer than last time. Mama-san had added another course to dinner—octopus! By now, I was doing much better with the chopsticks, and was developing a taste for Japanese food. The octopus was delicious.

When dinner was over, Kumiko said, "Papa-san wants to talk big business." He bowed, I bowed, and she said, "Papa-san say please follow him."

We went out through a door in back that connected to the warehouse. Papa-san flipped a switch, and several low wattage bulbs dimly light the cavernous interior. I could see where the damaged end had been temporarily repaired. The other end was filled with sacks that probably contained rice. The warehouse was a lot larger than I had at first thought and I could see there was a lot of space going to waste. I pointed to a rounded hump under a tarp and asked Kumiko what it was?

"Oh, that's our car," and she mentioned a Japanese name I'd never heard of.

When we removed the tarp I could see it was small, and reminded me of a 1937 Austin I saw once. It appeared to be in running condition; the tires were still inflated.

"Why don't you use it?" I asked.

"No gasoline since the war," she replied sadly.

I was wondering what would happen if I gave it a shot of 140 octane aircraft fuel?

"Kumiko, ask Papa-san if he would like to get it running again? I can get gasoline."

She translated and answered, "Papa-san say if you can get it going, you can use it all you want."

Great! I was starting to get excited.

"Jack, the car isn't what Papa-san wants to talk about."

"All right, Kumiko, what does he have in mind?"

"Papa-san say he hear United States is going to distribute much food here until farmers can raise crops again. Papa-san would like McArthur to know he has a complete distribution set up, ready to go. Papa-san would like you to stay here in Japan and be partner. He like the way your mind work. You take care of American end; he take care of Japanese."

Papa-san has been watching my face as she translated. He must have seen the offer came as a surprise. After a moment's reflection, I realized the suggestion had merit. It really was a most generous offer, with Papa-san already established.

I bowed to Papa-san and told Kumiko, "Tell him I consider the offer a great honor and I will give it very serious consideration." He bowed, and I bowed again and we returned to the house.

Papa-san and Mama-san disappeared while she was fixing my mat. This time there wasn't any hesitation and she came right into my arms. After I held her close for a minute, she asked, "Do you think you might stay, Jack?"

"I don't know, Kumiko, I already had some plans made and I doubt if I can be discharged in Japan. I'm almost sure I'd have to return to the States to get out of the Navy. Let me do some thinking about it."

This offer had thrown me such a curve I couldn't seem to mount my usual assault on her lips.

The next day aboard ship, I was leaning on the rail, looking at a bombed out portion of Yokohama, and wondering if I really would care to live here.

I heard a voice behind me. "Hello, Jack"

"Oh, hi, Lieutenant. I didn't hear you come up. I was just leaning here trying to decide what to do when I get discharged. It looks like my time is about up."

"That's one of the things I want to talk to you about, Jack, but first, do you think you might be able to make it to L.A. about three months from now?"

"I suppose so. Why?"

"It looks as if it will be at least two months before I can leave the ship. Right now there isn't anyone to replace me. Jill and I have the wedding planned shortly after I return and we'd like you to be best man."

"I'll be there!"

"Great! I'll have Jill keep you informed on the date. The other thing I wanted to mention is the letter from my brother. He says they are shorthanded at the yard, and there is a backlog of orders. This is post-war business, Jack, and the future looks good. Anyway, I know you are good with machinery and our college there has an evening marine engineering course. Jack, why don't you join us when you get out?"

"Wow! That's quite an offer, Lieutenant, I'll really give it serious thought."

It *was* quite an offer. Knowing the situation as well as I did, I knew Dan left a lot unsaid— like a closer family relationship with Niki, and when his brother retired, possibly a closer business one.

Dan didn't realize it, but all he had done was compound my original problem. What I really wanted to be was a single, Alaskan bush pilot.

It was time to service the flying boats. After we finished I asked the crew if they'd like to help me get a car running. It sounded more interesting than going back to the ship, so we pulled into the lagoon and tied up at Papa-san's dock.

Kumiko came out and I told her what we planned. She unlocked the big door to the warehouse and we trooped inside. When I pulled the tarp off the car I could see the others get excited. We pushed it out into the sunshine and gave it a quick going over. I'd stashed four quarts of oil from the inert gas machine, and I gave the car a quick oil change. Steve pulled the fuel hose over from the barge and filled the tank with 140 octane.

I connected jumper cables to half of the barge's twelve volt battery and the other ends to the car's six-volt one. We let the car battery have time to absorb some juice, and while we were waiting, Will found the tire pump in the trunk and brought the tire pressure up to normal.

Well, it was time to try it, so I got in, turned the key and mashed the starter. With all that amperage connected to it, the starter really took off. I pumped madly on the accelerator and one cylinder started to fire. In a second another joined and I shut off the starter before it overheated. I believed the engine was in shock from the 140-octane gas. The other two cylinders reluctantly joined, and I let it warm up before I adjusted the carburetor. The engine smoothed out, and we disconnected the jumper cables.

I told Kumiko we were taking it on a test ride; the others hopped in and away we went. The engine was very small, and with all our weight the acceleration wasn't much. Most of the other vehicles on the streets were trucks, busses and an occasional American Staff car.

We got a lot of attention as we went buzzing downtown, mostly from envious sailors.

It was getting toward evening; I was afraid the Warrant might be wondering what happened to the gas barge, so we headed back. Papa-san and Kumiko were there when we arrived. I believe I detected an expression of relief on Papa-san's face as he saw his car was still intact.

We topped off the gas tank, and I returned the car to the warehouse. Papa-san remembered the others from the first time we met, and Kumiko had been translating. She asked if I could stay, and we waved as the gas barge and the rest of the crew returned to the ship.

Mama-san was cooking dinner and tonight it was seafood. After dinner, Papa-san went to his room and returned with an officer's compact set of binoculars.

"Papa-san say that he will trade binoculars for what you bring last time."

I was happy to accept. I really didn't want to admit the offer of a partnership threw me so badly I forgot to collect.

"Please ask Papa-san to keep it for me, Kumiko."

"Papa-san want to know if you have thought about coming into business?"

"I'm thinking about it; it's a very great honor."

She and Papa-san talked fast for a few minutes and then she began. "Papa-san feel badly you haven't had a chance to see real Japan. Now the car is running he hopes that you will visit most beautiful inn in mountains."

"It sounds great, Kumiko, but not speaking Japanese, I'd probably never find it."

"Papa-san say I can come as guide," she replied, her face innocently downcast.

I knew this was no small thing—Papa-san was rolling out the big artillery.

"Ask Papa-san how long it will take."

"Papa-san say leave here in morning, reach inn early afternoon, come back next afternoon."

Wow! Papa-san wasn't kidding around.

"Please tell Papa-san I like the idea very much. When shall we go?"

"Whenever you like, Jack"

"How about tomorrow? That's Saturday and I should be able to get away."

"I'll be ready, Jack"

I caught the last liberty boat back to the ship, and located the Warrant. When he found out I had a weekend invitation to an inn in the mountains, he just shook his head and said I might as well. I knew he suspected I had something going on.

TWENTY-FOUR

It was a clear, spring morning, and I believe Kumiko was feeling as elated as I was. We waved goodbye to Papa-san and Mama-san and started out on the road to Tokyo. Kumiko had on her prettiest kimono and with the excitement showing in her eyes, she was really something to look at. I noticed she was getting considerable attention from two Army Lieutenants, passing in a staff car.

When we were about a half hour out of Yokohama, we cut inland and started to climb. Papa-san's car had a tendency to overheat and I suspected it might be the 140-octane gasoline. I didn't want to burn out the valves, so we stopped whenever we came to a scenic place. It was late afternoon when we arrived at the inn.

The scene was right out of a travel magazine. The inn was nestled into a gentle, pine-covered slope. A crystal clear brook curved around one side in a series of small waterfalls, with an arched, bright red footbridge where the pathway crossed the stream. The low-profile inn appeared to be made of cedar, with the wood darkened by age. We parked in the courtyard and slipped our shoes off on the veranda. So far we hadn't seen any other guests.

The manager recognized Kumiko as we entered. There was much smiling and bowing. She introduced me in Japanese, we each bowed, and the manager called a pretty little maid who led us to a spacious room on the view side. She carried two robes called yukatas and two sets of straw sandals, which she placed beside the low table near the open sliding window. I could hear the restful sound of water as it went over a falls. The maid said a few words and bowed as she left.

"She wished us a most enjoyable visit," explained Kumiko.

It was now obvious that we are going to share this room and I could feel the adrenalin start to flow. Kumiko walked to the open window to admire the superb view; as I came up behind her I slipped my arms around her waist. She leaned back for a minute and then asked, "Jack, have you ever had a Japanese bath?"

"I've heard of them but never had the chance. Why?"

"This inn famous for its bath—very special water. Before war Papa-san bring us here many times. You like to try?"

"Sounds great!"

"All right, Jack, we hang our clothes here," she indicated a low wardrobe, "and then we put on the yukata and sandals and go to bath."

Kumiko casually turned her back and slipped out of the kimono and whatever was underneath. She picked the yukata with the large sleeves and pretty embroidery, slipped into it and tied the obi to hold it together.

As she hung up her clothes in the wardrobe, I took the plunge and removed my uniform. While she was hanging it up, I removed the rest and tried on the plain yukata. It obviously was designed for a much smaller man. I pulled the obi tight and felt at least partially covered. We tripped down the hallway on our straw sandals with my toes overhanging the soles by at least an inch.

Kumiko turned into a steamy room with wooden benches and a big urn of very warm water. There were wooden pegs on the far wall.

"Hang the yukata here," she instructed, as she turned her back and demonstrated.

I noticed two hanging there already. While I removed mine and slipping off the sandals, she was already soaping up. I figured if she could be blasé about this, it sure shouldn't bother me. I got a good lather up and then watched her take the large dipper and pour water over herself. As the soap washed away, a profile view did things to my blood pressure.

Not only was Kumiko taller than most Japanese girls, she had well formed, slim legs, a nicely sculptured rear, and now that they were released, breasts that were an exciting surprise.

I quickly reached for the dipper, and tried to drown the thoughts about to get me in trouble. The water helped and I followed her through the entrance to what she called a bath, but was really a pool.

There must have been room for a dozen people, and there was one older couple already in the pool.

I'd have liked to get beneath the water as quickly as possible; however, I soon discovered it was just too hot. I finally made it under and began to relax.

The lady said something in Japanese, and soon Kumiko was introducing Mr. Kioshi and his wife from Tokyo. She told them my name and we all bowed our heads.

I could tell Mrs. Kioshi was asking questions, and Kumiko was reluctantly answering. I guess she found out all she wanted because soon she and her husband got up to leave. I noticed both of their skins were flushed from the warmth of the water. I also noticed Mrs. Kioshi was as flat-chested as most of the other Japanese women I'd seen. I appreciated my good fortune all the more.

My forehead was perspiring and Kumiko soon decided I'd had enough. It was strange how the bath removed all self-consciousness. We strolled back to the first room, where she found towels and we dried off.

As we were slipping on our yukatas and sandals I asked, "What were you and Mrs. Kioshi talking about?"

Kumiko became all flustered and dropped her head. "I tell you some time, Jack"

It must have been quite a conversation.

"This inn have girl who give very good massage—feels very nice after bath. Mama-san had her teach me each time we were here. Mama-san teach me from little girl all ways to make husband happy.

"Kumiko, if I have a massage I'd rather you gave it to me."

"All right," she smiled, "when we get back to the room."

The maid had been in while we were gone and I could see two futons had been placed side by side at the opposite end of the room from the table. The futons reminded me of sleeping bags without zippers. I stretched out on one and it was very comfortable.

Kumiko clapped her hands twice, and in a few seconds the maid arrived and bowed. She told her what she wanted and it wasn't long before the maid was back with a tray and warm body lotion. There was a small pot with two cups on the tray. Kumiko poured and handed one to me. I propped myself up on an elbow and took a sip.

"Wow! What is this?"

"Hot sake—very good to relax—now out of yukata."

I got up, slipped it off and while she hung it up I stretched out on my stomach. I could feel her pour the warm lotion on my shoulders, and then her busy hands went to work. She started with the neck and arms, skipped the back, then down to the toes. Just as I was ready to turn over I felt her return to the back and shoulders, only with a heavier pressure this time. I glanced to the side to see what she was doing and found she wasn't there. It suddenly registered that she was standing on my back and massaging with her toes, while she held on to a chrome bar above my futon.

She finished the back, spread a towel across my middle and had me turn over. Before she started I finished the hot sake. This side went even better.

As she leaned over me to work on my chest muscles, the yukata opened enough for me watch her breasts do their little dance. This, together with the hot sake was having powerful results. The towel had developed a life of its own. I cast it aside, reached up to encircle Kumiko's waist and bring her closer.

"Jack, I not finished with massage!"

"You're finished, Kumiko."

"Let me at least untie the obi!"

I released her so she could get the obi out of the way, then she came back to this delightful position. The yukata was open and covered her back.

She knew this was the moment of no return and whispered, "Jack, if you promise to do what I say—I try to make you happy. You very large and I afraid you hurt me if you move."

Well, when I thought back to what happened at Sasebo, I decided anything was better than nothing.

"All right, Kumiko, I promise."

I wasn't sure what all she was doing under the yukata; I saw the body lotion disappear. I felt warm moisture, followed by a slowly descending, delightfully tight, presence.

Unfortunately, the descent ended too soon. She had carefully resumed a semi-reclining position above me, which gave me access to the breasts that intrigued me so. Suddenly I felt the beginning of indescribably erotic, rippling, muscular contractions. My face must have registered my delighted surprise.

"You like, Jack?"

"Ooooh, I like, Kumiko!"

It was a completely relaxed, superbly pleased, Jack, who sat beside Kumiko at the low table watching the maid serve the evening meal. The thought crossed my mind that a young Kamikaze probably left for his one-way flight in much the same condition. Kumiko may not have kissed, but such exceptional expertise suggested she had not let that curtail life's other pleasures.

The dinner had several courses; each one served hot, and ended up with more hot sake. There must be something aphrodisiac about this drink because as I glanced at slim, bare legs, I felt a definite reaction.

After the maid left I asked, "Kumiko, what were you and Mrs. Kioshi talking about?"

She ducked her head, and laughed embarrassedly.

"Mrs. Kioshi feel much concern for me. She wanted to know how I'm going to take care of that big thing."

"What did you tell her?"

"I tell her—ask me that question tomorrow!"

I slowly rose from the low table, reached down and helped Kumiko up. She came into my arms and this time as I brought my head down, she let our lips meet. They were firmly closed at first, however, with a little encouragement; I could feel them begin to relax. I was just about to get them open when she ducked her head down to my chest.

We slowly walked over to the futons where I removed my yukata and hung it up. She hesitated a second and then did the same. Before she turned, I slipped my arms around her and slowly caressed this seductive, slim beauty. I could feel her breathing accelerate and her body start to tremble.

She turned to a facing position, and with downcast face said, "Jack, I hope you not be disappointed. My body feel all strange; I don't think I can make you happy that way again—tonight." She dropped her head further as if to apologize for her failure.

I lowered myself to the futon and coaxed her into lying beside me.

"Kumiko, you made me very happy. Now it's my turn, you don't have to do anything more, I'll take it from here.'

I began with soft exploratory kisses to locate the sensuous places, and soon I was getting increasing responses. We had all the time in the world, and when I got to her lips, this time they opened and met each gentle thrust. As we approached the universal position of love, Kumiko looked up into my eyes, and in a breathless little voice whispered, "Please don't hurt me, Jack!"

This more than reminded me it was her turn, and not to get carried away. I employed every bit of self-control and skill I possessed. Her quickening responses told me—soon, and then I was overjoyed to feel those erotic contractions begin—not as strongly as before—but enough we reached that ecstatic moment together.

She curled up in my arms and just before I drifted off to sleep, she kissed me on the lips and murmured, "You make me happy, Jack"

I awoke with the sun streaming through the window area. Kumiko was still asleep, and I pushed the futon aside to admire this lovely Japanese girl. Her lips were parted, as if asking for another kiss. A cool breeze touched her nipples and they became erect. My gaze reached the apex of those exciting slim legs and I could feel my blood pressure increase.

She opened her eyes, surveyed the situation, and said, "Jack, get that look out of your eyes!" She started to rise, and then fell back. "Oh, help me up!"

We got her up and she tried walking.

"I think I ruined. I must have bath now." She winced. We put our yukatas and sandals on and slowly made it to the bath. Fortunately, we were the only ones there this early, and she stretched out in the hot water.

"Oh, this feels good!"

She improved to the point where I could coax her between my legs and this greatly increased my enjoyment of the bath.

"Jack, stop that—someone might come!"

I decided I'd had enough hot water and headed for the towels. I took my time and when she joined me later, I could see she was walking normally.

We returned to our room where the maid had removed the futons, and the table was set for breakfast. I stuck to tea that morning. I knew what hot sake could do.

When we finished breakfast, Kumiko looked out over the pathway and the bridge over the stream.

"Jack, let's take a little walk—I want you to see how beautiful the inn."

"You sure I won't have to carry you back?"

"Oh no, Jack, I feel much better now."

I felt a little self-conscious walking around outside in the yukata, but by the time we reached the bridge I'd forgotten all about it.

The smell of the pines, the sounds of the splashing water, and especially Kumiko's happy exuberance, made the walk a delight. We reached a pine-covered promontory, where we could look back across the stream to the inn. I wished I was an artist; I'd like to paint this scene and take it with me.

We were slowly returning when we saw Mr. and Mrs. Kioshi approaching, wearing their yukatas; we stopped and bowed as we met.

Mrs. Kioshi fired off a few questions and seemed pleased with the answers. Mr. Kioshi didn't seem nearly as pleased. We all bowed again and continued on our way.

"Did Mrs. Kioshi ask what I think she asked?"

Kumiko smiled, "She asked."

"What did you tell her?"

A wicked gleam came into her eyes.

I tell her, "Merican very gentle, very great lover. She doesn't know what she is missing."

We return to the room and it was time we started back to Yokohama. As we slipped off the yukatas, I held her in my arms one more time; she could tell what was happening.

"Jack, what you doing?"

"Just being a very gentle, very great lover."

"You be that one more time, and I let you explain to Papa-san why I can't walk."

She did have a point.

I left a nice tip for the pretty little maid and we stopped by the office. Considering the exceptional service, I felt the bill was most reasonable. I had a feeling business was pretty quiet right then. The manager was very friendly, and I asked Kumiko to tell him I enjoyed my visit very much. He said he hoped I would be able to return. Kumiko translated, I bowed, he bowed and we were on our way.

TWENTY-FIVE

The ship was all-astir when I returned. When Steve saw me he advised, "Jack, go take a look at the list posted in the hanger!"

I located the list, and sure enough it had the names of the ones to return to the States on the next transport. Steve and I were among the lucky ones. On the bottom were instructions to report aboard the transport next Monday. This left less than a week to wind up our affairs.

I thought about Kumiko and Papa-San. I knew it was unlikely I would return and I wanted to help them before I left. I checked for the location of the Army occupational headquarters, found it was in Tokyo, and let an idea begin to form.

The next day I stopped at Papa-san's and broke the news of my leaving. The family looked so unhappy, I broached my idea. They began to perk up a little, and Kumiko agreed to come to Tokyo with me in the morning.

I slipped away on the early morning liberty boat, and Kumiko and I caught the early, high-speed passenger train to Tokyo. She wore her prettiest kimono, and it seemed I was the only round eye on the train. The Tokyo station was crowded. I had never seen so many people together.

We located a rickshaw, and Kumiko told the little man between the shafts to take us to the occupational headquarters. As we rode through the crowded streets, it appeared Tokyo had not been damaged as badly as Yokohama.

He stopped in front of a former insurance building, with American and Japanese streaming through the doors. When we went inside I asked for whoever was in charge of food distribution in the Yokohama area. We ended up in a cubbyhole office facing a young Army Captain and his Japanese assistant.

"Good morning sir," my name is Jack Barnes, and this is Kumiko Shurama."

He stood up from behind his desk, and I saw he wasn't much taller than Kumiko.

"I'm Captain Anderson, what can I do for you?"

"Miss Shurama's father was a rice merchant in Yokohama, with a large warehouse and a dock with access to the bay. He would like you to know he is available for any planned food distribution in the Yokohama area."

I sensed the Captain was interested—I just couldn't tell if it was the warehouse or Kumiko.

"How large is the warehouse?"

"Oh, I guess about seventy feet wide and twice as long. The roof must be thirty feet high. There is some bomb damage at one end, which has been temporarily repaired."

"You say a boat could deliver supplies right up to the dock?"

"That's right," I replied, "except at low tide."

"Does Mr. Shurama speak English?" the Captain asked.

"No, but Kumiko here is fluent. She can also keep books our way."

The Captain regarded me with a suspicious look.

"What's in it for you sailor?"

I didn't appreciate the question.

"Captain, these are friends of mine who have gone through a rough time. I'm trying to help them get back on their feet before I return to the States this week. There isn't anything in it for me!"

The Captain could sense I was ready to take Kumiko and leave.

"Nothing personal, I had to ask that question. Some sharp operators are already trying to set up with Japanese as fronts."

"Captain, I suggest you have someone check it out."

"Better still, I'll go myself. Miss Shurama, would it be convenient if I came tomorrow?"

Kumiko bowed, "Please do, Captain Anderson. Papa-san be most pleased to meet you."

The Captain returned the bow. "I should arrive on the noon train. Would you explain to my assistant how to get there?"

He then turned to me, "Thanks for coming, sailor. This could possibly fill a need in that area."

We started to leave, when I thought of something. "Captain, do you like Japanese food?"

"I do if the seafood isn't raw," he replied.

"Kumiko's mother is a fine cook. Why don't you plan on being invited to lunch? It will be worth the trip."

"Well thanks, I will."

Kumiko was all big-eyed on the return trip.

"Jack, you think he really come tomorrow?"

"Yes Kumiko, I really think so."

"You think he make Papa-san a distributor?"

"Maybe Kumiko—maybe not."

"Jack, that was very great thing you do today."

"I just hope it works out."

I felt as if I had given something away I didn't want to part with. I knew the Captain's interest was in more than just food distribution. Well, at least he was more Kumiko's size.

Papa-san and Mama-san got all excited when she told them what had taken place. Mama-san was worried about what to serve for lunch. I was glad I'd dropped off a couple steaks that morning, and I made a few other suggestions.

"You be here won't you, Jack?" Kumiko asked.

"No, I believe it will go better without me. I'll come by tomorrow evening."

I started to leave, and then turned, "Oh, Kumiko, why don't you serve hot sake during lunch?"

The next evening I caught the last liberty boat to the beach, and walked the short distance to Papa-san's. A joyous Kumiko met me at the door, and Papa-san and Mama-san were ecstatic.

I wondered who it was that said the Japanese were an inscrutable race.

I laughed, as Kumiko was so excited she lost her English. "Jack," she finally blurted out, "Papa-san to be distributor for whole area. Captain Anderson buy all Papa-san's rice—already!"

I finally got her to calm down enough to tell me what happened.

"Captain Anderson come, Papa-san and I show him dock and warehouse. When he see the rice already here he get very interested. He like Mama-san's lunch and the hot sake very much—soon he say government will buy Papa-san's rice at good price. From now on all food for this part of Yokohama come through Papa-san's warehouse and Papa-san be paid dockage, warehousing and distribution."

It was even better than I had hoped. The only question in my mind was whether the Captain had the authority to carry it through. I felt more reassured when Kumiko said Army engineers would be there to finish repairs to the warehouse, and Captain Anderson would be out each week to set up the food distribution.

Mama-san put on her second big meal for the day and I noticed the cup Kumiko brought me had something more exciting than tea.

After dinner Papa-san had Kumiko thank me for my part in the project and to say he knew it never would have happened without me. He repeated his wish that I join them as soon as I got out of the Navy. He said he liked the way I operate. I didn't believe he had Kumiko in mind with that statement.

When Papa- and Mama-san retired for the evening, Kumiko got out my sleeping mat and quilt. She joined me briefly on the mat, and there was no hesitation as our lips met. I would have liked to carry it to a natural conclusion but that would have been asking too much of Papa-san's hospitality.

In the morning on the ship, I asked Stan to print up all the remaining paper. I had heard there were several thousand troops returning on the flat top.

A supply barge pulled up alongside and our large crane hoisted aboard a massive cargo net, loaded with captured German and Japanese rifles. Everyone aboard ship was allowed to choose one for a souvenir.

Ever since the Skipper got his jeep, he had leaned overboard for the enlisted men.

The next day was Steve's and my last day on the gas barge, and before we returned to the ship we pulled into Papa-san's dock. I asked Kumiko to unlock the warehouse and our crew pushed the car and two, large, empty, gas drums out onto the dock. While we were filling them with gasoline she motioned me back into the warehouse where Papa- san waited, clutching a long, rag wrapped bundle to his chest.

Papa -san handed it to me with a bow and I was surprised at the weight.

"Jack," Kumiko translated, "Papa-san wants you to have this as a gift for what you do at Tokyo. Please don't let anyone see it until you are off the ship at San Diego. It is very rare ceremonial set, and was never intended to leave Japan. If it was discovered Papa-san gave it to you, he be in big trouble."

I could see the concern in her eyes. "Papa-san," I bowed deeply, "I will guard it carefully. Thank you, very much."

While the crew pushed the car and the filled drums back into the warehouse I stashed the present in the barge along with the other souvenirs Papa-san had been keeping. I asked Kumiko to tell Papa-san I hoped the gasoline would keep him going until it was available again.

She sighed unhappily, "You not coming back again, Jack?"

"I don't think I'll have the chance." I handed her a slip with my parent's address and told her to write if she ever needed anything from the states.

Mama-san, who had joined the other two, just stood there. All three looked as if there had been a death in the family. I didn't know what to say—I was too old to cry, so I climbed back aboard the barge and waved as we pulled out. I really wasn't much good for the rest of the day.

In the evening, I went off by myself and unwrapped the rag covered present. I could hardly believe the sight of so much gold, silver and jewels. No wonder it had been heavy!

The few samurai swords I had seen had a plain, two hand handle, with a dull wood sheath. This obviously was a ceremonial pair. The matching smaller sword was the one used for hara-kiri. The sheaths were silver with a decorative gold overlay. The butt of each handle was filled with a brilliant green stone, which I suspected was either emerald or jade. Each handle was covered with bright, interwoven gold wire.

I wondered how Papa-san got them, and suspected they were too hot for him to keep.

I knew it was going to take all the stealth at my command to get this pair to San Diego. With a little luck they might pay for the airplane I hoped to buy. I quickly rewrapped the swords and placed them in a small compartment that only I had the key for.

Deciding the best hiding place was in plain sight, I exchanged my Mauser rifle for one of the cheap Japanese rifle souvenirs. When I was sure I had privacy I removed the barrel and action from the rifle and threw it overboard.

I enlarged the area of the stock that had contained the action with my pocketknife. I retrieved the swords and fitted the hilt of the larger one into the stock, and strapped it into place with tape. I then taped the scabbard of the smaller one to the larger. I rewrapped the upper two-thirds with the dirty rags and secured them by tape with just the stock exposed. I then carved my initials deeply into the stock.

I leaned back to admire my handiwork. The scabbard now appeared to be the rifle barrel and the cheap gun had been further mutilated by carving my initials into it. No one in their right mind would want to steal it. I leaned it against the bulkhead near my bunk, along with all the Mausers.

TWENTY-SIX

Monday morning, two boatloads departed for the carrier that was to transport us home. The instant I saw it, I realized this was not going to be a fun trip. It was one of those small jeep carriers that were turned out in a hurry by mounting a flight deck over a transport hull. She would be top-heavy, with a shortage of facilities for the number of passengers she would be carrying.

Our group was the last to arrive, and all the bunks and even the mattresses were already taken. When I saw the overcrowded compartments, I really didn't mind. I doubted I could have slept there anyway.

Steve and I located an open area below the flight deck where we could lash our hammocks. I'd packed the hammock around for three years and this was my first chance to use it. The rest of our group followed suit, and we became an enclave in a sea of humanity.

The ship got underway, and as soon as we cleared the bay it developed such a nasty roll in the moderate swells, most of the soldiers and even some of the sailors got seasick. It was bad enough in our fresh air location; I didn't even want to think about the conditions below decks.

After a couple days chow became a continuous line, starting at dawn and ending after dark. I sure wouldn't have wanted to be a mess cook on this ship.

I worried about the safety of my precious cargo. I had lashed my sea-bag that contained the pistol, binoculars, and other souvenirs along with the rifle, to the same stanchion that supported one end of my hammock. At least I could keep an eye on it while I was there. I kept the clip of the pistol in my pocket so I couldn't be accused of having a loaded firearm aboard ship.

After the worst of the seasickness was over, I dug out the remaining pictures, and quickly sold out. I meant to keep one for myself, but I forgot. I was kept busy exchanging dollar bills for larger denominations so I could get them into my money belt.

Poker and crap games seemed to be springing up all over the ship. There really wasn't much else to do for entertainment. I had already learned the hard way—my facial expressions were too revealing to ever be a successful poker player. I didn't care much for craps, so I searched for a blackjack game—mainly because I knew if I could get the deal the odds would be in my favor. When I couldn't find a game, I spread a blanket and was in the gambling business.

I had over five hundred from picture sales to back me up, and it became a wide-open game. There was one big dogface I wished would fall overboard. Every time he lost he made disparaging remarks about the dealer's honesty. The game fluctuated. Some days I did very well, occasionally I was fortunate to break even. The gamblers were pretty well thinned out with just a few big winners as we neared the end of the trip.

One evening as I returned from chow, I noticed the top of my sea-bag was open. A hot searing anger began to rise as I discovered the pistol and my other souvenirs were missing. I knew the chance of recovery was practically non-existent. There had been a lot of thievery going on, especially with the three branches of service thrown together and everyone bringing home souvenirs.

Finally I decided to run one more blackjack game, just to get my mind off dangerous thoughts.

The game was going well for the house when the dogface with the big mouth showed up. I hoped he would mouth off about my honesty one more time. He reached into a sack, pulled out a Japanese officer's automatic pistol, and slid it onto the blanket.

"What will you allow on this?" he demanded.

It looked very familiar

"Where's the clip?" I asked.

"There isn't any,"

"Oh yes, there's a clip," I shouted, as I pulled it out of my pocket, jammed it into the pistol butt, and jacked back the slide. The cocked pistol was now pointed at his belly.

"Let me tell you something, you thieving son of a bitch. This model is famous for its hair trigger. That's why so many Japanese officers walk with a limp. Just one little jar and off it goes."

His face turned white, and perspiration was breaking out on his forehead.

"You have ten seconds to get the hell out of here before that happens."

The dogface was scrambling to his feet when I continued in a low, deadly voice, "If all my stuff isn't in the sea-bag when I get back—you're going to leave this ship in a box!"

After his hurried departure I let the hammer down on the pistol, unloaded it, and stuck it in my waistband. The other players were shocked, with mouths agape.

The game ended shortly after the confrontation, and I returned to my hammock and seabag. I untied the top of the seabag and reached inside. When I was sure it was all there I took a deep breath, replaced the clip to my pocket, and shoved the pistol to the bottom of the seabag.

The day we entered San Diego harbor, over two thousand men were mustered on the flight deck for roll call and inspection. I could feel the warm sun between my shoulder blades as I stood at attention. After we were dismissed, most of us remained on the flight deck for the view of the harbor and city.

A departing sailing yacht with three girls sunbathing on deck passed close to our port side. The servicemen on that side started to whistle and wave, and the rest of us rushed over for a look. The weight shift of several thousand men caused the already top-heavy ship to list so badly, I was afraid we might capsize. The loudspeakers were blaring, "ALL HANDS TO STARBOARD". With the scare we had just received, we obeyed too readily. The ship heeled to starboard with the momentum of the roll behind it. This was worse than the first roll. The next order over the speakers was, "ALL HANDS MIDSHIP!" The wild rolls slowly subsided.

I would bet no other returning servicemen put on so dramatic an entrance. I wondered if this was an omen of my future stateside life!

TWENTY-SEVEN

The war in the South Pacific had been over less than three months when our transport docked at San Diego. Several thousand servicemen, all eager for discharge, prepared to disembark. I had been in the Navy over three years with the last one overseas, and I was just as eager as the rest.

The Navy band in their dress uniforms was at the dock, pumping out patriotic airs. Even though I knew better, I straightened my shoulders and puffed out my chest—just a little. The next announcement over the PA system brought me back to reality.

"*Now hear this. Now hear this. All Samurai swords will be turned in to the Officer of the Day before departure!*"

I heard unhappy groans and saw a few sailors who had been lucky enough to acquire one, reluctantly bringing theirs forward. No one knew if it was the custom agents, or a ploy by the officers to seize the number one souvenir of the war.

When my turn arrived to line up for departure, I could see shore patrol on one side of the gangway and custom agents on the other. Each sailor was questioned, and then some were pulled from the line and their sea-bag searched. Most of the sailors from my ship were carrying a Mauser rifle in one hand; I was the only one with a Japanese rifle. With the rags wrapped around the upper part, only the stock was visible.

"Anything to report, sailor?" the customs agent demanded as my turn at the head of the line arrived.

"A kimono for my sister and a robe for my mother—oh yes, this." I beamed proudly at the rag wrapped rifle in my hand. After one glance, I could see suppressed humor in the shore patrols expression—pity in the custom agent's.

"Proceed, sailor." And I continued down the gangway.

The Navy band was still playing, and I could see Red Cross ladies in their fancy uniforms with paper cups of fresh milk and glazed doughnuts. Those were two of the three things we had missed most. A sweet, motherly lady handed me a cup of milk and a doughnut, and when I started to say thank you, she spoke first.

"That will be twenty cents, sailor."

I dug out the change and handed it to her. I ate the doughnut, and drank the milk, but somehow the welcome home had gone flat.

Those of us who were to be separated from the Navy in California were loaded into a bus and transported to a compound for the night. As we pulled up in front, two words came immediately to mind—concentration camp! The compound was surrounded by chain link fence with strands of barbed wire above. No one was to be allowed out until we departed at nine o'clock the next morning.

This was not the welcome home I had envisioned—especially with Jan and Cleo probably still in town! At this point, the Navy and I mentally parted company. Their rating in my mind was on a par with the Red Cross.

The only positive thought I could muster for Camp Shoemaker was its location. It was over halfway to my parent's new home in Sacramento. The five-day mustering out process could easily have been compressed into one, but that would have precluded the hard sell to sign up in the reserves. When my turn for the private interview arrived, I got to laughing so loudly the recruiter hurriedly ended the interview.

The following day I noticed a well-dressed Asian man circulating around, discreetly making inquires about Samurai swords. When he came my way I asked, "What do you want with a Samurai sword?"

"I have clients that collect them. I can offer up to a hundred depending on condition. You don't have one, do you?"

I smiled cynically, "I might but we aren't even in the same ballpark. The scabbard alone is worth five times that."

"What's so special about the scabbard?"

"It's silver with gold overleaf."

His face lost some of its inscrutability. I knew I had him hooked!

"Could I see it?" he leaned forward intently.

"Unless you could pay what it is worth, we'd just be wasting each other's time."

"I can pay what it is worth," seemed to come out reluctantly.

"You don't sound very positive."

"I can pay what it is worth," came out firmly this time.

"All right, follow me."

I lead him to my bunk and reached for the beat-up rifle leaning there.

When he saw "that" was it, he grimaced.

"I said Samurai sword."

"I know; come on."

I led him to a protected area where we wouldn't be interrupted. When I was sure we had absolute privacy, I sat on a lower bunk and slowly began unwrapping the dirty, bulky rags that protected the barrel and action.

The removal of the last cloth revealed to him this wasn't a gun at all but a beautiful Samurai sword with a smaller, matching hara-kiri knife and scabbard.

I could sense his quick intake of breath. I separated the gleaming knife with the jeweled hilt and its silver and gold scabbard from the sword and placed it behind my back. His eyes followed until it was out of sight. I removed the last of the tape from the sword and handed it to him.

He tried to suppress his excitement, but the way his hand shook told me this set might be even more unique than I had first thought. I decided to be creative and see what might come from it.

He looked the scabbard over closely and then withdrew the gleaming blade. I could see he was studying the characters engraved into the base of the blade and the large, green stone embedded in the butt of the handle. With a sigh he slipped the blade back into the scabbard and leaned forward.

"I could go three hundred on this one."

I laughed condescendingly. "Here I thought you were knowledgeable about Samurai swords and knew what happened in Japan."

He looked shocked. "What happened in Japan?"

"Oh, nothing much—just a jeweled, matching, ceremonial sword and hara-kiri knife set with silver and gold scabbards are missing from the imperial palace. There are no others like them in the world and they are considered national treasures. Both the Japanese and American governments are searching, and all Samurai swords are being confiscated on any ship that arrives from Japan. The only way I got these off the ship is as you see—and there won't be any others until the missing ones are located."

I suspected he had already heard about the impounding, as it had been angrily received. The rest of my story was pure conjecture.

"How did you get them?" he asked suspiciously. I believed he envisioned me sneaking into the imperial palace in the middle of the night, and was going to use that as a lever in the dealing.

"They were a gift from my trading partner, and his lovely daughter in Yokohama. I had performed a public relations service for them that resulted in a lucrative contract with the occupational forces. These were a thank-you, as well as a farewell gift. Papa-san didn't mention how he acquired them."

"Do you think these are the missing set?"

"I honestly don't know. I almost hope not, because I could sell them now without fear of repercussions. Should they be, whoever buys them will have to keep them out of sight until the search is called off. Of course, then he could start adding zeros to the value."

I watched the different expressions cross his face—sorrow for the end of his sword business—greed as he thought of the future value of this set.

"Might I see the hara-kiri knife and scabbard?"

"Yes, but it is not for sale now."

I watched as he reverently compared the smaller with the larger one, and acknowledged they were indeed a matching pair, right down to the large jewel in the handle butt.

He finally asked, "Why not sell them both now—they are worth more as a set, than singly?"

"That's true; it's sort of a hedge. Should they turn out to be the missing pair, I suspect the buyer of the sword will be contacting me when the time is right, and we will be talking serious money. If they turn out not to be, I believe he still will want to negotiate."

The Asian buyer did not look happy as he asked, "What value do you place on them right now?"

I paused in thought. It would serve me right if my fanciful story about the missing set should turn out to be fact—after I sold them.

"Twenty five hundred for the sword—five thousand for the set. If they turn out to be the missing ones, add a zero! If the green jewels in the handle butts turn out to be emeralds, add another."

It was difficult to believe an inscrutable Asian face could register so much pain.

"That's ridiculous."

I didn't say anything more, just started reassembling the rifle.

"I might go a thousand for the sword—twenty five hundred for the set."

I kept right on with my work.

"Oh, all right—three thousand for the set."

The gun was now as it had been before. I picked it up and started to walk away.

"Thirty five hundred and that's my final offer." He spoke to my retreating back.

I turned, "I don't take checks!"

He motioned me back and removed a money belt from around his waist. I watched as he counted out thirty-five, one hundred dollar bills on the bunk. I picked one up and held it to the light. It would be just my luck to end up with funny money. The bill looked all right, considering I wasn't used to denominations this large.

I placed them in my money belt, handed him the gun, and we went our separate ways

I left the main gate the next morning, a free and happy young man. The war was over and I was out of the Navy. I was not yet twenty-one and my money belt bulged with my gambling winnings and mustering out pay, added to the thirty-five hundred from the sale of the Samurai Swords.

All I had to do was locate a war surplus Stinson L-5, get my pilots license and fly to Alaska before snow fell. In my present frame of mind—no problem!

It was spring, the sun was warm, and I caught a ride to Sacramento with the first car that came by.

TWENTY-EIGHT

After a quick reunion with my parents, I took the downtown bus to look for transportation and civilian clothes.

My first stop was a branch of my bank in San Diego. I wasn't comfortable carrying all that cash.

The teller, who had been a little condescending about my request to open an account, changed his attitude as I pulled up my jersey, removed the fat money belt, and started counting out hundred dollar bills. I banked five thousand and transferred my account from San Diego. There still was over five hundred in the money belt.

A couple hours later I was sitting at the bus stop with two bags of new clothes. The search for a car had been a disappointment—too many returning servicemen and a limited supply. I was reconciled to resurrecting my fifty-dollar Model A Ford from the barn of our ranch at Placerville. It needed tires, but I only planned on being here long enough to get my pilot's license.

The street was quiet; the bus wasn't in sight, when I heard the sound of a fast approaching motorcycle. The rider was coming from a side street and really pouring it on. He just starting the turn to my street, when his front tire hit the streetcar track still imbedded in the asphalt. He lost it and went flying one-way, the motorcycle another.

The rider ended up in the gutter, more dirty than hurt, but the motorcycle was spinning circles on its side, the throttle wide open. It was a beautiful, customized machine, and to keep it from chewing itself up, I corralled the throttle and shut it off.

The rider showed up about the time I had it upright on the kickstand. Gasoline had been spilling from the tank and I was afraid it might catch fire. Even with the skinned up gas tank, it was a beautiful 1941 Harley Davidson. The finish was a gleaming mint green and nearly everything else was chrome. It had the large, leather, buddy seat and leather saddlebags.

The rider came over to my side and he was a mess. He must have picked the dirtiest gutter in town. Instead of thanking me for the help, he started cussing the motorcycle, then hauled off and gave it a kick. It was obvious he had been drinking, and this commotion was producing a circle of onlookers.

From what I could make out from his ramblings he spent all of his mustering out pay, plus six hundred more on the machine, and he never wanted to see it again. I suspected he was afraid to get back on.

"How much do you want for it?" I asked.

"Make me an offer."

"Have you got the title?"

He pulled out his wallet and displayed the title, which was free and clear. I pulled out my wallet and started peeling off fifties, depositing them on the buddy seat. When I reached eight, I showed him the wallet was empty.

"That's not enough money."

"Take it or leave it." I started to pick up the money.

The crowd was watching this with more interest than the accident.

"I'll take it," he said, and grabbed the money.

"Sign the title." I handed him my new pen.

I made sure he signed the right line and I got my pen back with the title. I started to fill the saddlebags with my purchases, when I discovered a half-empty bottle of whiskey. I carefully set it on the curb; it was a wonder it survived the crash.

I put the cycle in neutral, turned on the key, and reared back on the kick-starter. It fired right up and from the sound of the exhaust, I was almost certain the engine was in excellent condition. I dropped it into low and slowly let out the clutch. It started out smoothly and I was well pleased. I hadn't been on a motorcycle in years. I fooled around with it on the way home and felt confident by the time I arrived. It handled beautifully.

The next morning, I signed up for flight training under the G.I. bill. Not only would the government pay for my flight training, they would pay me for attending ground school.

Later, I swung by an auto body shop, and when they finished no one would ever know the motorcycle had been flopped.

Flight training started the next Monday in a sixty-five horsepower, Aronica trainer. It was similar to the cubs I had been in charge of on the flight line in San Diego, and where I had managed some unofficial flight time. The instructor soon found this out, and between us we revised the training program. We quickly finished the license requirements, and then worked on short field landings and take-offs. He knew my Alaska plans, and we concentrated on what I'd need up there. The Aronica didn't have flaps, so he showed me how to sideslip into short fields.

In the evening I started meteorology in ground school, and kept trying to locate a war surplus L-5. After bootlegging a flight in one from an Army pilot on Okinawa, I knew this was the plane for me in Alaska.

My training course was nearly over before I located the phone number of a dealer in the Los Angeles area who bought a dozen, and was modifying them for C.A.A. certification. I held my breath as I placed the phone call.

"Yes, we have L-5s for sale."

"How do the prices run?"

"With C.A.A certification, and a fresh annual, the A models go for $2000 to $2500."

"How about the Gs?" I knew they had the latest improvements with a larger engine, droop ailerons, and baggage space for a stretcher.

"They run from $3,000 to $4,000, depending on time and condition."

"What's the lowest time, G model, you have right now?"

"Let me see...we have one we are just starting on with less than 500 hours total time. It will be available for $4000."

"All right, I'll take it. My name is Barnes, and I can be there in a little over a week. Do you want a deposit?"

"We will hold it that long. It probably won't be finished before then."

"Do you include a check out?"

"Yeah, but I'm not going to teach you how to fly."

I bit my tongue, and hung up before I said something that blew the sale. This was a later model than I hoped for.

The next week I received my private pilot license, and the following morning pointed the motorcycle toward Los Angeles before the sun was up.

TWENTY-NINE

I arrived mid-day at a small airport and located the outfit with the L-5s. They were parked all over the place, and some looked beat. In one hanger a painter was masking out registration numbers on a nearly new G model. Over in the corner was a pile of the bulky, military radios that looked as if they had been ripped out by the roots.

Something about the operation nagged at my subconscious. There was no sign of any mechanical work being done. With this many planes to be certified, and an annual inspection performed, there should have been several mechanics hard at work.

I located the small office and asked the pretty girl inside for Mack, the guy I had talked to on the phone. She pointed to the pilot of an L-5 just taxiing in. I waited until he got it shut down and climbed out, then introduced myself.

"Hi, I'm Jack Barnes"

"Oh yeah, you wanted a G model."

Something about this guy was causing alarm bells to ring. He was tall, about thirty, pencil-thin moustache, wearing a fancy flight jacket and silk scarf.

"I want a specific, low time G model," I replied firmly.

His lips smiled, but not those agate eyes. "Don't get uptight; it's in the hanger with the new numbers being painted now."

I had secretly been hoping that one was mine!

"How soon will it be flying?"

"It should be ready tomorrow morning."

"Great, can I get a check out then and we'll wind up our deal?"

"Just as soon as I see the color of your money."

"Ok, I'll be here in the morning. If the log books say the same thing you do, you'll find the color is green."

I turned and left before we said any more and I lost an airplane I really wanted. I swung by the hanger for one more peek, but the spray fumes were so thick I gave up.

I had a dilemma to face. Should I play it safe and get a motel, or should I call Niki, a lovely girl I was afraid was in love with me, and who had marriage on her mind?

It wouldn't be fair to leave without seeing her, so when I knew she should be home from work, I placed the call.

She answered, and I said, "Hi."

There was a hesitant pause, "Jack?"

"Sure is."

"Jack, where are you?" I could feel the warmth right through the phone.

"Right here in Southgate."

"Oh, I just got home and I'm a mess," Niki wailed. "Have you had dinner?"

"Not yet."

"You come over right now. I'm starting dinner and then I'll grab a quick shower. I'll leave the door unlocked and if no one answers come on in; this is Jill's club night. Oh Jack, I'm so happy."

After she hung up, I had a feeling I would be welcome, even though I hadn't been much of a letter writer.

A little later, I parked the motorcycle in the driveway and rang the doorbell. No one answered so I came right on in. I could hear the shower running in the bathroom and knew I was early. I was about to find a chair in the living room when I heard the bathroom door open, and I glanced down the hallway. The vision before my eyes could have caused cardiac arrest.

Niki had come out with her blond hair piled on top of her head, and a rather skimpy bath towel wrapped around her middle. Even from where I was standing, I could tell there had been some changes during the year I had been away.

The emotional uncertainty, the sadness caused by her father's untimely death, were no longer visible. This was a warm, exciting woman. Her translucent skin had picked up a glow from the shower, two out-thrust breasts were holding up the towel all by themselves, and her lovely, slim legs, seemed to have acquired additional curvature.

Niki glanced down the hall, saw me standing there with my mouth open, hesitated, and then came running.

"Oh, Jack," she murmured and threw herself into my arms. I had two eager arms around my neck and as mine encircled her waist, our lips met. It felt so great neither of us noticed the towel heading south.

Suddenly I became aware my hands were stroking a sleek back and developing strong inclinations to drop lower. Niki wasn't aware of the towel's defection until the end of my welcome home kiss.

I could see the color rush to her face as she tried to retrieve the missing protection. This just added to my enchantment as with each movement of her body, different portions asserted their independence. Realizing that all was lost, Niki gave the towel a kick, and strode toward her bedroom. I decided she looked as good going, as coming.

"I'll be back in a minute. Pour us a glass of what's in the refrigerator," she called over her shoulder.

I checked the fridge and retrieved a bottle of champagne. There were two special glasses on the drain-board. I had a feeling she had been saving the bottle for this occasion.

I had them poured when Niki appeared. The weather was warm and she was wearing a sleeveless blouse, white shorts and high heels. The heels just seemed to accentuate those incredible legs. Her freshly brushed blond hair was loose around her shoulders. Niki came into my arms for a lingering kiss, I handed her a glass and we silently toasted each other.

"Jack, I had just about decided you weren't coming."

"I wanted to get my pilot's license so I could take you for a ride. The plane I'm buying should be finished tomorrow—course if I had known what kind of a reception I was going to receive, I'd have made it sooner."

She laughed. "You are just as terrible as ever."

Niki checked the casserole in the oven, retrieved the salad from the fridge, and I brought the champagne while she took care of the rest. I hadn't forgotten how delicious her casseroles were and I had to use rigid control to leave enough for Jill when she arrived.

"What's the latest on the wedding?" I enquired.

"I'm glad you are here now. Jill was going to call you. Dan is due early next month and the wedding is scheduled for the following Saturday."

"That's cutting it pretty close, isn't it?"

"Dan is anxious to get to Bremerton as quickly as possible. They are way behind in his marine engineering business. Jill has the house sold already, and right after the wedding we are moving. You can stay that long, can't you, Jack?"

"I would love to but I don't have time. Snow flies as early as September in the part of Alaska where I plan to do my flying. I have to get up there, get skis on the plane and be ready for business. I wrote you I planned on hunting wolves from the air this winter. They are decimating the caribou herds and there is a fifty dollar bounty as well as fifty dollars for the pelts."

Niki's eyes started to puddle up so to change the subject, I told her about the motorcycle. She came outside to see it and got so enthused I took her for a ride.

She sat on the back of the big buddy seat, with her arms tightly wrapped around my waist. I had a hard time concentrating with two firm breasts caressing my back.

Jill was back by the time we returned and I received another friendly welcome. When Jill found out I wasn't going to be able to stay for the wedding, she looked almost as unhappy as her daughter. I finally agreed to stay until I found a buyer for the motorcycle.

Early the next morning I joined the girls for breakfast, and was on my way to the airport.

My L-5 was out of the hanger, and parked on the flight line. No one was around, so I gave it a very through, pre-flight check. With the bulky military gear removed, it was much roomier than I had expected. I was pleased to see the rear seat was almost wide enough to accommodate two passengers.

I slid into the front cockpit to familiarize myself with the controls, and then cranked down the droop ailerons to be sure they worked. The plane's fabric was like new.

I was feeling great until I got to the engine. There was water and sediment in the fuel strainer, and as I pulled the prop through I discovered a soft cylinder.

I was so angry and disappointed I could feel my perverse personality start to take over. I glanced up and there came Mack with the logbooks. He didn't seem any happier to see me than I was to see him.

"I see you found it."

"That's right. Is it completely ready to go?"

"Yeah, fresh annual and certification. Those are your new numbers painted under the wing."

"Could I see the log books?"

"Here they are-only four hundred eighty hours total time, just like I said."

I checked the logs and saw where an A and E mechanic had signed off the annual inspection.

"Now, when you give me the four thousand, the plane is yours."

"Is the mechanic here that signed off the annual?"

"No, he works at a shop down the line."

"What about the C.A.A. inspector that certified the plane?"

"He left yesterday. Why?"

"Well, I'll tell you, Mack. All of you are in big trouble. You had better get the A and E back here as fast as you can. I'm calling the C.A.A. office and requesting their investigator gets out here right away."

"What in hell are you talking about?"

"I'm talking about criminal negligence and fraud. I don't know what kind of sweetheart deal you have with the mechanic, but I do know the engine on this plane hasn't been touched and it has serious problems, including contaminated gas tanks and a bad cylinder—yet the logs show a fresh annual. This will get the license of the A and E lifted, and no telling what it will do to your business. You must have been dumb to believe the paperwork those dogface mechanics put out. Some lie as bad as you do."

"All right, wise guy, hand me the logs and hit the road; I don't have to take your crud."

"Sure, Mack, I'll hand them to you just as soon as the C.A.A. arrive. Right now they are evidence."

I had them in my right hand, my best punch is a powerful left hook, and I was hoping he would make a grab for them. He started to and then changed his mind. I headed for the public phone booth, closed the door, and looked up the CAA number.

I was just placing the call when a subdued Mack asked me to open the door. I cracked the door, and jammed it with my foot.

"What's it going to take to make you happy?" he asked.

"Getting what I'm paying for—an airplane in top condition."

"O.K. Hang up the phone. We can work it out."

"Mack, the least you're going to get by with is a top overhaul and purging both fuel tanks. I have until Monday—I don't think you can make it." I picked up the phone again.

"Hold it, Jack, it will be done." Mack's voice had a panicky note. "I'll have that lying mechanic back here today, and he will only leave to eat and sleep. It's his license that's on the line."

I hesitated; I now felt like I was back in control of myself.

"All right, I'll tell you what I will do. I am going to get on my motorcycle and go have lunch. When I get back if the cowling is off and someone is working, I'll talk about it. Otherwise forget it."

I put the logbooks in the saddlebag and fired up the engine. When I returned an hour later the cowling was off, and a heavy-set, disgruntled mechanic was running a compression check. I could tell he was angry, and that I was the cause. That was all right, I wasn't feeling friendly right then either.

"There isn't anything wrong with this engine except maybe a piece of carbon under an exhaust valve. It will clear on the first run-up." He snarled.

"You may be right—too bad you didn't use more than a pencil on the annual. We might not be having this conversation."

"Well, I'll pull the jug and clear the valve."

"No, you will pull them all and do a complete top overhaul—that's providing we don't find a reason to go all the way. I'll be looking over your shoulder; I'll do the final compression check, and buddy, it better be right on the money."

"Who the hell do you think you are—ordering me around?"

"I'm the guy that's probably going to save some lives by having your license lifted. Now, you got any more cheap talk?"

He muttered something and went back to work. I really would have liked to help. It would have sped things up, and I would have become more familiar with the engine, but I knew it wouldn't work; before the day was over one of us would have wrapped a wrench around the other's head.

"I want to check those jugs in the morning," I curtly snapped. "When you purge the fuel tanks, if you put the contaminated gas back in, you'll have it to do all over again."

I had visions of Mack trying to save thirty-eight gallons of aircraft fuel by filtering it. I got on my motorcycle and pulled away, noticing Mack had stayed out of sight.

The mechanic worked straight through the weekend and Monday morning the L-5 was really ready to go. He had completed a top overhaul, including new plugs and magneto points. I didn't like the looks of the tires and battery, couldn't find Mack, so I installed new ones from his supply.

I had checked with the young man who dispensed fuel on the flight line and confirmed there was new fuel in the tanks. In the process I found a buyer for the motorcycle. The line boy had been eyeballing it every time I rode by. He didn't blink an eye at twice what I had paid. No new motorcycles had been sold yet since the war, and a customized one was at a premium.

The mechanic had taken off like he wanted to put a county between us. Mack was still in hiding, so I decided I might as well fly it before I paid for it. I might find something else wrong. I was so disillusioned with Mack I didn't want a check ride with him anyway.

I climbed into the front cockpit, flipped the magneto switch, shoved the mixture control in and hit the starter. The new battery gave the prop a great spin and the engine fired right up. I taxied out to the end of the runway, set the altimeter, ran my magneto checks and waited for a green light from the tower. I didn't plan on using flaps, as I wanted to know how quickly it would get off without them.

I got my green light, made a running turn from the taxiway, and opened the throttle wide. I was pushed back in my seat by the thrust, the tail was already up and the torque was turning me toward the tower. I booted hard right rudder and then I was angling toward a cow pasture. I barely had flying speed when I horsed back on the stick and floundered into the air. I shoved the stick forward before I stalled, and was on my way. Not the prettiest take-off, but there is a big difference between a sixty-five horsepower engine and one with a hundred and ninety.

As soon as I was out of the pattern I could feel my rapport with this superb machine begin to establish itself. It responded to my every wish without conscious thought. I was so entranced; I headed out over the ocean where I could have some privacy with my new love.

It was an unbelievable three hours. Crossing the coastline coming back, I glanced down at Howard Hughes's monster flying boat; I wouldn't have traded straight across. I had complete confidence in my ability to fly this plane to Alaska.

I entered the pattern, got my green light and brought her in as smooth as silk. The gas was about used up so I taxied over to the pump, and while the line boy was pumping gas, I checked the engine for oil leaks; no problem. The line boy asked if he should charge the gas to Mack, and I nodded my head. It was still his airplane.

As I taxied back and parked, I could see Mack angrily pacing in front of my motorcycle.

"Well, you decided to come back."

"Yeah, I wanted to see your smiling face one more time." I replied as I climbed out.

"Listen, wise guy, another few minutes and I was calling the sheriff."

"Too bad you didn't—that would have opened up a whole new can of worms."

"Who authorized you to fly this airplane? You haven't even been checked out in a L-5."

I could feel my euphoria from the flight begin to dissipate.

"Well, I'll tell you, Mack, I figured if your flying was as bad as your business ethics—I'd be better off checking myself out."

His face got so red I thought he was going to blow a blood vessel.

"Listen you bas—" He didn't get a chance to finish. I edged up close where I could get in that important, first lick.

"All right you B.S. artist—either take that swing or deliver the airplane. You can't stay on dead center the rest of your life."

I could see the mental debate.

"You finally ready to put up the money?"

"Just as soon as the title is taken care of."

He took a deep breath, exhaled and muttered, "Follow me."

We went into the office, completed the paper work, and I handed over a cashier's check for four thousand.

I could see he had a list there of the extra parts I'd installed plus the mechanic's labor and would have liked to have tried for more money. He saw the expression on my face and handed over the documents.

"I want you to get that airplane off my property—now!"

I knew this was a face-saving gesture for the benefit of the office girl.

"Gladly, Mack. The way you operate, it probably would have been picked clean by morning!"

For a moment I thought I was going to be lucky enough to get both the airplane, and the pleasure of beating the hell out of Mack. His face got red, and then white, as he stormed out of the office.

I taxied over to the transient tie-downs, paid my fee, and asked the same young man who was buying my motorcycle to keep an eye on it. He didn't ask why, just nodded his head like this had happened before.

To be on the safe side, I located an agent, and insured the plane.

I didn't leave the next morning because I had promised Niki an airplane ride. She took the day off from work, and we got an early start for the airport. She was all excited about flying—this would be her first time. She wore those distracting white shorts and a bandanna over her hair.

We pulled up beside the L-5, and when the young lineman saw Niki, he hurried over to help untie the plane. He knew I was leaving tomorrow, and I suspected had hopes of getting more than just my motorcycle.

Niki seemed properly impressed with the plane. I got her buckled into the rear seat and we taxied out to the runway. The takeoff was smooth—I'd learned a lot about this plane. I glanced back to see how Niki was doing and when I received a happy smile. I headed out to the coast and it was two hours later before we glided back to the runway. We had seen a lot of country, from high up to right down on the water. I gassed it up and had help on the tie-down from the eager young lineman.

As Niki climbed out, she stretched those distracting legs, came over and gave me a passionate kiss. "Jack, I loved it, flying does something for me."

Judging by the sexy kiss, I believed her.

We stopped for a leisurely lunch, and when we returned to the house I stretched out on the sofa for a quick nap. I soon gave up on that idea, as Niki had something else in mind.

"Jack, I wish you were coming to Bremerton with us. Alaska is too far away."

"Hey girl, look at it this way—from here, Bremerton is halfway to Alaska."

Niki sighed; she had been sitting on the edge of the sofa. She turned and lay beside me in my arms with her back to me, spoon fashion. My free hand was on her midriff, and everywhere I put it there seemed to be bare skin. I resisted the temptation to slide it further north. I suspected Niki was now braless and had unbuttoned her blouse. In a moment her hand was guiding mine to a firm young breast. The nipple had already risen to attention.

I turned her so I could see her face. "Niki, aren't you the girl that wanted to be a virgin on her wedding night?"

Niki's face flushed. "I'm afraid I'll never see you again."

"Niki, Bremerton is only a five hour flight from Anchorage. I plan on spending my first vacation with you and Jill and Dan."

"Really Jack?" Niki asked tremulously.

"Really. Now get straightened up before Jill gets home. We wouldn't want Dan shooting me for fooling around with his new daughter."

Niki laughed, and I knew it would be all right. Phew! That had been close.

I said my final farewells at breakfast, and was on my way to the airport. I completed the sale of the motorcycle, and as the lineman helped me untie the L-5, he asked about Niki.

"I'm barely getting away in time." I said apprehensively, "Her father gets back from overseas this month, and he packs a big .45!"

THIRTY

My stop in Sacramento was just long enough to make a few modifications to the rear seat and to the cabin width with a hydraulic jack. It was ridiculous to have an airplane with all this power that only carried two people. The civilian version carried four with a smaller engine. My modifications may not have been strictly legal, but were so well disguised they weren't readily visible. After the installation of an extra long seat belt, I could easily carry two medium-sized people in the rear seat.

I took the family for a ride and early in the morning I was headed north.

The flight went well until I reached Ely, Nevada for a fuel stop. This was my first landing at altitude and I flared out just like I did at sea level. I must have been ten feet in the air when the wing lost its lift and dropped so hard the gear spread out like a ruptured duck. I was sure I'd sprung it, but no, it came right back. This Stinson was really built; I guess this was one of the reasons the government paid so much money for them.

I made a mental note to come in hotter at altitude, especially with a load. I already discovered this plane had a taste for gasoline.

The next excitement occurred on the leg to Montana. I was making such great time I didn't stop for gas at Butte as I planned.

The airport at Great Falls is perched on a windswept plateau and when I turned into the wind to land, I discovered why I had been making such great time. I must have had at least a sixty-mile an hour tail wind. I lined up with the runway and then couldn't believe what was happening. I was descending and going backward at the same time. I checked the airspeed indicator and it showed a respectable sixty miles an hour.

Well, I couldn't let the airport disappear so I gave the engine more throttle. The wind was steady and it was like coming down in an elevator. I knew if I landed on the runway it would be impossible to taxi to the hangers without being flipped over. I didn't have enough fuel to go anywhere else, so I picked a concrete slab in front of a large hanger and descended straight down. I prayed the wind would hold steady and the hanger wouldn't cause any wind deflections. When the main gear touched, I held it there with the tail up, brakes on and lots of throttle.

When the hanger door opened and the surprised mechanics came out to manhandle the plane inside, I chopped the throttle and relaxed.

"Man, you've got guts bringing this light an airplane in today," commented one of the mechanics.

"Check the gauges, "I replied. One tank was empty and the other was bouncing on a quarter.

I heard comments about never seeing a landing like this before, and realized they had watched my approach through the windows in the large hanger door. I thanked the mechanics for the help, and bummed a ride into town with one. After the day's trauma, I deserved a good dinner and a soft bed.

In the morning, the air was calm; I refueled and flew to Lethbridge, where I went through Canadian Customs. The flight to Edmonton went well until I approached the city, and found it a lot larger than I anticipated. I wasn't sure where the airport was so I kept a sharp lookout.

Ah! There it was; I could see a major airdrome with twin runways. Right then a two-way radio would have been nice. All I had was a little portable Airboy that received the dots and dashes of the low frequency, navigational beam. I saw a twin-engine military plane approaching a runway, so I fell in behind and landed.

This created all kinds of excitement. Jeeps with rotating, colored lights on top pulled up alongside as I turned off onto a taxiway. I throttled back and waited to see what all the commotion was about.

"By what authority have you landed at an R.C.A.F. base?" demanded a sergeant with a Scottish accent.

"R.C.A.F. base? I thought this was the municipal airport."

"Look at your charts, mon—this is restricted territory!"

"My charts ran out in Montana. I'm following a road map from there and it shows an airport right here—see!"

This produced a few snickers and I guess they decided I wasn't an enemy invasion after all. The sergeant radioed the tower and received permission for me to take off from where I was. He explained the civilian airport was several miles further on.

I arrived at the correct airport only to discover that before I could continue I had to buy three hundred dollars worth of survival equipment and dehydrated food.

This really set my finances back and didn't do much for the plane's center of gravity. I ended up strapping the rifle and shotgun to the overhead canopy. This helped the balance, but deflected the magnetic compass. I bought some Canadian charts so I wouldn't end up on any more restricted airports.

I had to file a flight plan following the Alcan Highway, so if I went down they wouldn't have trouble finding me.

I wasn't adverse to that, only from Edmonton to Fort St. John, my next fueling stop, the highway made a big bend. This would take extra gas and push my range to the limit.

The airline path was a straight shot with a beam all the way. Even better, a railroad ran over halfway to a small lumber town on a river. I didn't see how I could get lost with all those navigational aids and decided to take the shortcut.

I filed the flight plan the R.C.A.F. demanded, and flew the route I wanted. The forecast was for scattered clouds at four thousand feet and by the time I reached the end of the railroad, it was solid and down to less than three. I switched over to the beam and continued on.

Something very strange was going on up ahead. There was a solid wall rising from the ground. As I got nearer, I realized it was smoke from a massive forest fire. The smoke almost reached the clouds. This gave me a narrow corridor to fly through—clouds above, smoke below.

Well, I still had the beam, and St John couldn't be much more than an hour ahead. The clouds were lowering, the smoke was rising, and then the beam quit! It was only then that I realized I had forgotten to put new batteries in the Airboy receiver. I continued a little further, dodging clouds and smoke, before I realized I would never make it.

I made what I figured was a hundred and eighty-degree turn; it was hard to tell with the magnetic compass deflected by the guns. I checked my fuel and knew I didn't have enough to make any known airport. It was going to be a forced landing at best, a crash at the worst.

I finally reached the river the railroad intersected—then was the lumbering town upstream or downstream? I gambled on upstream and with both gauges sitting on empty, I reached it. If I crashed at least someone would be there to pick up the pieces.

I remembered today was my twenty first birthday and I wondered if I was going to die on the same day I was born?

Expecting the engine to quit at any second I saw the town had a wide and empty main street and decided to set down there. At the last crucial second I could see power lines crossing the street and kept on going.

A fellow came running out of a building, pointed to himself and then to the pickup sitting there. I could almost shake his hand as I went by. He jumped into the pickup and went charging out of town. I could see which way he was heading, and searched ahead until I spotted a green alfalfa field.

With my crucial fuel supply I didn't wait for my guide to arrive. I swung around to land, only before I could touch down the pickup pulled into my path. I was beginning to feel a little hostile about then, but when I saw him line me up on a different heading, I figured he might know what he was doing.

I quickly swung around, and this time got it down. From a ground view I could see my landing was between two irrigation dikes, several feet high. If I had touched down the first time, I would have wiped out the gear and probably flipped over on my back. I don't know why the dikes didn't show up from the air.

I had the engine shut down when the pickup pulled beside me.

"Hoot mon, am I glad to see you," the slim, middle-aged driver exclaimed as he climbed out of the pickup. "You are the first airplane to ever land at Whitecourt."

I was just thankful to get down in one piece.

"I want you to fly me and the fire warden up and around the fire so we will know where to send the firefighters."

"Hey, thanks for guiding me in, but I'm completely out of gas."

He had walked over to the plane—I'd crawled out and he offered me a cigarette. I took it and searched for a match. When he saw I didn't have one, he handed me his. I discovered I was having difficulty getting the match and the cigarette to meet. It was then I realized I didn't smoke. I wasn't spooked—not much!

Malcolm introduced himself and I discovered he was the owner of the sawmill, the timber that was on fire, and the alfalfa field we were standing in.

"Jack, I'm calling Edmonton and having two barrels of aviation gasoline sent out on the morning train. I'll pay you a hundred dollars to fly me and the fire warden up over the fire."

"All right," I agreed reluctantly, "better include a clean barrel pump and four C batteries."

I figured with the beam back in action and the guns removed which were messing up the compass, we might possibly find our way back. The thought of a flight tomorrow was way down on my priority list.

"Can I give you a ride to town? There are plenty of empty bunks in the bunkhouse and the cook will fix anything you want."

"I really need to close my flight plan. I don't want them starting a search."

"No problem, the radio station is just outside town. Check with me after you eat."

I slipped the guns into the pickup, Malcolm said he would keep an eye on them, and he dropped me off at the radio navigational station.

The radio operator's eyebrows rose as he realized I was closing a flight plan prematurely, from a location I shouldn't be anywhere near.

I explained, "The smoke was so bad over the highway; I got lost."

"When are you reopening your flight plan?"

"Not until the smoke clears. One forced landing in a cow pasture was enough for me."

I didn't know how long I would be there and I suspected the R.C.A.F. might take a dim view of my flying for pay in Canada.

With that, I hiked to the combination mess hall and bunkhouse of the sawmill. The air was so pungent in the bunkhouse, even with most of the men out fighting fire, I decided I'd rather sleep out by the plane. The cook threw a big steak on the grill and the dinner was great. After dinner, I wandered over to the office to see what else Malcolm wanted.

He tossed me the keys to an older Buick parked outside. "Use it as long as you're here, Jack"

"Thanks. I believe I'll camp out at the edge of the field if it's all right with you? I'll feel better about the airplane."

"Sure, I should be out with the gas about ten in the morning."

I drove out to the alfalfa field and discovered a wooded campsite where the field cornered with the river. This was the irrigation pumping station with an inviting, large, clear pool. I taxied the L-5 to the campsite and as I spun it around, the engine died. I knew why!

I unloaded my sleeping bag and camping gear and then walked the few steps to the riverbank. Although the sun was setting, I knew after today I badly needed a bath. I located my soap and towel and headed for the pool.

My morning coffee was just finished when the pickup arrived with two barrels of gasoline. Malcolm pulled right up to the plane and he and the fire warden got out of the pickup. I was pleased to see he was also slim. Malcolm hooked up the barrel pump. I crawled up on a strut and we filled the tanks, which took about two thirds of the first barrel.

I slipped the new batteries into the Airboy, while Malcolm pulled the pickup out of the way and unloaded the two drums and pump. I was hoping he would do that.

The fire warden showed me his grid map and designated the area he wanted to cover. The two squeezed into the back seat and because there wasn't any wind, we started the takeoff run from right there between two dikes. I popped a notch of flap and we were off.

It took an hour to map out the grid. As they crawled out after the flight Malcolm said in a relieved voice, "Finally I know where to send the firefighters."

He peeled off a hundred and commented, "Jack, it was cheap at the price. If you can stay longer, keep the car and eat at the mess hall. I might need another flight later."

After they departed, I stretched out on my sleeping bag for a siesta. I didn't even get to sleep before a cavalcade of vehicles began to arrive. They had seen the airplane land and this was their one chance for an airplane ride.

Well, there was all that airplane gas left over!

By evening there was only enough remaining to top off my tanks. By carrying two in the rear seat, up over town and back, at ten dollars each I had made nearly two hundred. I now had a wallet full of Canadian money.

I drove into town, checked with Malcolm, and explained I planned on leaving the following morning. He happily reported that the fire was under control and thanked me again for the flight. I picked up my guns. We shook hands— neither of us mentioned the remaining airplane gas. I was sure when Malcolm saw the plane flying over town all afternoon he had figured it out. I just hoped all the traffic on his alfalfa field wouldn't be reflected in the volume of his next cutting.

I swung by the radio station to reopen my flight plan.

"Glad you came by." The operator reported. "My last message from Edmonton was if you aren't out of here by this weekend they are sending an investigator on the Monday train. They are suspicious of your activities."

I had forgotten the radio operator would have viewed all the flying activity.

"Well, I just came by to report the smoke has cleared enough for me to leave. Please reopen my flight plan for Fort St. John at six a.m. tomorrow."

THIRTY-ONE

The smoke had cleared and I resumed my flight to Fort St. John. With the beam coming in loud and clear, it was an easy flight.

I topped off the tanks and continued on toward Fort Nelson, but before reaching there the Alcan Highway rose right up into the clouds. I didn't have much confidence in either my instruments or my blind flying ability, so I landed on the highway, pushed the plane off to the side, unloaded my sleeping bag and crawled in.

Several hours later, a passing truck woke me. I saw the clouds had lifted, the pass was clear, so I continued on my way.

From Ft. Nelson to Watson Lake was my longest hop. It was beyond my range and the only hope for gasoline was at Big Delta, the storage area for the remains of the Alaska pipeline project built during the war. There was a landing strip and thousands of gallons of automotive gasoline, stored in fifty-gallon drums.

Because I didn't know how good it would still be after years of storage, I had deliberately drained one fuel tank first on the flight. I filtered the car gas into that tank with a chamois. If it would burn I could make the next fuel stop, and if it wouldn't, I had enough good gas to make it back to the airstrip.

The watchman gave me a form to sign for the gas and I took off. As soon as I had altitude I switched to the car gas. The engine didn't miss a beat so I kept on going. This far north it didn't really get dark at night so I continued on until I finally arrived at Fairbanks—where the customs agent was unhappy with my midnight arrival. I was so beat; I spread the sleeping bag beside the plane and curled up right there on the concrete.

I cleaned up in a hanger the next morning and located a place for breakfast. I was uncomfortable leaving all my gear in the plane but I had been told people didn't even lock their doors.

Later, as the fixed base operator gassed the plane, I asked about the wolf hunting further north.

He laughed, "You must have read the article in the sporting magazine over a year ago. Last winter there were so many planes up there at Nome, they were practically having dogfights over any wolf they could find. The government pulled the bounty before the wolf became extinct."

Blast—so much for that dream. As I took stock of my situation it didn't look too great. Winter was almost here, my money was low and I didn't have a job.

"What's the job situation like?"

"Not good, the mines and practically everything else closes down for the winter. Oh, I did hear the Alaska Railroad was hiring firemen. Their office is in Anchorage,"

"Do you know what a fireman does?"

"Yeah, he shovels coal into a coal burning locomotive about twelve hours a day. That's probably why the job is hard to fill."

I thanked him for the information and after seeing what a meal cost in Fairbanks, I figured the sooner I got out of town the better. I could follow the railroad to Anchorage without getting lost and it was south.

I passed the base of Mt. McKinley, the tallest mountain in the country, on the flight and admired the impressive lodge with its own landing strip. In a couple of hours I could see Cook Inlet and the city of Anchorage. I located the airport, landed, made arrangements for permanent tie-down and checked my gear into a storage area. I still had enough money to fill the tanks, and buy food for a few more weeks.

A bus came by and the driver told me where to get off for the railroad offices. An inquiry produced the information that the road foreman of engines did the hiring and firing of engineers and firemen. I found his office and after an hour wait I was called in for an interview. He was an unfriendly, crusty old bird, who didn't pull any punches.

"Barnes, these are hand fired, coal burning engines. The fireman may have to shovel coal for as long as sixteen hours a day with a number two scoop." He glared at me. "This isn't a job for weak-kneed Cheechakos."

I didn't know what a Cheechako was and sure wasn't about to ask.

He continued. "It takes about a week to cover the entire railroad as a student fireman. The regular fireman shows you how it's done and each one you travel with turns in a report. When all the reports are in, you are either hired or not. If not, you put in a week's work for nothing."

I asked, "How soon can I start?"

"There is a freight leaving for Curry tonight; better pick up a handbag, long sleeve shirt, bib overalls, cap and neckerchief and heavy, gauntlet-type leather gloves. The railroad supply store on Central has what you need."

"What about eating and sleeping? I'm running low on money."

"The railroad has bunkhouses and mess halls everywhere except Anchorage and Fairbanks. Meal tickets are seventy-five cents each. Here is enough for the first week," he said as he handed them over. "Be at the roundhouse by six o'clock, ready to go. Ask for the fireman of the Curry freight."

I knew I was dismissed and as I headed for the door he finished with, "I don't think you are going to make it, Kid."

I hated being called Kid, and I had already figured out this old man and I were not going to get along. I located the supply store and by six o'clock I was at the roundhouse wearing my new gear with a fresh change in the bag.

The roundhouse foreman pointed out an older, heavyset man as the fireman of the Curry freight.

I walked over and said, "Hi, I'm Jack Barnes. This is my first run as a student fireman."

He groaned, "How did I get so lucky—well, come on?"

I followed him over to a locomotive, steaming quietly with the stack under a large hood.

"The first thing you have to do is get the engine ready," the fireman muttered.

I followed him up the steps to the cab. He checked the sight glass mounted on the boiler, saw the water level was in the center and then checked the steam pressure gauge. He appeared unhappy, as the pressure was just over a hundred pounds.

"Damn hostler helpers are getting lazier all the time."

He stepped on a button on the floor and the two firebox doors opened wide. I could see a dull glow inside. He cracked a valve and I could hear the rush of air. The fire seemed a little brighter before the doors closed. The fireman then picked up a heavy, four foot long, iron shaker bar with a rectangular hole in one end and fitted the hole over one of the metal stubs on the floor of the cab. He propped open the firebox doors and pushed the bar gently back and forth. I could see grates tilt in the firebox and ashes fall through to the pan below.

He warned me to do this very carefully, or the burning coal could also be dumped into the pan and that would be the end of the fire.

The fireman took the big scoop, shoved it into the coal in the tender behind us and with a practiced movement swung the loaded scoop toward the firebox doors, which opened just in time. He banged the scoop on the steel doorsill in passing, and the coal sprayed into the firebox in a fan shape. The next scoops were tucked into the rear corners of the firebox.

"That's called building a heel in the corners. You can't' reach them with the spray, and if they aren't kept plugged up, you pull cold air through the grates. If you don't spray the coal into the firebox, the mineral content melts and runs together and you have a clinker, which is hard to get rid of. I hope I don't have to demonstrate on this run," he said as he sprayed several more scoops into the firebox. I could see the steam gauge rising.

I followed him up another ladder to the top of the tender, where he checked to be sure we had a full load of coal. He lifted a steel lid on top of the water tank to be sure it was full. When we returned to the cab, he lifted the cover to the fireman's seat and rooted around inside checking what he called flares and torpedoes. We were supposed to have a certain amount in case of emergency. He handed me a canvas water bag and long neck oil can and told me where to fill them.

I had just returned when the engineer and head brakeman arrived, and in a moment we were slowly backing out onto the turntable. It turned until we were lined up with the right track and shortly we were steaming down the track backward to our northbound train. The head brakeman made the connection, cut in the airbrakes, and the compressor on the front of the locomotive went mad trying to pump up the air tanks on each car.

When the compressor finally calmed down, the head brakeman threw a switch and motioned us forward. The engineer cracked the throttle and the engine slowly moved forward taking the slack out of the cars. The head brakeman swung aboard and forced the fireman to share his seat. The fireman wasn't doing much sitting anyway.

There was a slight uphill grade leaving the yard and I watched the fireman get busy with the large scoop. As quickly as the steam pressure reached over two hundred pounds, he pulled out the injector handle and I could see the water level in the sight glass rise slowly. I could also see this caused the steam pressure to drop. The fireman sprayed more coal into the firebox and heavy black smoke belched from the stack.

The fireman explained it was a fine balance between steam pressure and the level of water in the boiler. The harder the engine worked, the more coal and water were required. He added as an afterthought, that if the water ever dropped out of sight in the sight glass, the boiler would probably explode killing everyone in the cab! If the water level went out of sight from too much water it would cause a liquid lock and do serious damage to the engine. I could hardly keep my eyes off the glass for the rest of the trip.

The steam pressure was just below 220 pounds, the water level was in the center of the glass, when the fireman handed me the scoop.

"It's all yours," he growled as he sprawled on the seat next to the brakeman.

Everything looked under control so I just stood there. The fireman got a pained expression on his face as the steam pressure started to drop. I filled the scoop with coal and started my swing. I hit the button with my foot, the doors swung open, but I missed the sill and all the coal landed in the middle of the firebox in a black heap.

The fireman looked even unhappier. My second swing was a little better. I bounced the scoop off the sill and some of the load sprayed and some didn't. When I checked the steam pressure gauge I saw it was dropping, so I quickly began adding more coal to the firebox. I was improving with each swing. Black smoke was pouring out of the stack when I noticed the steam pressure was rising very rapidly. I quit shoveling and pulled out the water injector handle. This slowed the sudden rise in pressure but the water glass was rising toward the top. I shut the injector off before the dread liquid lock occurred.

The steam pressure resumed its climb and I watched fearfully as the gauge passed 220 pounds. Suddenly I heard such a deafening roar, I was afraid I might have blown the boiler. The engineer, who up till now had acted as if I didn't exist, glared at me like I had broken his engine. The steam pressure was coming down and soon the horrible noise quit. I realized it must have been a safety valve that popped open. I decided to govern the amount of coal a little more carefully.

My problem then was with the first scoop I had thrown into the firebox. It had formed a clinker about two feet across and it was right in the middle. Every time I sprayed coal with the scoop, the clinker seemed to get larger.

The fireman got up, looked into the firebox, motioned for me to sit and then he pulled a long iron rod out of the tender. He propped the firebox doors open and then hooked the clinker with the prongs at the end of the rod. He pulled it back to the firebox door, shoved the scoop inside and pulled the clinker onto the scoop. He balanced the clinker on the scoop, eased it out the firebox door, quickly tossed it out the open gangway and then retrieved the rod, which was now glowing red at the end. As the fireman slipped the rod back into the tender I could see his gloves were starting to smoke. He handed me the scoop and quickly removed his gloves.

Well, we had lost twenty pounds of steam pressure with that maneuver so I sprayed another coating of coal and even remembered to build up the heel in the rear corners. The pressure came back nicely and when I glanced at the fireman he gave me a grin. I must have been doing all right because the fireman remained on the seat and I did the work. I was getting both hungry and tired when we finally began to slow down. I stuck my head out the gangway and could see we were approaching a small settlement with a large water tower beside the tracks. Fortunately, I hadn't shoveled a large slug of coal into the firebox recently. When the engineer closed the throttle I could control the steam pressure rise with the water injector.

The fireman came to life and motioned for me to follow him. We climbed to the top of the tender, where he stood on the engineer's side and guided him to the waterspout with hand signals. They had it well rehearsed, because the engine stopped with the nozzle of the tower directly above the lid to the tender tank. The fireman flipped the tank cover open, pulled the rope on the nozzle until it descended to the tender and commenced filling our tank. With the size of the nozzle and the pressure from the large tank, it only took a few minutes. The fireman released the nozzle, closed the tender lid, and we returned to the cab.

The engineer backed the train into a siding because we had a meet here with a southbound freight and we went into a mess hall to eat. The food was served family style and was surprisingly tasty, with meat, potatoes, a vegetable and a skimpy, fresh salad.

I had worked up a man-sized appetite and was just getting started when the others finished and started to leave. I quickly gulped a few more mouthfuls and then made a dash for the engine. The engineer was already pulling the throttle as I clambered aboard. The southbound freight had arrived and pulled by far enough to clear our siding.

After shoveling coal for over four hours, I was hoping the fireman would take over, but no such luck. Well, I had already learned enough to conserve energy and in another five hours we arrived at Curry. This was the end of the run for this crew and tomorrow they would take a freight back to Anchorage. I would pick up the next northbound freight. I hadn't had any more difficulties and hoped the fireman would turn in a satisfactory grade on his report.

Curry was a railroad settlement with a repair shop and guest hotel. I happily discovered train crews were treated as guests—even student firemen. I was assigned a private room and found I could order from the menu in the crew dining room. After being short-changed on the last meal, I ordered a massive dinner.

The next northbound freight wasn't until tomorrow so I had time for a good rest and was first in line when the dining room opened for breakfast. I had already met the fireman on this crew and found out there wouldn't be any more food until we arrived at Healy, our next stop.

This fireman was only a couple years older than me and he was friendly. On this run he showed me all the ways to make the job easier. I was glad he fired part way as my muscles were in spasms from yesterday. He also warned me the trip from Healy to Fairbanks wouldn't be fun—something about the sadistic engineer and the Johnson bar. I should have asked what a Johnson bar was but didn't want to appear that dumb. He did temper the bad news with some good.

"Today is a hot day," he said with a smile.

"Ok, what's so great about that?"

"Wait till we get to the Cantwell native village," he replied.

We pulled into the Cantwell siding to drop off supplies for the section gang, and I noticed the section crew working on the main line. They were stripped to the waist and I suddenly realized they were broad-shouldered, well-endowed, young native women. These amazons swung the heavy iron spike maul with ease and ignored their attentive audience. The young, white, section gang foreman watched with a satisfied expression.

The fireman told me the elders of the native village sat in front of the trading post, smoking and drinking beer. Their sons trapped and hunted when they felt like it, and the daughters worked on the section gang. Visiting white men were discouraged, he added with a smile. The section foreman hadn't taken a vacation in years.

Healy was a barren railroad outpost servicing train crews. I again had a room to myself and the food was good. I found out there was a dormitory at Fairbanks but no mess hall. I didn't know how long I might be stuck there so I talked the waitress into packing an extra large lunch in a paper bag.

The fireman on this run was almost as green as I was. This was his first assignment after working the extra board, and he hated it so much, when we arrived at Fairbanks he was quitting. I started to ask why, but just then the engineer staggered aboard and the fireman clammed up. The heavy-set engineer appeared about fifty, and it was obvious he had been drinking.

The first part of the run was downhill and the engineer no sooner had the train out of the yard, when he cushioned his head on the arm holding the throttle and went to sleep.

I looked out and we were already going too fast to jump. The cab got to bouncing so badly it woke the engineer, and he drew some air off the air brake. Just before we stopped, he woke again and released the brakes. That's the way we went down the grade, all the way to Nenana, the halfway point and where we stopped at a mess hall.

After a good meal and several cups of coffee, we continued on toward Fairbanks. The engineer appeared refreshed after his sleep and the coffee, and dropped the iron bar with a lever on the end into the forward position. It was mostly uphill the rest of the way to Fairbanks and the fireman and I took turns shoveling coal.

I soon realized there was something drastically wrong. We were using twice the coal and water on any previous run, and I finally figured out why. The iron bar in the forward position must be the infamous Johnson bar. This was similar to a combination gearshift lever and spark advance on a gasoline engine. The other engineers had hooked it toward the center as soon as we got rolling. The speed had picked up and the steam usage dropped. Not so with this sadistic engineer—he liked to watch the fireman sweat.

The reason the fireman was quitting was obvious. In the cab, the engineer is king, and whatever he wants he gets. Between the two of us we made it to Fairbanks, and I could see we had gone through a massive amount of coal. Every muscle in my body ached. I decided then and there, I wasn't making any more runs with this engineer.

There was a dormitory in Fairbanks, but no mess hall. I still had the large lunch from Healy, and I decided to wait for another southbound freight—after this engineer departed.

After a good night's sleep, I finished the sack lunch for breakfast, and wandered to the roundhouse to find when there would be a second, southbound freight. When I met the roundhouse foreman I received a shock. The other fireman had indeed quit and because there wasn't anyone else to take his place, I now was assigned to the freight with the miserable engineer. I was on the payroll and my seniority started immediately.

Talk about good news and bad news! Instead of completing more days without pay and perhaps not being hired at all, I would start immediately on an assigned run. Normally I would have had to work the extra board out of Anchorage for months before garnering enough seniority to bid in a regular run.

The roundhouse foreman had contacted the road foreman of engines, and received permission to grab me. He explained that I really was assigned off the extra board, and the job would be put up for bid. He added with a grin that he didn't think there would be a large list of applicants.

The bad news, other than the miserable engineer, was the pay car had just left, and there wouldn't be another payday for a month. I explained I was flat broke, and almost out of meal tickets. He supplied the meal tickets, to be taken out of my first check, but that was as far as he would go.

I decided to make the best of it, and returned to the dormitory for my gear. I tried to remember all I had heard about getting the engine ready, and when the engineer arrived it was ready to go. At least he didn't appear to be drunk, and although he seemed surprised to see a green student as his fireman, he didn't say anything.

The trip went fairly well until we left Nenana, and began the uphill portion of the run. The Johnson bar was in the way forward position, and I was shoveling coal as fast and as hard as I could. By time we were halfway up the grade, I was tired and angry. I could feel my perverse personality start to take over, and I knew something ugly was going to happen.

I decided I wasn't going to give the road foreman the satisfaction of calling me a quitter; instead I was going to break this engineer of some bad habits, or get fired.

With my next swing of the loaded scoop, the firebox doors failed to open. The scoop glanced off the doors, and the coal kept right on going. Most of it ended in the engineers lap, and only his neckerchief kept some of it from going down his neck. I didn't know he could move that fast. He jumped to his feet, dumped the coal out of his lap, and stood there glaring.

"What was that all about?" he demanded.

"Sorry, my foot missed the door button—something distracted me."

He brushed as much coal off as he could and returned to the engineer's seat.

"Don't let it happen again,"

I quickly threw more coal into the firebox; I didn't want to get behind with the steam pressure and water. When I got caught up I glanced at the Johnson bar. It was still in the same position, and I knew this was going to get violent.

Another scoop of coal landed in the engineer's lap and some in his face. He leaped up again, and I could see he was looking for the iron shaker bar. I had already hidden it and the only possible weapon in the cab was the big scoop, which I was holding like a baseball bat. He could see I was ready to use it! I watched the color leave his face.

"You get distracted again?"

"Yeah."

"What distracted you?"

"The Johnson bar!"

"Oh."

He returned to his seat, and hooked the Johnson bar back up to where it belonged. The coal consumption returned to normal, and it was an easy run the rest of the way to Healy.

We bailed off the engine, another crew took over, and we continued on to the dormitory. I watched to see if he stopped at the office of the station agent. If I was fired, he would have to wire for another fireman, as there were no students at Healy; instead he headed for the showers. I let out a large breath and headed for the crew dining room. Ever since I had been doing heavy physical labor I was continually hungry. The bag lunch I took with me from Healy just wasn't enough.

The return trip next day was something else. The engineer was so drunk two brakemen had to help him up in the cab. He managed to get the train out of the yard, and then resumed his favorite position; his left hand on the throttle, and that arm cushioning his head. I remembered enough from the first trip, that when the wildly swaying cab didn't wake him, I reached over and drew some air from the air brake. There is a delayed reaction, and when I didn't release it quickly enough, we almost came to a stop. He had his hand on the throttle, so I had to wait for gravity to increase our speed. The next time I didn't draw off as much air and that was the way we continued to Nenana

He woke just before we came to a siding, where we had a meet with the southbound passenger train, and appeared all refreshed and happy—what a way to run a railroad!

After lunch, we started the uphill portion of the run with the Johnson bar in its old position. I was just about to dump another scoop of coal, when the engineer glanced over, and quickly hooked it up. The engineer and I developed a silent truce; he slept on the downhill part of the Healy to Fairbanks run, and I did both our jobs to Nenana. On the uphill part, he kept the Johnson bar hooked up.

I was beginning to enjoy the job when a serious problem surfaced. I had run completely out of money. I could barely survive on the lunches from Healy during the week, but on the weekends in Fairbanks, there was no food at all. I knew that something was going to have to give—and soon!

THIRTY-TWO

I discovered that the lumberyard was good for four hours work whenever we had a load for them. I shoveled coal for twelve hours and then unloaded lumber four hours more, trying to put enough aside to be able to eat on the weekend. The injustice of it all was beginning to get to me. I was down to muscle and bone by the end of the month, and when the pay car finally arrived there was a check for everyone, except Jack Barnes.

What was even worse, I didn't have money for laundry, or even soap, toothpaste and razor blades. I quit showering because I couldn't stand putting filthy clothes back on. I let my beard grow, and even quit brushing my teeth. My hair grew long, and I didn't attempt to comb it. The engineer moved out of our shared room at Healy, and I noticed most people gave me a wide berth. It was surprising how quickly man can revert to a primitive state, without money.

I had the station agent fire off a telegram to the disbursing office in Anchorage every week, with no reply. Finally at the end of the second month the pay car arrived. There was a check for everyone but me. That did it!

The passenger train was leaving for Anchorage in an hour, and I headed for the roundhouse. The roundhouse foreman backed up as I burst into his office.

"No check again; I'm headed in on the passenger."

"You leave without a replacement and you're fired!"

"Good, if I'm not going to be paid—why work!"

I stalked out with a full-blown attitude, and climbed aboard the passenger train with my little bag of worldly possessions. This was the prestige train on the Alaska Railroad with a dining and bar car. I chose a seat and soon I had that part of the car all to myself.

I glanced at my reflection in the window and could understand why. I didn't recognize the creature staring back. All I could see was wild hair, a thin bearded face, a body dressed in filthy clothes and wild, red-rimmed, angry eyes staring back. It scared me, and I knew something ugly was going to take place in Anchorage.

The conductor came by for tickets. "I'm deadheading into Anchorage to get paid," I muttered, and hoped he wouldn't like the answer. He liked the answer just fine, and hurried on.

It was evening when we arrived in Anchorage, the disbursing office had already closed, and the only ones around were the station agent, and the dispatcher. The thought of no money for food increased my simmering rage. I entered their office, slammed the door behind me, and angrily advanced. They looked alarmed as I strode forward.

"My name is Jack Barnes, and I just came in on the passenger. I haven't been paid in two months, and haven't eaten in two days; I'm going to eat tonight. I want five dollars, and I want it now!"

I could tell the station agent was about to start that song and dance about not having anything to do with payroll, so I started for him. He quickly reached for his wallet, and seemed aghast to find he only had three dollars. He turned to the dispatcher, who speedily supplied the other two.

"Thanks, now what's the name of the disbursing officer?"

"Mr. Roberts," the agent faltered.

"Good, that's the bastard I'm looking forward to meeting tomorrow. When I get mine, you'll get yours." I slammed the door again as I left.

I stopped at the first restaurant, and blew the whole five on a steak dinner and a couple beers. My stomach quit thinking my throat was cut, so I stopped at the first vacant lot and curled up in the weeds with my bag for a pillow. It was after nine o'clock when the sun woke me the next morning. I stretched, and headed for the railroad offices.

When I reached the pay window of the disbursing office, I suspected they had already heard of me. An office girl with a scared expression on her face slowly came to the teller's window, after a quick look at me; she hurriedly backed off a couple feet.

"Can I help you?" she asked in a squeaky voice.

"Yes, I would like to speak to Mr. Roberts. Would you tell him that Jack Barnes is here?"

"Mr. Roberts is busy right now."

"That's too bad, would you tell Roberts that if he isn't here in thirty seconds, I'm headed for the general manager's office."

"Yes, Mr. Barnes, I'll tell him." I watched her scurry around a corner and out of sight.

I glanced around the massive office where there must have been at least six typists, and they were all staring at me with horrified fascination. I hadn't heard a typewriter click since I arrived.

I heard approaching footsteps from around the corner. If this was Roberts, he was a real dandy, about thirty, my height, with a fancy sport coat and color coordinated necktie. Something about him reminded me of Mack, the crooked dude I had trouble with when I bought the airplane. He even had the pencil thin moustache. He stopped several feet back from the teller's window.

"Roberts?"

"Yes."

"I'm Jack Barnes—where are my payroll checks?"

"Oh yes, Barnes, why we sent your checks to Seward."

"Why did you send them to Seward, when I was at Fairbanks? Didn't you receive the four telegrams I sent?"

"I don't know—anyway all your checks will arrive at Fairbanks with the next payroll," he announced smugly.

That did it! I felt something snap. I lowered my voice and motioned him closer. He advanced a foot; my right hand snaked out and grabbed his pretty necktie. I yanked him partway through the teller window until I had him balanced on the ledge with his face up. His arms were trapped beside his body with his feet churning the air. I kept wrapping my fist around his tie, until there wasn't any slack left. I placed my filthy, bearded face, right above his freshly shaved, sweet smelling one, and tightened the tie a little more. He tried to turn his head; my breath was potent after not cleaning my teeth for weeks.

"Roberts, I've been shoveling coal on an empty stomach and living like a pig for two months, all because of your lazy incompetence."

The more I thought of it the more incensed I became! I emphasized each following remark regarding his ancestry with another twist on the necktie, and I could see drops of spittle raining on his face.

"Now Roberts, you are going to go to your cash box, and get me every cent this Mickey Mouse railroad owes me. If those checks even exist, you can use them to wipe your ass! If I don't have my money in five minutes, I am going to get really pissed!"

I unwound the tie, and gave Roberts a mighty shove. He slid out of the window like a cork out of a bottle, and landed on his butt and back. He just lay there for a moment trying to get air back into his lungs. He must have seen me pull out my watch to check the time, because he scrambled to his feet and disappeared. I figured it was fifty-fifty, as to whether he went after the money, or the cops. The way I was feeling, I didn't much care. I'd been thrown into jail before, and I knew they fed prisoners.

About five minutes later the same scared girl came out with a fat envelope. She cautiously pushed a paper to the counter.

"Mr. Barnes, you need to sign this."

I glanced at it, saw the amount was just over eleven hundred dollars, which was about what I figured I was owed. I counted the money, and signed the paper. I dropped off a five at the station agent's office and told them to give it to the nightshift.

What a way to end a railroad career!

THIRTY-THREE

I was hungry again, so I returned to the same restaurant and ordered a double helping of ham and eggs. Later, I picked up a complete change of clothes, toothbrush, and shampoo, and headed for a sauna to sweat the dirt out of my pores.

After a sweat, shower and hair wash, a barbershop was next. I was about to trash my filthy clothes, when I saw a Chinese laundry. I told the man if he could get them clean in the next hour I would pay him double.

At the barbershop I ordered a shave and haircut, and when the barber finished, I felt almost human. I checked at the laundry and not only were my clothes clean; the Chinaman had even removed the pitch from the lumber.

I had decided to fly to Bremerton and see if Dan, my former engineering officer, still needed help. There were two negatives with this idea. It would be necessary to fly back the way I came and I knew the R.C.A.F. wasn't happy with me.

The other problem was Niki. I would be in serious danger of being married before my time, as Dan was now Niki's stepfather.

I caught a cab to the airport, loaded up my gear and pointed the L-5 toward Fairbanks. When I passed over Curry and Healy, I felt a touch of nostalgia. I had enjoyed my overnight stays there.

A little further down the tracks was a roadhouse called Lignite, where a spur line took off to a coal mine, and the miners came here to drink and party. I was flying along five hundred feet above the tracks, when I saw a girl in white shorts standing in front of the roadhouse, wildly waving her arms.

I circled to check out a very small meadow in front of the roadhouse, and decided to try it. I cranked in full droop ailerons, full flaps, and brought the L-5 in, hanging on the prop. I taxied up to the roadhouse, where she was waiting on the front porch.

"Hi," she called, "I was hoping you would land. Come on in; the drinks are on me."

I shut the engine off—this was one good-looking woman. She introduced herself, and also the chubby gal that ran the roadhouse. After several beers, I learned her name was Bobbie and her business was delivering pleasure to lonely men. She was here visiting her girlfriend, and she wanted a ride to Fairbanks.

She was the first hooker I had met socially, and I was forced to throw out some preconceived ideas. Bobbie had a happy, outgoing personality, and was fun to talk to. We both had a glow on by the time we took off and she brought a six-pack to keep it going.

Once we were airborne she asked if she could fly, and judging by her competence, I suspected she had more hours in her flight logbook than I had in mine.

When we came to Nenana, I took the controls back. I could see the railroad bridge over the Tanana River, and every time I had crossed that bridge, I had wondered about flying under it. When Bobbie saw what I was going to do, she handed me another beer and cheered as we passed under. We must have had twenty feet to spare.

A little further on, I spotted a freight train headed north, and it took a moment to realize this was my former train. At the first clear stretch I dropped down beside the fireman's side of the cab. When the fireman stuck his head out the window, I realized it was the roundhouse foreman who fired me. I got to laughing as he scowled, and wondered where the engineer had the Johnson bar set.

I took a big swig of beer and he shook his fist. Bobbie was feeling no pain and she waved. I climbed a hundred feet and when I was set up, I told Bobbie to drop the empty beer bottles out the window. The trajectory was perfect and they shattered on the top of the cab. I thought that pretty well expressed my feelings for the last two months.

I refueled at Fairbanks and talked the fixed base operator into storing my gear. It was much too late to continue on today. I was hungry and when I told Bobbie I was going to go eat, she wanted to come with me, however, there was a bartender friend she wanted to check on first. She had heard a jealous husband was looking for him with a forty-five.

We found Dave, the bartender, cowering in his apartment. He seemed pathetically pleased to see Bobbie and told her if he couldn't get out of town tonight, he was a dead man. When he found out I had an airplane, Dave begged me to fly him to the Mt. McKinley resort hotel where he had a friend.

I told him I was too hungry to go anywhere, and besides it would be dark soon. The days were now much shorter.

Dave countered, "If you will fly now, I will pay all expenses at the resort hotel for both Bobbie and you, and will give you a hundred dollars besides."

I glanced at Bobbie. She smiled and said, "The food is really good at the resort dining room, Jack"

The sun had already set as we three stealthily reached the airport. I quickly took off while there was still some light, and before someone started shooting.

It was pitch black by time we arrived. My only landmarks were the lights from the hotel and moonlight reflecting off steel rails. I knew the landing strip was some distance away. Unless someone turned some lights on soon, I was flying back to Fairbanks.

As I circled someone flipped a switch, and I could see two rows of lights defining the airstrip. What a relief! I hadn't mentioned to my passengers—this would be my first night landing. I don't know who was the most relieved when we set down—the bartender or me. He feared I would return to Fairbanks where the furious husband would be waiting.

We three had a delicious and expensive dinner in the dining room; now that he wasn't afraid of being shot, the bartender's appetite returned.

After dinner, we retired to the bar where his buddy was on duty, and the drinks were potent. The bartender left for the front desk to get us rooms for the night; it was getting near closing time.

Two young studs recognized Bobbie, and came over promoting. Bobbie was friendly with her turn down, said she was on vacation, and I noticed their disappointed expressions. Bobbie must have been very good at what she did.

Dave, the bartender, returned with our room key, and said he registered us as Mr. and Mrs. Jack Frost. He slipped me the hundred, and thanked me again for saving his life.

Bobbie and I located our room, and I noticed it had both a double and a single bed. As Bobbie started to undress by the double, I got a glimpse of her superb body, and knew we weren't going to need the single. I slipped into the inviting bed, and as my hand explored some northern territories, hers took a more southerly direction.

"Oh, Jack!" she happily exclaimed, "If you do what I ask, we are going to have fun tonight."

I was more than ready to follow instructions, when I heard the sound of our door being gently closed. I glanced that way and in the dim light from the transom I saw the two young studs sneak over to the other bed and stretch out. I realized that in my haste to get into Bobbie's bed, I had neglected to lock the door. It was obvious what they had in mind. The more I thought of it the more furious I became, especially as they had disturbed my concentration at a crucial moment.

I leaped out of bed, grabbed the two handles of the single mattress and gave a mighty heave. The young studs flew through the air, crashed against the wall, and slid down into the narrow space between the wall and bed. The mattress flopped back onto the bed, and I leaped on top. My head was practically touching the ceiling, and a distended member was waving over their heads as I moved.

"Out!—Hit the road!" I roared.

They acted as if they were in a state of shock; their eyes followed the waving member like they were hypnotized. I was really getting angry and was about to throw them out bodily, however, they acted more concerned about what I was going to do with something else. Finally they got their minds in gear and hurriedly slunk out.

I carefully locked the door this time, and as I returned I could feel the bed shaking. Bobbie was laughing, and trying to be quiet. I was afraid I'd blown the whole thing, but after a few minutes of Bobbie's skillful attention, I realized I had been unduly concerned.

During breakfast the next morning, I found out how Bobbie came to be in her present profession. She came from a good family in Seattle, married right out of high school, and discovered sex. Her husband couldn't keep her satisfied, so she started adding volunteers. Finally she decided that if she liked it so much, she might as well be paid.

She divorced her husband and moved to Alaska, where her services were greatly in demand. She charged premium prices, and only accepted those willing to follow her instructions. Bobbie figured in another five years, her investments would allow her to be financially independent for the rest of her life.

I still planned on leaving for the states, so we got an early start to Fairbanks. We parted friends at the airport, and I taxied over to fuel up. I had just finished when the fixed base operator came over. He said the roundhouse foreman had called, and wanted to see me as soon as possible. Damn! I mentally debated, and finally decided to find out what he wanted.

I trudged to the roundhouse, and located the foreman in his office. He looked completely beat.

"Jack, you are going to take the freight out this afternoon, aren't you?"

"Hey, you fired me—remember? I'm flying to the states today."

"Jack, you weren't fired. I didn't turn in the paper work, and I'm too old to shovel any more coal. Hey! Did you really collect your pay the way I heard?"

The foreman had a big grin, and I realized that while I had been flying with a friendly hooker, drinking beer, and throwing the empty bottles at him—this old man must have been covering for me.

"Depends on what you heard."

I knew the railroad had a grapevine that was superior to the telegraph and the stories seemed to grow as they were passed from crew to crew.

"It's all over the railroad. Everyone feels now there is a better chance their checks will be delivered on time. I wish I could have been there to see it."

We got to laughing when I told what actually happened, and I realized I didn't really want to quit. I agreed to take out the freight and went back to transfer my gear. I halfway expected to be fired later for what took place in Anchorage.

THIRTY-FOUR

Life settled into a pleasant interlude. I had made my point in the necessary places, and no one seemed inclined to give me a hard time anymore. My next checks arrived like clockwork. I was getting enough to eat and with the steady coal shoveling, I was developing a massive set of shoulders.

Winter had arrived at Fairbanks, and no one on the extra board wanted my run. When I found the temperature could drop to fifty below, I understood why. I invested in some extra cold weather gear, wool long handles, down-filled mummy bag to go inside my extra-heavy outer bag, felt boots to fit inside regular ones, and a down-filled parka with hood and insulated gloves. I also picked up a wool scarf to wrap around my face, to breathe through when the temperature dropped low enough to freeze lungs.

I had discovered early on the railroad operated on a seniority system. The day you were hired was your seniority date, and all job choices were determined by this system. In a way I was fortunate. Some of the firemen above me had quit or been promoted to engineer, and there was a shortage of firemen.

When I checked the bulletin board in the roundhouse, I saw posted for bid: two firemen on the snow-fleet. I wasn't sure what a snow-fleet did, but just for the hell of it I tossed my name in. A week later, I saw my bid had been accepted and I was to report to the roundhouse in Anchorage.

I didn't want to leave the L-5 in Fairbanks for the winter, so I paid to have it parked overnight in a heated hanger to melt the frost and ice.

My replacement had arrived on the passenger, so the next morning I said goodbye to my old crew and flew south. I arranged tie-down at the Anchorage airport and checked in at the roundhouse. The hostler showed me where the snow-fleet was parked and I wandered over to check it out.

The fleet consisted of a massive rotary wheel about eighteen feet in diameter, powered by an enclosed steam engine and operated by a fireman and engineer. Behind it was the locomotive that pushed it and also pulled an outfit car and caboose. All were stone cold.

I checked the outfit car and saw it was a bunkhouse with a large table, chairs, bunks, and a pot-bellied coal stove with a large coffee pot on top. The coal bin had been filled so I decided to move in. There was a shower and toilet in the roundhouse, otherwise I would have to find a place to stay in Anchorage like the rest of the crew, and pay rent while I would be gone most of the winter. We were all on call and on the payroll while we waited for our services to be needed.

Two days later it started to snow, the hostlers fired up both boilers and the rest of the crew arrived. We were all young bachelors with low seniority. The old hands wanted to be home with their families in the winter. It was a congenial group, and we swapped duties just for the hell of it. I managed some experience on the engineer's side of the cab, and up front running the big wheel. Our crew consisted of two firemen, an engine watchman, two engineers, a brakeman and a conductor.

The winter was one of unusually heavy snow and we worked almost around the clock keeping the rails clear. Some weeks we would go on overtime as early as Wednesday and be on time and a half the next four days.

We tried to tie up at one of the hotels or section gang shacks for meals and a shower, as all we carried were emergency rations and coffee. We all slept in the outfit car and each morning, on a rotational basis, some unlucky person had to slip out of his warm mummy bag and build the fire in the pot-bellied stove. The others waited until it warmed up. The temperature had been dropping, the further north we worked, and we had to chip ice from the water in the outfit car to fill the large coffee pot.

Shortly after Christmas, the snow slacked off. On New Year's Eve we checked into the Curry hotel and threw a party at the hotel bar. We invited all the single waitresses, and pretty well took over the place. We had our own bottles and mix, as well as hats and noise makers. The jukebox had recently been restocked with some good dance music records, and the party was off and rolling.

The wives of the employees that lived in the hotel perched on the bar stools to watch. We were their entertainment for the evening and I could imagine the gossip that would flow later.

After a couple hours I realized I wasn't enjoying the party. I had been drinking beer from the bar and had danced with each of the single waitresses. They all were so short I had a crick in my neck.

I believe the thing that really got to me was their attitude. The ratio of men to women was seven to one in Alaska, and worse on the railroad. With so much attention from desperate young men, they all had acquired a condescending manner—like they were Miss America.

I finally had enough and wandered out to the dimly lit, hotel lobby, which appeared deserted. I located a magazine and parked under a reading lamp. I could hear the music and laughter from the bar. I detected movement over in the corner and saw it was Raggedy Ann, who worked in the basement laundry and was usually so quiet you didn't know she was around. Her first name was Ann and she probably got the rest of it from the long, shapeless dresses she always wore—tight around the neck and wrists—loose everywhere else. I'd seen her face in the light and it was a mass of fine lines, like in an old painting. I had guessed she might be in her late fifties.

I didn't think anymore about it and started to return to the magazine. It was then I noticed she was crying. Every few minutes she wiped her eyes with a handkerchief. I tried to concentrate on the magazine, while all the time I was thinking it was a shame for anyone to be crying in a deserted Alaska hotel lobby, on New Year's Eve.

I finally couldn't take it anymore and walked over and sat in the adjoining chair.

"Hi Ann."

"Hi Jack." I was surprised she knew my name. She had put the handkerchief away and tried to pretend there was nothing wrong.

"Why are we sitting here with a New Year's Eve party going on?"

"I don't know about you, Jack, but I wasn't invited. Who invites an ugly old woman to a party?"

"That's not true; I'm one of the hosts and we invited all the single gals—besides, you are not ugly."

Ann hesitated, "How come you aren't in there?"

"The gals are all so short I can't dance with them." I appraised her figure, "I'll bet you are tall enough."

"Jack, I haven't danced in years, I've probably forgotten how."

"There's one way to find out. Come on."

I took her hands and pulled her from the chair. She was taller than I'd remembered, and by tucking her arm under mine, I got her to come with me.

I found seats at the snow-fleet table, mixed Ann a drink, and got another beer from the bar. Paul, my engineer, came by to welcome her, and I could see she was beginning to relax. The jukebox started a ballad I liked and I turned to Ann.

"Jack, I have rubber soled shoes on, they won't slide."

"Slip them off—I will too-then when I step on your toes it won't hurt so much."

That brought a smile, and we slowly headed for the dance floor. Ann was hesitant and held herself away. I started out real easy, and hoped she would relax, or this was going to be as bad as the earlier dances.

"Ann, you are going to get lost out there; I won't bite—honest."

She hesitantly moved closer, and I used all my skills as a leader, until soon she began to relax. I drew her in closer yet and our dancing improved greatly. Ann was light on her feet and could follow. When the dance ended I got her another drink, and when another slow one began, I coaxed her back out on the floor. We started where the last dance left off, and improved from there.

Ann was just the right height, and once she relaxed, was very good. I tried a few of my variations and she followed them all. I realized I was enjoying the party.

The next record was a hauntingly beautiful ballad, and as we danced a surprising thing occurred. Ann came all the way into my arms and slipped her arm around my neck. As my arm slid around her slim waist and brought her even closer, the dance became a moving embrace. Her body certainly didn't feel like that of an old woman! When the dance ended, we seemed reluctant to part. Just then it must have been midnight—all the noisemakers were going off, and most of the couples were kissing. Ann hesitantly raised her lips and we were engaged in a surprisingly warm, moist kiss.

We didn't leave the floor; the music began again and I danced with my eyes closed. I had a warm glow from the beer, and with a tall, slim, partner in my arms, I was happy. We didn't miss another dance, and before I was ready, it was closing time.

I was reluctant to part, and escorted her to her basement room. We stopped at her door and she turned to me.

"Thank you, Jack, you have truly made this a happy New Year's Eve."

"Hey girl, there were two of us in the lobby feeling miserable; thank you."

I pulled her close for a good night kiss, and then something unexpected, occurred. Ann's arms slid around my neck and she molded her body to mine. The response was immediate on my part, and when I turned the doorknob with my free hand, we were inside. When I closed the door Ann returned to our embrace. The next thing I did was lock the door!

There was enough light coming through the transom window to watch as Ann slowly removed her clothes. I started on mine and then I became entranced with what I was seeing. Beneath the baggy, shapeless dress, was a slim, supple body. From her neck down her skin was milk white, without a blemish. When she unsnapped the flat restraining bra, two lovely breasts asserted their independence. Ann unpinned her red hair and shook it out over her shoulders. When she turned to me she was a completely different person.

I hurried to complete my undressing, and when she returned to my arms, it was even more exciting. A few caresses later we were in each other's arms, on the bed, and my eager hands were exploring this sexy body. As our lips merged in a passionate kiss, I felt her hand go timidly exploring. The kiss ended abruptly, and I knew the moment of truth had arrived.

"Jack," Ann said in a scared little voice. "I don't think I can. I haven't in years, and you are so large."

"Don't panic, it will be alright—really, I wouldn't hurt you."

Our lips merged again and I employed all the skills I had perfected for just such a situation.

At the climactic moment, Ann was so excited; I believe she had forgotten all about her concerns. Later we lay beside each other, with her head on my shoulder, and her arm across my chest; I brought up the subject I knew she was sensitive about.

"Ann, do you mind talking about your skin?"

"I haven't discussed it before, but I don't mind telling you, Jack I have skin that can't tolerate sunlight. I lived all of my life in Seattle where the sun hardly ever shines. When I married, after a few years we moved to Arizona. The damage was done in a year, before I even realized what was causing it. My husband was so revolted by my appearance he divorced me. When I saw this job advertised by the Alaska Railroad, I just wanted to find a hole, and crawl into it—away from the stares of people. I'm only thirty four years old and I look sixty."

"Is there a reason you dress the way you do?"

"Jack, I'd rather have everyone believing all my body is this way, than having some fat conductor sniffing around, wanting to do me a favor. The only reason I broke my rule, is because you were so nice to me, even when you thought I was old and ugly."

"Ann, you are the nicest thing that has happened to me since I have been in Alaska."

"Tomorrow, I will be back to being Raggedy Ann, and this won't happen again. The gossips will already have a field day."

I already felt a sense of loss. Fortunately, the edict didn't start until later; we still had the rest of the night!

The snow-fleet left the next morning right after breakfast. The wind had come up, the snow was drifting at Hurricane Gulch, and we needed to clear the track for the passenger.

It was two weeks before we returned to Curry, and Ann had been on my mind. As exciting as it was to know a passionate woman here liked me, my concern had really been for Ann. It didn't seem fair to have something like that happen at such an early age and I wondered if something couldn't be done.

After a shower and dinner, I checked the lobby and lounge—no sign of Ann. I had a beer at the bar and was ready to call it quits. I started to my room when suddenly I found I was in the basement knocking on Ann's door. I could hear the lock click and she opened the door a crack.

"Jack?"

"Hi Ann."

She hesitated and opened the door wider.

"Come in."

Ann was wearing an attractive robe over her nightgown and her hair was down around her shoulders. She removed a magazine from the chair and motioned for me to take it. She sat on the bed with her legs curled up beneath her.

"I missed you, Ann. I checked around the hotel and didn't see you anywhere."

"I heard the snow-fleet come in, and came to my room early."

"Any special reason?"

"I didn't want the talk to start up again. It was pretty bad after the party. Those biddies perched on the bar stools saw us kiss.

"So?"

"So now the latest story is you are turned on by old women, and I am by young men."

I laughed, "Ann, they're just jealous—they thought they had someone they could look down on and feel sorry for. There you were—having a ball while all they were getting was a sore butt from the barstool. You ruined their whole night."

Ann gave a relieved smile, "You mean you don't mind what they said?"

"Not about me, I hope they didn't get to you."

"I feel better now, Jack, I'm glad you came."

"I better get going; we both have to get up early."

I stood up and had one hand on the door. Ann came over for a good night kiss. It started as just that, and then it changed. Our minds might be saying one thing but our bodies were sending a different message. Ann took my hand and led us to the bed.

That night was different from the first time; more relaxed—more sharing. We went to sleep in each other's arms and woke up the same way. I slipped out early, before there was a possibility of an audience.

From that night on Ann and I were together every night the snow-fleet stopped at Curry. She wouldn't join me at the bar but would be waiting after I had my single beer. Our desires seemed perfectly matched.

The next few months were pure pleasure. It was exciting to push the big wheel and watch it throw the massive stream of snow to the side. Paul let me run the locomotive while he fired, and I found I liked that just fine. The paychecks were substantia,l and because I didn't have any place to spend them, I already had more than three thousand in the bank. The best of all was having a warm bed and a loving woman waiting at Curry. The snow-fleet had been getting back every week.

Spring came, the snow was diminishing, and in two weeks the snow-fleet would be retired for the season. I desperately watched the bulletin board for a run that had Curry for a terminal. The only job that showed up was a work train, operating out of a gravel pit fifty miles to the south. It appeared there would be lots of overtime, and Paul and I both placed a bid.

Morrison-Knudsen had the contract to replace the worn, ninety-pound rail with new, one hundred ten pound and re-ballast the track. The railroad supplied a locomotive, train crew, and the dump cars as part of the contract. M-K had a short time and a lot of work to do while the weather cooperated. They planned on working twelve hours a day. The long hours must not have appealed to the men with higher seniority, because both Paul's and my bid were accepted.

I had a couple free days between the two jobs and made the most of them. After a sauna and massage, I bought some new clothes and moved into the best hotel in Anchorage. I had my meals in the fancy dining room and checked out the nightlife. I knew that for the next five months I was going to live with a shovel in my hands.

I checked with the railroad doctor about Ann's skin condition. He had read an article in a medical journal about a process a dermatologist in Phoenix had developed, and he said he would find out and send me the information.

The hotel room was well supplied with crested writing paper and I put it to good use. I got a letter off to Niki bringing her up to date. Her last letter had questioned why I was working on a railroad when I went to Alaska to hunt wolves.

I wondered about Papa-san's and Kumiko's new business and got one off to her.

In my letter home, I thanked dad for sending his gold railroad watch. It was mandatory for engine crews to have a lever set watch. At one time, dad had been a station agent on the Southern Pacific and he was pleased that I had gone railroading.

I felt I had touched most of my bases and was ready to go back to work.

THIRTY-FIVE

Monday, I arrived on the new job. M-K had built a special siding to hold the gravel and outfit cars, as well as a spur line to the gravel deposit and crusher. There were sleeping cars for both M-K people and the train crew; a kitchen car, dining car, and an office car completed our camp. M-K paid our salary.

Shortly after I reported to the work train, Tom, the construction superintendent, called the railroad crew together.

"Fellas, I have a problem—I have a lot of track to replace in a very short time. If you will hi-ball your runs from the gravel pit to the track, I'll make you a deal. We will work all the overtime you can handle and the cook will serve steak every day."

That sounded good to us. We were all there to make as much money as possible in the short summer, so we elected to work seven days a week with a later start Sunday morning. Saturday night was beer and poker.

The first week sailed right on by. Unfortunately, there was no train connection to Curry. It was only fifty miles away but it might as well be five hundred.

I had noticed the M-K people had been flagging down the passenger going to Anchorage and an idea began to form. I suggested the idea to Paul and he was all for it, so I waited until I could talk to the superintendent alone.

"Tom, would it be of any advantage to M-K to have an airplane here, available for immediate flights to Anchorage?"

"Yeah, it would, Jack, but where would it land?"

"Right there by the gravel pit. I have an L-5 and all it needs is a couple hundred yards of fairly smooth surface. I bet the cat skinner could do it in a couple hours."

"What's in it for M-K?"

"I'll fly your people wherever and whenever they want. I can carry two passengers and luggage for whatever price you think is fair. If it's during working hours you will have to pay the engine watchman to take my place. The only time I won't be available is Saturday night. I have a lady friend at Curry."

"Jack, you've got a deal. I'll talk to the cat skinner and you show him where you want it."

The next day while the steam shovel was loading the cars I got together with the cat skinner and we laid out the strip. It was mostly flat already, and all he needed to do was remove some brush and smooth it out.

Friday afternoon, the engine watchman fired for me and I caught the passenger to Anchorage. Eight hours later, I was landing on the new strip. This time of year, one could read a newspaper at midnight, so I didn't have to worry about runway lighting.

As soon as we tied up Saturday evening, Paul and I bundled up our dirty laundry, threw it in the luggage compartment and took off for the short landing strip at Curry.

We packed our laundry into the hotel basement, prepared to use the slow, coin-operated machines; however, as we walked down the hall Ann saw us and motioned us over. She was running a load of hotel laundry and offered to throw our clothes in with it. We were happy to unload and before I continued on to the showers, I dropped back and told Ann I would see her as soon as I got cleaned up. After the makeshift shower at camp, a real shower with hot water was a luxury.

It was great to be back in that cozy bed with Ann. It had been a month and we spent a long time catching up.

This pretty well defined my summer activities and I was happy. I was getting lots of overtime, lots of good food and lots of loving. I was even getting quite a bit of flying. M-K personnel were going to Anchorage several times a week and Tom was paying seventy-five dollars round trip. I could make a round trip in about an hour and a half if I didn't need to gas up. I noticed on my next paycheck that Tom didn't even dock me for the time I was away from the engine.

A half-starved black bear cub started showing up to search our garbage, and before we realized it, he had become a camp project. Something must have happened to his mother, and we saved scraps from our evening meal for him. With the cook serving steak every night, the cub was eating well, and starting to fill out. He figured out our dinner schedule and timed his visits to coincide. This little cub added something pleasurable to our day, and we looked forward each evening to his visit. By mutual consent we agreed not to feed him by hand, so he wouldn't be too friendly toward humans later in life and get into trouble.

A newly hired track worker arrived with a suitcase and a fancy hunting rifle in a sheepskin lined case. After work he proudly pulled it out of the case and showed off the expensive scope and custom stock. All he wanted to talk about was the big game he was going to kill.

We had just finished dinner and were gathering little tidbits for our friend, when we heard the shot.

I had a horrible premonition and rushed out of the dining car to the place we fed the cub. He was sitting on his haunches with his paws folded over his belly where he had been shot, and was crying like a baby. The second shot finished the cub.

I was stricken; tears were running down my cheeks. I yanked the rifle out of the hands of the great hunter, took it over to the railroad track and beat it to pieces on a steel rail.

I don't know what the rest of our camp told him about me, but when I looked for him, I saw him running down the tracks with a hastily packed suitcase. The nearest civilization was thirty-five miles ahead; the mosquitoes were fierce and the bears hungry!

I knew Tom wouldn't pay him for the day he worked; Tom had also been feeding the cub. We buried our friend, and never brought the subject up again.

It was about the middle of the summer when I received the letter from the railroad doctor. He enclosed the article from a medical journal describing the new method developed by a Phoenix dermatologist. A special process removed the old skin and the new skin came back as smooth as a baby's. The article went on to say it was developed in Phoenix because of the sun damage there to certain types of complexions. The article did mention that if the new skin wasn't protected from the sun, it could also be damaged.

I sent a letter to the Phoenix doctor describing Ann's condition and requesting all the information about costs, pain and length of recovery. Three weeks later I had a response.

The cost was five hundred dollars, there was considerable pain, and Ann would need to stay in Phoenix a week to ten days for follow up. It would be several more weeks before she would be completely recovered. From my description the doctor was very optimistic.

I was disappointed to discover a selfish side to my nature. I didn't want to tell Ann. She was the bright spot in my week and I would be miserable without her. I wrestled with my dilemma right up to late Saturday night, when the better side of my nature finally triumphed.

Ann was lying in my arms after an especially passionate loving, when I reached for the letter I had placed on the nightstand.

"Ann, there is a letter here I would like you to read," I said quietly, and handed it to her.

She took the letter from me reluctantly, like it might be bad news for our relationship. I watched the expressions on her damaged face. It showed interest, a gleam of hope, excitement and then her face assumed a pleased, but kind of wistful expression.

"Hey, why the sad look—this is good news."

"It's exciting news, Jack, I didn't know there was any hope. Maybe someday I can think about it. Thank you for finding out."

"Why not now?"

"I don't have the money."

"I never see you spend anything; I figured you must have a nice savings by now."

Ann smiled sadly, "When my father died, all he left my mother was a house with a mortgage. Her health is failing and all my spare money goes there. It won't be long before I will have to move in and take care of her. I look on our time together as a wonderful and unexpected gift."

What a compliment, and what a grim future.

"You know afterwards you could get a good paying job anywhere you wanted to."

"That's true, Jack, are you trying to get rid of me?"

"No, Ann, I've got rocks in my head for even bringing it up ... only for my own personal satisfaction I would like to see you as the good Lord intended you to look. If you will go, I will pay for it."

I watched the reflections of her emotional turmoil. Two big fat tears slowly coursed down her cheeks. She came into my arms and whispered, "Jack, that's the nicest thing that has ever happened to me. Thank you for offering."

"Well, are you going?"

"I'll think about it."

The following Saturday night she completely ignored the subject. I finally brought it up as we were lying in bed.

"Have you made a decision yet?"

"Are you sure you still want me too?"

"Yes, Ann."

"When does the work train get pulled off?"

"When the first snow arrives, probably another four or five weeks."

"All right. I'll go then."

I smiled with relief. "I'll make the arrangements and get your plane ticket."

Ann turned and expressed with her body the tender emotions she was feeling. It was a thoroughly grand night.

The next time I flew to Anchorage, I wired the Phoenix doctor's office, and made an appointment for a week after when I expected the work train to be pulled. I wired the five hundred and also ordered the plane ticket.

The work train had been pulled. The snow-fleet was still in Anchorage, I had bid it in again and there wasn't enough snow yet to fire it up. I was on salary, and still available to meet the passenger when Ann arrived.

I guess I wasn't fully conscious of Ann's concern about appearing in public, until I saw the fright in her eyes as she searched wildly for me at the station. I quickly came over, took her bag and escorted her to a waiting taxi. He drove us to the quiet hotel where I had reservations. It wasn't until we were in the pleasant room with a view of Cook Inlet, that Ann could relax.

She didn't want to leave the room, even for dinner. I knew she liked Chinese food so I placed our order by phone and then talked the manager into delivering it. After dinner we lay on the bed watching the lights of the city blink on below. Ann had been very quiet.

"Jack, am I ever going to see you again?"

"I sure hope so, Ann. Seattle is only five hours away by air. When the snow-fleet is pulled off, I'm taking a vacation. After all winter without your being there at Curry, I am going to be very lonesome, and probably very amorous."

Ann smiled and slowly began to disrobe, I did likewise and soon we were in each other's arms, trying to store up enough loving to last the winter.

The next morning, at the airport, before Ann boarded, I slipped an envelope into her carry-on bag.

"Ann, there is enough there to live on while you are in Phoenix and a little extra. I want you to buy some new clothes to show off your pretty figure. No more raggedy Ann!"

Ann was wiping her eyes as she slowly climbed the stairs to the entrance. She stopped at the top, we waved and she was on her way. It was starting to snow and I was glad. It would give me something to do.

THIRTY-SIX

During our heavy snow, the big rotary stayed busy for several weeks. When I finally reached Curry, a letter had just arrived from Ann.

"Jack, the procedure is a complete success. The doctor and I are very pleased. My face is still pink and tender, but there is no trace of the previous damage. Phoenix is a western town and I am wearing jeans, a long-sleeve shirt, and a cowgirl hat to protect my face. I am not taking any more chances with this sun.

Something very interesting took place yesterday. It doesn't lend itself well to a letter, so I will tell you when you come on vacation. I know you will be pleased."

After a heartfelt thank you, she concluded she would return to Seattle and apply for a job. Ann and I wrote back and forth all winter, and no matter how I tried, she wouldn't divulge what occurred in Phoenix after the operation.

Niki was also a faithful letter writer, and before I realized it, I promised both girls, as well as my parents, I would be down as soon as the snow-fleet was pulled off. Niki worked in Seattle and had her own apartment.

When the season ended, I checked the bulletin board in the

roundhouse for a possible job after my vacation. The Anchorage-Curry freight had just come up for bid and I applied. With my seniority climbing, I might just have enough to swing it. The bids would be awarded about the time I returned.

The next day, I caught a flight to Seattle, and five hours later we were taxiing into the terminal at Seattle's new international airport. If Ann hadn't written she was still wearing western gear, I wouldn't have recognized the slender redhead in the form-fitting jeans and shirt. A cord around her neck attached her hat, pushed back. She looked about twenty-five and the radiant smile directed my way made my toes start to curl.

I couldn't believe the transformation—not only in appearance, but also in body language. She projected the inner confidence of an attractive and happy woman. In a moment, I had barged through the crowd and Ann was in my arms.

"I hope I've got the right girl," I whispered. "Otherwise some husband is going to be mighty upset."

"It's me, Jack. Do you like the change?"

"Wow! I'm speechless—finally I get to see the real you. You're lovely."

Ann and I chatted happily as she drove to her home, and she slowed as we passed a large, neighborhood market.

"This is where I work, Jack. It's close to home where I can be available in case of an emergency. Mother's health is failing, and soon I will have someone stay with her while I work. Fortunately, the owner likes me and already made me assistant manager. The pay is good, and I'm happy again, meeting people."

A few blocks later, Ann pulled into the driveway of a modest, two-bedroom home, and I reached back for my luggage.

"This is it—nothing fancy," Ann announced.

Her mother was sitting in a rocker doing something with yarn and large needles.

"Mother, this is Jack—Jack, this is my mother."

She gave me a sweet smile and said, "I've heard a great deal about you. Thank you for helping Ann."

"It was really my pleasure, Mrs. Martin. Ann is very special to me."

"Jack, you can put your luggage in here." Ann opened a bedroom door.

I could see a double bed inside, and I looked at her inquiringly. She turned so her mother couldn't see, and gave me a wicked smile that answered my question. Ann had apple pie in the kitchen, and we three settled there for pie and milk.

A little later, Ann's mother said it was her bedtime, and retired to her bedroom.

When I finished my pie, I asked Ann, "Are you going to tell me what happened in Phoenix—what you wouldn't put in a letter?"

She smiled mysteriously, "All right, Jack, I think you are going to like this story. A couple days before I left Phoenix, I called Sidney, my ex, to find out why I wasn't getting any rent from my half of a cheap rental that hadn't been spelled out in the divorce settlement. The rent barely covered the payments and repairs, and he wanted to sell it to raise some money. Without my signature on the papers, he was stuck. Our equity was worth about three thousand dollars.

Sidney wanted to meet at a lawyer's office to sign some papers. I laughed and said I was flying back to Seattle, and if he wanted my signature, to meet me for lunch at a certain prestigious restaurant with the papers and a cashier's check made out to the name I mentioned, in the amount of fifteen hundred dollars—otherwise the house could rot as far as I was concerned.

Sidney didn't want to come up with the fifteen hundred, and he especially didn't want to be seen with me at that famous restaurant. I laughed at him, and said, 'Fine, forget it!"

He changed his mind and we made the date for the next day."

"I'll bet you were quite a surprise."

"Jack, I deliberately looked my best for that lunch. Most of the red was gone from my face by then, and it was easily covered with makeup. I had my hair done, and was wearing a new cocktail dress I bought with your money. I arrived early, had the maitre d' seat me at a secluded table, and ordered a double martini. I was really primed when the maitre d' escorted Sidney over."

"How did he handle the new you?"

"He just stood there—like he couldn't believe it was me. I could hardly believe it was him. Sidney is forty now, with a potbelly, and very little hair. All through the expensive lunch, Sidney raved about my new looks, and tried to make a date for that night. I just laughed and said, "Married, fat, bald-headed men, turn me off."

He finally produced the papers and cashier's check. I signed the papers, picked up the check and flitted away, leaving Sidney to pay the bill. I don't know if Sidney has a notary friend, but if not, he won't be able to record the documents I signed. He may be stuck with that shack forever. All in all, Jack, that day was one of the better days of my life."

"What was the best day?"

"A New Year's Eve in a certain Alaska hotel." Ann rose and came into my arms. "Let's go to bed."

We closed the bedroom door and Ann went to the top drawer of the dresser.

"Before we get distracted, Jack, I have something for you," and she handed me a fifteen-hundred- dollar cashier's check made out to Jack Barnes. "I didn't want to chance sending it by mail."

"Ann, this was a gift."

"I know, Jack, it changed my life—and now I'm returning it. Please take it, and then we can both feel good, and forget it."

Ann started to disrobe; I acknowledged defeat, and tossed the check to the top of the dresser. I didn't want to be left behind. As the last garment dropped to the bedroom floor, Ann did a slow pirouette for my approval. She was a breathtaking sight, but even more exciting was the behavioral change from the girl I had known before.

Ann took the lead in such inventive and passionate lovemaking that, after a long, cold winter, I wasn't sure my heart would survive. It was early morning when Ann murmured, "Oh, Jack, I've missed you," curled up in my arms and went to sleep. The stories I'd heard about redheads were obviously true.

Ann had the next day off and she came with me as I shopped for a sport coat and slacks. I was out of luck on the sport coat. Two years of shoveling coal had developed my shoulders to the point that coats in my size wouldn't fit. I chose the next size larger and then I had to pay a tailor to take in the waist. He demanded extra money for one-day service.

I took Ann to dinner at one of Seattle's plush restaurants. Ann wore the cocktail dress that demoralized Sidney, and I wore my new sport coat and slacks. I even wore a color- coordinated shirt and tie, in honor of the occasion. We spent more time admiring each other than we did with the dinner.

The next morning, Ann drove me to the airport for an early morning flight to Sacramento, with the understanding I would spend the night with her on my return flight.

It was a grand family reunion, and during it I casually invited my sister to come for a visit when she graduated from high school. It was almost a year away and I felt safe.

While I was in Sacramento, I looked up Roger, who had been on the same ship in the Navy. Roger was now the assistant sales manager of a Ford agency and while I visited him at work, he showed me pictures of the new 1949 Ford to be introduced sometime in the near future.

It was a streamlined beauty, completely different from any post-war automobile on the market. I wanted to be the first person in Anchorage with this unique automobile. I left a sizable deposit with Roger on his promise to send a wire the moment a sport coupe was to arrive, and I would fly down to pick it up.

THIRTY-SEVEN

On my return trip, I called Niki from the Seattle airport and caught her at the office, just as she was leaving.

"Jack, I'll meet you in the lounge of the airport in about forty five minutes. I have a car—oh, I'm glad you are here!"

I watched the entrance, spotted her as she came in, and had a chance to observe the changes in the last two years. The biggest surprise was her hair. The shoulder-length blond hair had been replaced with a boyish cut. After the first shock, I realized on her, it looked good. The hair no longer drew attention from her striking facial features, and there was nothing boyish about her body.

I watched her face light up when she saw me, and in a moment we were holding each other close. We walked hand in hand to the car. Niki's one bedroom apartment was high up in a new building, with a view of Puget Sound. After a real welcome kiss, Niki suggested I hang my garment bag in the bedroom closet.

We were both hungry, and she wanted to take me to an exclusive restaurant she saved for special occasions. While she was calling for reservations, I took my new clothes from the garment bag and laid them on the bed. Niki returned, removed a sexy cocktail dress from the closet, laid it beside mine, and started removing clothes. Well, if she could be blasé about this, so could I. When I was down to shorts and tee shirt, she discovered the change in my upper body.

"Oh, my," she marveled as she ran her hands over my shoulders. "Jack, what have you been doing?"

The fact she was down to panties and a bra didn't seem to bother her.

"Shoveling coal—that's what I do for a living."

Niki smiled, "On you it looks good."

I quickly slipped on my new shirt and slacks, which was a good thing, because Niki began connecting silk hose to a black garter belt. There is something about that combination that does things to me. I hurriedly concentrated on my tie and sport coat. I didn't want to blow our best friend relationship, and get her thinking about marriage again.

The maitre d' seated us at a choice table in the prestigious restaurant. A cocktail waitress brought us martinis; Niki was old enough to partake now. We placed our order, and I asked her about her job.

"I stayed with Jill and Dan for over a year, while I attended a special secretarial school for executive secretaries. It's a fairly new position and demands far more business training than a regular secretary. It pays better, too. I was already a good typist with office skills. My job description now is executive assistant to the shipping manager of the large company I work for. That's how I can afford the car and apartment. I've been here nine months and my boss seems to like me. Unfortunately, he only sees me as his efficient assistant."

I brought her up to date on my job and we were just finishing an excellent meal when a tall, slim man in an expensive suit, walked by with two others. He glanced our way, paused, then waved the other two on.

"Niki, I almost didn't recognize you in that lovely gown. I didn't know you dined here." He didn't seem too pleased seeing us together.

"Hello, David, it's a special occasion. Jack just flew down from Alaska. David James, I'd like you to meet Jack Barnes."

I stood and we shook hands. I was glad I had acquired the tailored clothing.

"Jack, David is the manager I work for."

David just stood there looking unhappy, so I invited him to join us.

After he was seated, he asked in a slightly condescending manner, "What do you do in Alaska, Jack?"

I paused, "I'm in transportation."

"Oh, what type? As Niki probably told you, we are in shipping."

Something about this guy's attitude was getting to me, yet I didn't want to get Niki in trouble. Unfortunately, my perverse personality chose this moment to surface.

"I'm in rail and air."

Niki ducked her head and took a quick gulp of the wine we had with dinner. David didn't seem to like that answer. I knew he was trying to put me down, and suspected he had suddenly developed a territorial thing over Niki. I decided to help that along.

"I didn't know there were regional airlines in Alaska?"

"If you don't count Sig Wein, you are correct. I have my own air service."

David seemed to like this answer even less. Niki was emptying the remainder of the wine bottle into her glass.

"How long do you plan on being in Seattle?"

"Long enough to accomplish what I came for," I replied with a confident smile.

"Might I ask what that might be?" David seemed suddenly apprehensive.

"Certainly, I'm searching for an exceptional, executive secretary, willing to relocate. I would like her to be young, attractive, and preferably blond; I can be very generous for the right person."

I smiled at Niki.

David looked ill! I rose, tossed a twenty on the table, and after assisting Niki with her chair, I held out my hand.

"Nice meeting you, David."

He reluctantly shook my hand. Niki said good night and we left.

"Jack, let's get out of here before you have David convinced you own Alaska!" Niki had hold of my arm and was guiding me. "You are just as terrible as you ever were. I should have run the other way at the dance the night we met—when you came up with that monk trainee routine."

"I'm sorry. He was so upset seeing us together, I couldn't resist it. Have you ever been out with the guy?"

"No, but only because I haven't been asked—of course, he hadn't seen me dressed up, and with a handsome man before."

"I'll bet you get the third degree about me tomorrow, and probably a substantial raise. Just tell him I get angry if anyone pries into my business, and I have a violent side to my nature."

She checked the refrigerator when we returned and located a bottle of champagne. She always seemed to find one when we had been apart. We toasted each other and after a few sip Niki said she wanted to get into something more comfortable. I had already removed my tie and jacket.

I never could understand why I preferred Niki as a best friend, and not as a lover. I believe it started when we first met, when she was emotionally fragile from her father's unexpected death. Her mother, Jill—she was something else!

She returned in a robe and we chatted while we finished the champagne. I told her about Ann, and my feelings for her. She took it well, and agreed to drop me off in the morning.

"Niki, if you will find a blanket and pillow, I'll curl up on the sofa."

"No, you won't—I've tried for years to get you in bed with me. I know I don't appeal to you that way and we will end up only friends, but at least I can be held."

After a quick shower in the early morning, I woke Niki in time for her to drive me to Ann's before work.

She asked during the drive, "What's going to happen to us, Jack?"

"You hold a very special place in my heart, and no one will ever be able to take that place. I guess we're going to remain best friends. When I come to Seattle again, if you want me to, I'll call you."

"I want you to."

We parked in front of Ann's house. She gave me a farewell kiss, and after I got out, with my back to her, I hurriedly wiped my lips with my handkerchief. When Ann's front door opened, Niki drove away.

Ann was pleasantly surprised and gave me a welcome kiss.

"Jack, I thought I was to pick you up at the airport?"

"You lucked out. A friend with a car gave me a ride."

She was a little suspicious, but did loan me her car while she was at work. That night she was happily surprised by my rampant desire. The following morning, Ann drove me to the airport in time to make my flight.

THIRTY-EIGHT

On my return from the states, I was pleased to find my bid on the Anchorage-Curry freight had been accepted. This meant I needed to find a place to live in Anchorage, and a car to get around. I had no idea when the Ford I had ordered would be available.

Used cars were not usually a problem in Anchorage. Eager young men drove up the Alcan Highway every spring, expecting to find a high-paying job, and not realizing that living expenses were even higher. By the end of summer many were broke, and had to sell their car for an airplane ticket home.

I wanted one ruggedly built, because the pot-holed roads and freezing weather took their toll. I found a 1937 Packard coupe in very good condition for three hundred fifty dollars. I had to replace the failing battery with an oversize one for below-zero starts. All I could find for living quarters was a boarding house, where, with my being gone so much, I would be paying for a lot I wouldn't receive.

My first day on the job was full of surprises. The crew had been together on this run for over a year, and were pretty set in their ways—on top of which, the two brakemen were the young studs that interfered with my romantic night at the Mt. McKinley hotel. They didn't recognize me, and I didn't say anything—their day was coming. Both the conductor and the engineer were soft and overweight.

Everything went well until we stopped at the section-gang mess hall for lunch. This was the halfway point of the longest run on the railroad—one hundred and thirty four miles. I was the only one on the crew doing heavy physical labor, and by the time we arrived, I was famished.

The engineer and I filled the engine water tank, pulled up and let the conductor and brakeman off in front of the mess hall, then backed the train into a siding for a meet with the southbound freight. By the time the engineer and I reached the mess hall, the train crew were already well into the meal. The meals were served family style and what was left looked like dregs. I could see tomato and cucumber in the salad on their plates, and all that remained was some limp lettuce in the bottom of the salad bowl. Fresh vegetables were expensive and scarce in Alaska, and the train crew had them all. The meat had been well picked over, also.

The engineer didn't seem to mind. He hadn't done enough to work up an appetite. After the engineer was served, I scooped the pitiful remains on the table onto my plate and started to eat. In a few minutes the train crew and the engineer rose, and the conductor said, "Let's get going." I had been feeling anger slowly building, and that did it.

I knew why they were in a hurry. The railroad paid by the union rule that one hundred miles equaled eight hours pay—hence one hundred thirty four miles equaled close to eleven. If we made it in eight hours we still received eleven hours pay, which made this a desirable run. The crew could hi-ball and spend the extra time and money in the Curry bar. They didn't take into consideration that the fireman was forced to shovel coal a lot faster and harder. I burned calories at an alarming rate!

I continued eating. I knew the time to get this untenable situation straightened out—was here and now!

"I said let's go!" the conductor growled.

I looked up at him. "Have a nice trip," and went back to eating.

The conductor wasn't used to having his authority challenged.

"If you don't come now, we'll leave you behind."

"Fine. The scoop is in the cab—start shoveling."

The rest of the crew returned and were watching. The cook came over to find out the problem. The other train crew had arrived, and there was only one dining table. They were standing, expectantly waiting.

I told the cook and his helper, "I want another complete meal—salad, meat, potatoes and vegetable. If you keep putting the meal out before the engine crew arrives, you are going to be serving two meals to this crew."

I was angry, and looking for a confrontation.

The cook gulped, hurried back and came out with what I demanded. It had to have come out of the south bound's meal, and I suspected they realized it. I continued eating while my crew, and the southbound crew, stood and watched in amazement.

I looked up and told my crew, "This is the way it's going to be from now on—unless you wait for the engine crew to be seated before you start. I don't shovel coal on leftovers!"

I took my time with the second meal. The cook's helper apprehensively set up the meal for the new crew at the opposite end of the table. I believe he was afraid I was going to continue eating the rest of their meal. Finally, a very subdued crew returned to our train.

Curry was a lonely place without Ann. After a generous meal in the crew dining room, I had a beer in the bar, and returned to the room I shared with the engineer. A quick shower and I was down for the night.

When we stopped at the same mess hall on our return trip, it became a completely different story. The train crew patiently waited for the engine crew to be seated. The cook increased the amount of food, and all dishes were passed to me, first.

As soon as we returned to Anchorage, I started looking for other living quarters. I noticed an ad in the Anchorage daily paper describing five acres near Lake Spenard, with a partially finished log cabin. The asking price was fifty-five hundred dollars. This was an area just starting to be developed, and the prices were still reasonable. I went with the real estate agent to check it out.

It was an interesting property, heavily wooded, only a quarter mile from the lake, with a dirt road to the cabin. The electricity was already connected, and an outhouse was located behind the house in the trees.

The cabin looked strange; I had never heard of a flat-topped log cabin. It soon became obvious the builder had done good work, up to the point he ran out of time and money. I could see where a portable mill had been set up, and twelve-inch timbers trimmed on three sides. With a flat strip of caulking, they formed an airtight bond. This also provided a smooth surface on the inside for further finish. The logs overlapped about a foot on each corner. It would have been very picturesque, if he had continued with a conventional roof.

The cabin was twenty-four feet by twenty feet, with a storm entry facing the road. According to the real estate agent, when winter arrived, and there wasn't time or money to do the roof, the owner laid one more log across the front to supply a slope, and then cut two by twelve's and laid them on edge every twenty-four inches, with an overhang front and rear. He sealed the bottom with plywood, filled the spaces in-between with sawdust for insulation, and covered the top with more plywood, followed by rolled composition roofing with the seams tarred. There was no evidence of roof leakage. The fact the ceiling had the same slope as the roof did take a little getting used to.

Inside, a bedroom with a closet had been finished, and the bathroom with a shower was complete. Unfortunately, there was no septic tank, and no water. A well had been dug about fifteen feet deep, but he had not reached water before he gave up. I figured the five-gallon jugs inside were what he used to transfer water from the lake to the cabin.

I was intrigued—with a little furniture, I could move in and work on the place in my spare time. I was glad I had saved my money from all the overtime on the work train and snow-fleets. There was a lot to do yet, so I made an offer of five thousand and returned to my job. The owner was in California, and I had no idea how long it would be before I had a response to my offer.

Two weeks later, the real estate agent had the signed acceptance, and had set up an escrow at the title company. I checked the title report to be sure it was free and clear, turned over the five thousand to the title company, and prepared to move in. The real estate agent said I wasn't supposed to do that until escrow closed, and I asked, "Who is going to complain?" He didn't have an answer, so I started my move. I would be glad to get shut of the boarding house.

I attached a tow-bar hitch to the back of the Packard, picked up a utility trailer, and used it like a pickup to haul furniture and building supplies. I bought a new double bed with a good mattress, a large chest of drawers, along with bedroom accessories, and a kitchen table with four chairs. When I moved in the camping gear I had in storage, I was really quite comfortable.

I camped there until escrow closed, and then got serious about improvements. I discovered I enjoyed working on a cabin that was my very own. I checked out how-to-do-it books from the library and took them with me to Curry. The time spent there didn't seem like such a waste, that way. By midsummer, I realized I wasn't going to have the well and septic system completed before snow flew, and I begrudged every night I was stuck at Curry.

I noticed a bid opening for the Anchorage-Whittier freight, which returned to Anchorage every night. It was also a long run with good pay. I had by then worked my way up to near the top of the fireman's seniority list, so I placed a bid on it.

After that session in the dining room, the current crew and I hadn't meshed very well. They almost acted as if they were afraid of me. I think the two brakemen had finally figured out who Jack Frost was that night in the hotel. Then there was that thing with the disbursing officer that was still being talked about, and the mess hall confrontation. With the smashed rifle added to the list, I was becoming infamous, with a reputation for violence.

THIRTY-NINE

There was a gap in time when one job ended and the other began. While waiting, I decided to check out by air the lake a friendly old-timer had drawn a map to. The old-timer came to the Curry hotel occasionally from his mining claim, and he and I had become friends.

The lake was ninety miles from civilization, and according to him it was filled with hungry trout. He said there was an old trapper's cabin there with a wood stove, and added that it was a ten mile hike from the railroad tracks to the lake, and to take a gun—there were a lot of bears back there! The passenger train would let off, and pick up fishermen at the trail.

I threw my fishing and camping gear into the plane on the off chance I might find a place to land, and managed to locate the lake from his map. There was a ridge above the lake without any trees or brush, which looked possible as a landing site, so I decided to try it.

The second the wheels touched I knew I was in trouble. The ridge was covered with deep moss, which swallowed the wheels, and stopped the plane so fast it was a wonder it didn't flip over. I shut the engine down and eyeballed the situation. The only possible way to take off was to turn the plane ninety degrees, point it down the steep slope, and hope I had flying speed before I came to the brush along the lake. I lifted the tail and managed to get it pointed downhill. I removed as much moss as possible from the path of the wheels for about a hundred feet with my trenching tool, and then called it quits. I was tired and I wanted fish for dinner.

I packed my fishing and camping gear to the cabin, and was pleasantly surprised by its condition. The roof was good and the wood cook stove appeared serviceable, with dry wood in the wood box. Someone, probably the old-timer, had been keeping the cabin in repair. There was a shuttered hole in the wall where a window had once been, overlooking the lake. I opened the shutters, tossed my sleeping bag onto one of the two bunks, and went fishing.

The lake indeed was filled with hungry lake trout, which ran in size from eighteen to twenty inches. I caught and released several, and then hiked to the creek, which fed the lake. The old-timer said the creek had small rainbow trout that, fried crisp in bacon grease and eaten bones and all, were utterly delicious.

I caught and cleaned a couple frying pans full of five and six inchers and returned to the cabin, where I fried up enough bacon in the cast iron skillet, to supply the bacon grease, and then started frying trout. The old-timer was accurate—they were indeed delicious.

I knew tomorrow's takeoff was going to be dicey, so I prepared for bed early. I latched the door and left the shutters open for fresh air. Sometime during the night I was awakened by a lot of grunting over by the window opening. I aimed my flashlight that way and was shocked to see a massive, brown bear's head and one paw and shoulder through the opening.

I yelled—he seemed determined; I didn't want company, so I hit him on the head with the heavy, cast iron skillet. Instead of discouraging him, all this did was make him mad. When he took a swipe at me with his paw, my friendly feeling toward bears changed dramatically. It appeared he would soon enlarge the opening enough to get inside. I shifted to where he couldn't reach me—stuck the barrel of my automatic pistol into his ear, and let off a couple rounds.

The whole cabin shook with the aftershocks! When I was reasonably assured he was dead, I crawled back into the sleeping bag, and then couldn't get back to sleep—something about that bloody head facing me, and then later waves of an unpleasant aroma.

I knew I had to get him out of the window if I was going to get any sleep. My feet were bare as I went to pull him out. When he wouldn't budge, I placed one foot on the cabin wall, grabbed a front paw, and gave a mighty heave. He popped out and then I discovered I was standing ankle-deep in a rapidly cooling pile of bear scat. I knew then where that horrible smell had been coming from. I cleaned up as best as I could at the lake, and this time I closed and latched the shutters before I crawled back into my sleeping bag.

The next morning, I fried up the rest of the trout and made coffee. After I ate, I cleaned up the frying pan and coffee pot at the lake and left them in the cabin. I didn't want heavy objects loose in the L-5 if the takeoff didn't work out. I left the sleeping bag, also. I didn't think I would ever want to sleep in it again, after the smell of bear poop. I replaced the firewood I had used, and threw the remaining bacon far away. I believe this attracted the bear in the first place.

I got a good look at the bear as I departed the cabin, and felt a clammy chill. He was a lot larger than I expected. I realized I had been fortunate to escape.

I let the engine of the L-5 get well warmed up, cranked down the droop ailerons, and opened the throttle wide. By keeping the wheels in the two trenches I had dug, I was rapidly picking up speed down the steep slope. I popped a notch of flap at the last possible second and was briefly airborne. Unfortunately, the wheels caught the top of the brush, and then I was upside down with smoke filling the cabin.

My fear of fire caused me to pop the latch on the safety belt prematurely, forgetting there was a considerable drop to the top of the canopy. I was groggy from the blow to my head, but still managed to get the door open wide enough to escape.

I got away from the airplane and when the smoke dissipated without it catching fire, I surveyed the damage. The brush had poked holes through the top fabric, but had also cushioned the descent. The prop was chewed up and one wing strut was snapped, other than that the plane seemed in fair shape.

I gathered up my fishing gear, pistol and flashlight, and headed down the ten-mile trail to the railroad. I knew if I missed the southbound freight, it would be another day before the passenger train came by.

Fortunately, I arrived before the freight train, and when it approached I stood on the engineer's side, and gave the railroad signal for slow. He did slow somewhat, but freights don't pick up passengers. When he recognized me, he slowed enough so I could swing aboard the cab. I then entertained the crew with the story of my fishing trip from hell!

FORTY

While waiting to start my new job, I drew a run off the extra board. This was a test of coal from a new mine, and it turned out to be the worst run of my life!

We took off for Portage, about fifty miles south of Anchorage, with a tender load of the test coal and only a caboose. What was most unusual was the road foreman of engines, dressed in a suit and tie, rode in the cab with us. I suspected the rumor that the road foreman and the general manager had bought a coal mine—and planned on selling the coal to the railroad—was indeed true.

The road foreman and I had discovered an instant dislike for each other the moment we met. It must have been chemistry. He was the one who had sent me out on my student run with the statement, "I don't think you are going to make it, Kid." I hate being called that. I knew union membership had something to do with my still having a job.

I considered myself an excellent fireman; I liked firing, and continually experimented with better ways to get more steam with less coal. We weren't out of the yard before I knew we were in trouble. There was something wrong with this coal. It wasn't putting out the heat, and as I checked the firebox, it was already starting to clinker. There were way too many minerals mixed in the coal. When they melted, clinkers were formed, which cut out the draft through the grates.

The only thing that kept the steam pressure up was my rattling the grates with the shaker bar and the fact we were only pulling a caboose. I knew we would never make it up the first grade on our return trip with a heavily loaded train.

Carl Banner, the road foreman, was sitting on the fireman's seat with the window wide open and a smile on his face. I suspected he was already counting millions from the sale of the coal. He looked my way.

"Damn good coal isn't it, Kid?"

I shrugged my shoulders. I was desperately trying to figure a way to avoid firing the return trip—a sudden heart attack...a fall and a damaged arm...

We were already into the turn-around and tying into loaded cars. Carl bailed out of the cab to drain his bladder and I leveled with the young engineer. He had been watching me use the shaker bar and had guessed why. He was on his first run off the extra board as an engineer, and wasn't about to tell Carl anything he didn't want to hear.

Well, when we stalled and plugged up the whole southern portion of the railroad, I didn't want Carl to be able to say, "The fireman never told me there was a problem."

I bailed out of the cab, and located Carl talking to the conductor.

"Mr. Banner, could I speak to you privately for a moment?"

He scowled and came my way, "Yeah, what do you want, Kid?"

"Mr. Banner, we have a serious problem. This coal has so many minerals in it that we are never going to get over the first grade. If you plan on getting this train back to Anchorage, we need to take on some good coal here."

I thought Carl was going to have a heart attack. "What are you talking about; we came sailing here in good shape."

"Yes, just pulling a caboose. Even then it was touchy. I had to use the shaker bar to keep the clinkers from forming with what little coal we used. Can't you imagine what it will be like with a heavy load, on a grade?"

Carl was thoroughly angry; "There isn't a thing wrong with this coal. You just don't know how to fire, Kid. Get back to the cab, if you can't fire it, I will!"

The conductor had been watching with a curious expression, so I motioned him over. He wasn't under Carl's authority like me, and he was in charge of the train.

"For a matter of record, I want to tell you what I just told the road foreman. The coal is no good. It has so many minerals it will clinker solid before the train gets halfway up the first grade. The road foreman refuses to take on some good coal here, so we can make it back to Anchorage. The train is your responsibility, and you are the one that will have to hike back to Portage to call another engine to tow us in. You also will be responsible for tying up the southern half of the railroad for God knows how long. It's up to you two to work it out." I stalked back to the cab.

The engineer and I watched the heated conversation between Carl and the conductor. There was a lot of arm waving, and an occasional gesture toward the cab. Finally, a brakeman cut the engine loose and guided us back to the clamshell that loaded coal. The operator removed the back portion of the faulty coal from the tender and replaced it with the good stuff. I figured there was barely enough to get us home.

Apparently they had compromised. The test coal was still first out and if it failed there was a backup of good coal—the conductor was a diplomat! We hooked back up to the train and Carl climbed aboard. He was furious.

"Kid, give me your gloves—you are relieved. I don't want you screwing up the test of this coal any further. Stay out of my way—I'll fire this engine back."

I tried to look disappointed and chagrined.

Carl took off his suit coat and tie, and tossed them to the fireman's bench seat by the window. I stood in the gangway on the engineer's side, out of the way. Carl went to work and I could see he knew what he was doing—with good coal.

I had heard that he had been a fireman and engineer before he became road foreman. He laid an even bed of coal and the steam pressure began to rise. The engineer eased the train out of the yard and we were slowly gaining speed. A couple miles later we reached the grade.

We slowed and Carl sprayed more and more coal into the firebox. The steam pressure went down instead of up. I knew exactly what was happening, and I was concerned. If the whole firebox clinkered over and became too thick, we wouldn't be able to break it up and even good coal won't burn without a draft through the grates.

Carl opened the firebox doors and I could see the sick expression on his face as he realized what had happened. He pulled the long iron rod with the prongs on the end, out of the tender and began breaking up the massive clinker. When he had pieces small enough to pass through the firebox doors he pulled them onto the scoop and tossed them out the open fireman's window. Had I been in his position with my suit coat on the fireman's seat, I would have tossed the clinkers out the gangway as I had in the past; however, he was the road foreman!

All this activity with the firebox doors open had cooled the firebox to the point the train slowed to a stop. The last clinker was larger than the rest and, as Carl tried to throw it out the window, one edge hit the window casing and it dropped back onto the fireman's seat.

The seat and Carl's coat both burst into flames. Carl stood there—stunned. I grabbed the canvas water bag. Carl had my gloves and the scoop, so I shouted, "Throw the clinker and coat over the side."

I wasn't going to waste water on them, with fire dropping through the burning seat to the flares and torpedoes stored below for emergencies. Torpedoes were made mostly of gunpowder and were set to explode when an engine's drivers ran over them. This was to warn the engineer there was trouble ahead. If they went off in the cab it was going to become very explosive indeed. I had to use all the drinking water to get the fire out.

The long rod in the firebox was white hot and had to be removed before anything else could be done. This would ruin a pair of gloves and wouldn't be beneficial to the hands inside. All the worthless coal had to be thrown overboard before anyone could get to the good stuff. Carl surveyed the situation—and handed me my gloves and scoop.

"Carry on, Kid."

He left the cab, headed for the caboose. He had just lost his dream of millions and had some humble pie to eat from the conductor.

Seven hours later, we limped into the Anchorage yards, the end of the run from hell. As Carl trudged past the engine headed for the roundhouse, I leaned out the gangway.

I couldn't resist calling, "Hey Carl, you owe me a new pair of gloves."

FORTY-ONE

The Whittier run started out in the same direction as my ill-fated one with the road foreman. When we reached Portage, the rail line divided, each line going to a seaport: The one on the right to Seward, the left to Whittier. Portage is a very small community with a section gang, mess hall, and coal and water for the engines. It is also home of the famous Portage glacier.

We ate at Portage, and this crew must have heard what took place in the mess hall of the Curry run. We all sat down together and the dishes just seemed to be placed in front of me first.

Just before we reached Whittier, there was a long tunnel through a mountain. The engineer advised me to get up a good head of steam and water before we reached it, and not to shovel any more coal than necessary until we were through. The air in the tunnel could get very bad, and we would be coming back through it. The minute we broke out of the tunnel we were in Whittier, a deep-water port surrounded by steep mountains. The whole port seemed to be built on pilings. We dropped off the empties, picked up the loads, and were on our way home.

It was a good crew, good food, and I was back in time to work on the cabin every evening. I was feeling better, even with my hormones in rebellion. Whenever I could spare a moment, I wrote to Ann and Niki. I had a picture of each on the kitchen table I used as a desk. I was finishing digging the well and it was slow going.

I complained in my letter to Ann about the difficulty of digging through permafrost to get a bucket of dirt, then climbing the ladder, pulling the bucket rope up hand over hand, emptying the bucket, and then doing it all over again. The shaft was four feet by four feet to allow room to swing a pick and to have storage capacity when I hit water. I wasn't worried about the shaft collapsing. The permafrost was like concrete. My progress was measured in inches. I knew now why the builder had given up at the permafrost line.

My last letter from Niki mentioned she had received a second raise since my visit. She also mentioned David was very interested in my quest for an executive secretary. She and David were dating.

I returned to the cabin one evening to find I had company. Ann had arrived unexpectedly, and was cleaning up the mess I had left. The cabin was much improved, and Ann was most welcome. Our reunion ended up in the bedroom.

I was glad the cab driver had located the cabin so easily. When she mentioned it was a flattop, log cabin, he already knew where it was. I guess the cabin was a topic of local conversation. As far as I knew it could be the only one in Alaska. Ann had taken some time off to help me finish the well.

I proudly showed her around the property, and when we strolled down the seldom used, grassy road to the crystal clear lake, I carried a bag. There was one five-acre parcel between the water and me and I had the real estate agent checking out the possibility of a purchase. I was already using it like I owned it for swimming, bathing and drinking water. If it were thinned properly, I would have a lake view from the cabin. Over on the other side of the lake was a seaplane operation and I realized if I had floats on the L-5, I could dock it right here—then I remembered where the L-5 was.

We stopped at a driftwood log on the sandy beach and I started removing my clothes.

"Jack! What are you doing?"

"Getting ready for my bath and swim. The shower in the cabin isn't hooked up yet. Come join me."

"Won't someone see us?"

"As far as I know, there isn't anyone living around here. I haven't seen another soul in the evening."

This was all the invitation Ann needed. In moments we were using the washcloths and soap in the bag, followed by a relaxing swim. The long summer sun had heated it to a temperature that was just right in the shallow water. Ann was an excellent swimmer, and seemed to enjoy this opportunity. When we finally tired, we dried off with the towels, dressed, and returned to the cabin.

Ann wanted to know what she could do while I was at work the next day, and I could think of a lot. It was difficult to get into stores while they were open with the hours I was keeping, so we made up a shopping list. I needed a pulley and axle for the well, including a longer rope.

I had gotten a bid from the man that built and installed septic tanks and had planned on doing the drain field installation myself, but with Ann here I wanted indoor plumbing now. I asked her to swing by his place and order the complete job done as soon as possible. He already knew where I wanted it located. I also asked her to keep her eye open for a propane range. I wanted one with the chrome griddle between the burners. I liked pancakes in the morning. I was tired of restaurant food and I knew Ann was a good cook. There already was a large propane tank behind the cabin and it was full. I also needed a refrigerator and told Ann to use her own judgment. I was afraid it would be necessary to have the kitchen cabinets, drain-boards and sink, custom built and I didn't know how long that might take. Ann was beginning to look a little bewildered so I stopped, signed some blank checks, and located a hundred dollars in cash. We figured out where the range and refrigerator should go, and then retired early. We wanted time for leisurely loving.

Early the next morning, Ann drove me to the roundhouse. I noticed she was wearing western gear and was covered up, even to gloves. I had forgotten how sensitive she was to sunlight and the long Alaska summer sun was powerful. I wanted to be sure she wouldn't have any difficulty with the Packard and I had drawn a rough map to the different areas she would be going. When I kissed her good-bye, I felt almost domesticated.

I told her to listen for the train whistle in the early evening. The railroad track wasn't far from the cabin, and the engineer always whistled for the road crossing. If she started when she heard the whistle, she would arrive at the roundhouse about the time I was ready.

Ann was parked and waiting when I finished. She was behind the wheel, so I let her drive. She needed to become familiar with the area and besides—I was tired. I asked how her day went.

"Jack, I spent a lot of your money. Wait till we get there and then you can either smile or frown. It's too late to change your mind."

When we returned, a backhoe was still parked out back and the septic tank and drain-field were completed, connected and covered. All we needed was water. When I opened the cabin door, the cabin was now a home with the range and refrigerator installed and working. The refrigerator was stocked with food. The biggest surprises were cabinets, drain-boards and a double sink, perfectly positioned between the range and refrigerator. Ann already had the top cabinets filled with plates, saucers cups, glasses and bowls. There was a set of stainless silverware in a lower drawer, as well as a set of carving knives. A matching pantry-like cabinet was installed on another wall and stocked with dry food, canned goods and other necessities. I was overwhelmed.

"Ann, how did you ever manage it?"

She smiled when she knew she hadn't overstepped her bounds.

"I lucked out. There is a new building supply store in town that also handles appliances. They had the stove and refrigerator we needed and also a new line of pre-built cabinets at half the cost of custom built. I told them if they could deliver and install today, I would take all three. They didn't think that was possible, so I said I would shop around and started to leave. They changed their mind and here it is. I think they shut the store down to do it.

"Did I do alright?" Ann asked apprehensively. "I had to pay extra for the copper pipe from the propane tank to the stove."

"Ann, you did wonderful. I'm so happy; I won't even ask how much it cost. The way I have been dithering around, it would have been winter before I got it done. How did you get the septic tank man to move so fast?"

"I told him if he could get it in and hooked up today, I would pay for it. If not, you would probably nickel and dime it the rest of the winter. He got to laughing, and said all right he would do it, and really laughed after he finished. He saw you made out the check. He just left and will pick up his machinery tomorrow. Now we can concentrate on the well."

I wandered over to the new range and turned a knob. It was a pleasure to watch the blue flame pop on. I checked the refrigerator with the cooling goodies inside—then the well supplied pantry cabinet. I picked up a five-gallon jug of water and filled the tank on the toilet in the bathroom.

"Voila! We now have indoor plumbing; no more treks to the woods."

We both smiled happily.

I drove the Packard, with the trailer filled with empty jugs, to the lake. We would be using a lot more water now that the toilet was hooked up. We filled the jugs first, then after a bath and swim we were hungry. Ann fired up the new griddle, made steak sandwiches, and found a bottle of wine to celebrate our improved home.

Ann had cleared the kitchen table of my correspondence and placed it in a new folder with several compartments. I saw she had labeled them with one for Niki, one for Ann and one for my folks. I hadn't ever mentioned Niki. I was feeling mellow from the wine, when Ann asked.

"How are you coming with your search for an executive secretary?"

Uh-Oh! She had read Niki's letter.

Well, Ann had always been up front with me; I could do no less, so I told her the whole story, from the time Niki and I met.

"It's alright, Jack, I know with our age difference, and the fact I can't have children, that we aren't marriage material. Now let's put it away and forget it. I want to enjoy this time with you."

That night Ann slept in my arms without our making love.

The next evening, I mounted the pulley about six feet above the surface of the shaft. When I threaded the new rope through, I could hoist the bucket from the bottom and all Ann had to do was guide it to the wheelbarrow, where the bucket practically emptied itself. It was many times faster and easier than the old way.

The following day was Sunday, and we really got serious about well digging. At the end of the day, we were three feet deeper and the bottom was beginning to show moisture. After our swim, I took Ann to my special restaurant for dinner with wine. That night Ann's passionate nature was in full recovery.

The next evening, the pick intercepted a vein of water that came spurting from the bottom of the well. I quickly scooped up any loose dirt and placed it in the bucket. A couple more swings with the pick and I had the vein fully broached. I used my hands to find any more loose material, filled the bucket and quickly climbed out. The icy water had already climbed over my ankles. The next morning, there was four feet of crystal clear water in the well.

I built a platform just above the permafrost line and installed the electric pump and pressure tank. I placed an insulated top on the well, much like the cabin roof, and added an insulated trapdoor for pump access. In less than a week, we had abundant hot and cold water in the bathroom and kitchen sink. I attached the sink outlet to a hose and ran it behind the cabin, where I planned on putting in a garden next year. The nutrients from the sink would make good fertilizer, as well as supplying water.

Ann and I appreciated the hot shower when the lake became too cold for swimming. Winter was fast approaching, and I still had lots to do outside. I was working on an exterior, concrete block chimney to supplement the propane heater, with a Franklin fireplace. There was lots of firewood on the five acres, as the former owner and I both had been judiciously thinning. He had left behind an old chain saw that still worked.

Ann was laying tile in the bath and the kitchen area over the plywood sub-floor, to define it from the living area. The way it was coming out, I suspected she had done this before. When she finished, I asked her to order thick, wall-to-wall carpet with the best padding—for the barefoot effect in the living and bedroom.

It all came together at the same time—the thick carpet and the fireplace. That night we made love on the carpet with the bright glow from the fireplace painting our bodies. It seemed to add an extra, sensual dimension.

The only thing left was living room furniture. We needed a sofa sleeper for unexpected company. I believed my kid sister might arrive as soon as she finished high school. We also needed two comfortable chairs and a reading lamp. Both Ann and I enjoyed reading, and winter was here. I had a lot more confidence in Ann's judgment than my own, so I delegated the job to her.

The next day was decision time. The furniture was delivered, and we both loved it. It truly made the cabin a complete home. I arrived with a telegram from my Ford buddy in Sacramento, notifying me the new Ford would arrive in two weeks. I had arranged earlier for time off to go after it.

Ann had originally arrived with the intention of helping with the well and returning home. That kept being put off, and I knew she was receiving letters from both her mother, and the owner of the market where she worked. I brought a bottle of wine home with me and we had it with dinner. I had discovered it took wine to get Ann to reveal what was truly in her heart.

"Ann, what are we going to do?"

"Jack, are you going to drive straight up the Alcan with the new car, or are you going to detour through Seattle?"

I had a feeling my answer would have a lot to do with Ann's and my future relationship. I didn't want to part with her.

"Straight up the Alcan."

"All right, I'll fly out with you and then see what can be worked out at home. I've paid off mother's mortgage, and she and her widowed sister seem to be getting along. With both social security checks and no house payment, they should be able to make it. Matthew, my former boss, checks on them and brings little extras from the store."

"Ann, is there something special in your relationship with Matthew?"

"He wants to marry me. I don't love him, and we have never made love, but I feel sorry for him. He is fifty, his wife died three years ago, and he is very lonely. He has the big market, the big house, the big car, and it's not enough. He knows about you and says he will wait however long it takes."

Damn! It seemed our lives were becoming entangled with others.

We only had a few days to enjoy our completed home, and then it was time to depart. Our last night together was especially poignant.

FORTY-TWO

I parted with Ann at Seattle and continued on to Sacramento. I had time for a very short visit at home, before my former shipmate called and said the new Ford had arrived. I instructed him to have it completely winterized, as I could be going into temperatures below zero. He agreed to have the shop do it, and that afternoon I went down to pick it up. It was a beautiful, blue coupe with lots of chrome. The body had a sleek, racy look that made other new cars look like boxes. I paid the balance of the twenty-four hundred for the car, waved goodbye to my buddy and proudly headed home.

Dad and Mom admired the car, but my sister demanded a ride. She wanted her friends to see her riding around in this special new model. I did notice we were receiving an unusual amount of attention.

Early the next morning, I headed north. I had heard on the news that a cold front was approaching from Canada. It was November, and this wasn't unusual; there had already been snow in Canada.

Everything went well until I stopped for the night at a hotel in Great Falls, Montana. I had to park on the street, and during the night the cold front arrived. It was well below zero, the car was covered with ice, and I couldn't even get the key into the door lock. I called the Ford garage and they towed it to their heated facility. I had breakfast while waiting for them to get it thawed out enough to get inside and start the engine.

They wanted to charge me for the tow, and I told them to send the bill to the Sacramento dealership. I showed the receipt for winterizing. The shop manager was really a good guy, and he told me quietly to keep it running until I got to Edmonton—only the Canadians knew how to winterize a car.

I followed his advice and this time it was really winterized. I believe there was more kerosene in the crankcase than oil, and 100% anti-freeze in the radiator. They let me leave the car in the Edmonton shop overnight, and the next morning I was on my way. When I reached the gravel portion of the highway, the snow had been graded until it was like blacktop. The cold had formed a rough surface on the top and it wasn't slippery. There was little traffic, and I batted along at seventy-five miles an hour.

The further north I went, the colder it got, and further apart were gasoline, food, and sleeping facilities. I tried to always keep at least half a tank on the gasoline gauge, and a bag of candy bars handy. An error here could be fatal. This was not normal weather for November. One night, I let the engine run all night; I was afraid it wouldn't start in the morning. I noticed several other guests at the roadhouse did the same thing. There were no heated garages, and a frozen car would sit until the next thaw. Some of the roadhouses had a man that went around every hour, and started the engines until they warmed up.

I was one happy young man when I finally pulled up into the driveway at my cabin. This had not been a fun trip. The temperature was ten above, and it felt balmy. I anxiously checked out the plumbing, and found nothing amiss. I was glad I had sealed off the crawlspace beneath the cabin and had left the thermostat on the propane heater set at forty. This cabin was really insulated and the more snow that accumulated on the roof, the better the insulation. I built a fire in the fireplace to warm the place up, placed the car cover I had bought in Edmonton over the Ford, and drove the Packard to work. I dropped a quick note off to Ann telling her I arrived safely, and how lonely the big double bed was without her. If anything would prompt her soon return, that might. When I returned to work, the crew was unhappy I wasn't driving the Ford, so I promised to bring it to work the next day.

Ann finally arrived, and she explained, between kisses, that she had only received my letter five days ago. I believe she was pleased that I had so obviously missed her. She hadn't eaten on the plane, and although I passionately desired to take her home and have my way with her—I took her to our favorite restaurant instead.

I deliberately ordered a bottle of wine with the filet. I wanted to find out what Ann really wanted to do. After the second glass, Ann commented, "Jack, I have, at least temporarily, all my ducks in a row in Seattle. The sisters are getting along well and mother's health actually seems better. Even without encouragement, Matthew is prepared to wait until you fall by the wayside."

This was more frankness than I had anticipated—I was cutting off her wine!

"The manager of the market here, where I had been buying our food, offered me a job before I left. I could work day shift, and the pay is higher than Seattle. I like the work, and we both would have evenings off. The cabin is finished and perfect. Jack, let's have some fun this winter. We have the new car, we both like to ski and dance, and with my working, we shouldn't have any financial problems. I just turned thirty-five, and I've never had a fling."

I could see the tears she was trying to hide.

I decided then and there, this was to be Ann's winter fling!

The next morning, after a passionate reunion, we went our separate ways. I insisted the Ford was for her use. I figured driving the most desired car in Alaska would be a boost toward her first fling.

That evening, Ann was ecstatic. The job was even better than she hoped, and the Ford was great for business. It drew a steady crowd to the parking lot and she had already been offered five thousand for it. Even the Anchorage Ford dealer hadn't received one yet and they were sending eager buyers over to view it. Ann was already famous.

It was Saturday night; there was a good band at one of the clubs so we went out on the town. It had been a long time since we had danced and Ann remembered the cheek-to-cheek position I liked, with her arm around my neck. After a couple beers, I was in my usual blissful state and could have danced all night. The word must have spread that the Ford parked in front was ours, because our table became very popular with friends, and some who were not. The two young studs had the guts to drop by all friendly, wanted information on the Ford and foolishly flirted with Ann. That did it—I started after them. These were the two that interrupted my romantic night at the Mt. McKinley hotel and I had wanted an excuse to tangle with them ever since. One of them overturned a chair in their rush to leave.

Paul, my former engineer on the snow-fleet came by. Ann remembered how his kindness had helped her return to society that New Years Eve, and she rolled out the red carpet. I didn't even get jealous when she took him out for a guided tour of the Ford. Paul was out at the car before he realized she was the former Raggedy Ann. I believe this made Ann's evening.

The music wound down and we drifted to the door. As we came out, I could see a circle of viewers around the Ford. The new model must have magic; they just stood and watched as we drove away. Maybe they wanted to hear the deep rumble of the v-eight engine.

As I drove back to the cabin, Ann snuggled up close. "Jack, I think I'm going to like this fling."

FORTY-THREE

The next morning was Sunday, and we slept in. Later in the morning, Ann cooked pancakes and eggs on the new range grill, and we decided to go skiing at the ski run outside Anchorage. Neither of us had the opportunity to do much skiing, so we rented skis and began at the rope tow of the beginner's hill. By afternoon, we had it mastered, and were determined to take the intermediate lift next time. It was so much fun that I bought us both our own skis and ski clothing. That night, we made love on the carpet before the glow from the fireplace.

This pretty much described the way the winter of Ann's fling unfolded. We took in each new movie or event during the week and it was the club Saturday night and skiing on Sunday. The Ford still was the center of attention everywhere we went.

This all ended with the first thaw. Potholes blossomed throughout the poorly paved streets of Anchorage, and the Ford's body literally began disintegrating before our eyes. The first time we attempted to roll down the side windows, the mechanism inside the doors snapped off. Both windshield wipers stripped out. The innovative front coil springs that supplied the smooth ride collapsed, and the front end was so low the car rode like a truck.

I returned it to the Ford garage for warranty repairs, and all they could do was look sick. They hadn't received any parts yet for the new model. I stuck boards inside the doors to hold the windows up and continued to drive it. Ann was driving the Packard with no problems at all. The final straw was when the door hinge snapped on the driver's side. I suspected the forty-below weather I encountered on the Alcan had done something to the temper of the metal. I tied the door to the body with a rope, and entered and exited through the passenger door.

I had Ann contact the dealership and strongly suggested the owner, shop foreman, and sales manager stay over until I got off work. They were there when I drove the wreck into the service area. I pointed out the different disasters.

"Gentlemen, I paid twenty-four hundred for this junk heap six months ago. It cost another couple hundred to get it up here. It is under warranty, and Ford seems to be unable to live up to their end of the contract. This car is famous in Anchorage. The smart thing would be to get it off the street, ship it back to Dearborn in the dead of the night, and let the Ford engineers figure out where they went wrong. Write out a check for twenty-six hundred, and it's on its way."

The owner started to protest this was a company matter, not a dealer one, especially as he hadn't sold it.

"Fine, remember it was your decision. I'm going to paint a big lemon on both sides and list all the things wrong you can't repair. I have another car, and I am going to leave this one parked across the street from your showroom. If I don't have my money this week, I am going to take pictures, and send them with my story to the editor of every major newspaper north of Kansas. If the newswires pick up the story, Ford's new model will be dead on arrival everywhere except southern California and Florida."

The sales manager's face turned ashen. He and the owner retired to an office for a hurried conference. The sales manager came out.

"Do you have anything against last year's model? We have a new coupe just like yours. I believe I can get the owner to trade straight across. We have the parts to back up the new warranty."

Actually I didn't have anything against this model except its boxy look. After a couple years, I knew most of the bugs would have been worked out. I did know with its heavy frame and springs it was a lot better suited to Alaska's roads. Ann was waiting when I drove to the cabin in the new, old Ford.

"Jack!" she cried in mock horror, "does this mean my fling is flung?"

"Depends on which car you drive in the morning." I commented, deadpan.

Ann wasn't foolish; she chose the new one.

I had been involved for months in mail negotiations with the insurance company that insured the L-5. I had written to their home office, described the location of the crash site and the condition of the plane, and told them I wanted them to, either get it out and fix it, or send me the four thousand it was insured for.

Their position was that there was a clause in the policy that I couldn't remove the plane from the United States without their permission, and because I had, they didn't owe me anything.

My rebuttal was that they may have added that to the new policies but it wasn't on my copy. I told them if they didn't send a check, my attorney would sue them. I added, when they lost the case, they would find out how expensive Alaska attorneys are.

One day I told my sad story to John, who ran the repair shop at the airport. He had done the last annual on the plane, and agreed it definitely was worth salvaging. He had me pinpoint the location of the plane on a map and describe the exact amount of damage. His repair business was slow just then and he agreed to salvage and repair it. We would sell the repaired plane and split anything over his repair costs.

John was in charge of the Civil Air Patrol and he threw a training exercise for his group. Four planes on skis, filled with bodies, plane parts, and beer landed on the frozen lake, dug the plane out from under several feet of snow, flipped it right-side up and went to work. A new prop and skis were installed, the worst tears in the fabric were patched with fabric and dope, and a piece of angle iron was attached to the broken wing strut with bailing wire. When gasoline and oil were added, the engine fired right up. They pushed the plane to the frozen lake, and John flew the L-5 back, with the others keeping a close watch. John added one hundred dollars to the repair bill for the flight and I felt he deserved every cent.

John was well into the repair job when I received an offer from the insurance company. They would pay three thousand and I could keep anything I could salvage off the airplane. I quickly accepted, before they discovered I was salvaging the whole plane.

With all new fabric, a new prop and wing strut, the L-5 was in better shape than before the accident. John's repair bill, including the salvage flight, came to eighteen hundred dollars. There wasn't much interest in used airplanes that time of year, and John had considerable time and money invested in the L-5. He knew I had received an insurance settlement, and suggested I pay the repair bill and keep the airplane. I was glad he brought it up—I was about to broach the same offer.

Spring arrived, the snow melted, and one Sunday, Ann and I went trout fishing. We followed a dirt road in the Packard to where it intercepted Willow Creek, upstream from the railroad bridge. I had a new fly rod and was determined to become a fly fisherman. Ann stuck to bait. After an hour, Ann's creel had both rainbow and Dolly Varden trout; mine was still empty. In disgust, I hiked downstream to a long, clear pool, with shallow rapids at each end. After fruitlessly casting again and again with the fly, I gave up, and peered into the pool to see if there were any fish in there.

There was something in there, long and dark, that looked like a submarine; it had to be a monster king salmon. The run wasn't supposed to start for weeks yet, and I wanted that fish. There were enough salmon steaks there for all summer.

I had one large spinner in my bag so I removed the light end of the fly rod, tied the spinner directly onto the line, and when I managed to get it across ahead of the salmon, he hit it. I had an automatic reel with fifty feet of line, and he immediately had it all. He took off down the pool with me running on the path alongside; when he came to the shallow end he turned and charged back upstream. I ran as fast as I could, expecting the line to snap any minute. He did the same thing at the other shallow end, and we charged back downstream. It was becoming an endurance contest.

All this commotion attracted another fisherman, and after watching my speed slow down, he asked if I really wanted to get that fish—no matter how? I was so out of breath, I just nodded my head.

"OK, his back comes part way out of the water when he makes his turns. I'll put a couple twenty-two slugs in his back. That should slow him down."

He had his pistol ready and it took both shots before I could feel any difference.

The sound of the shooting brought Ann down to see what was going on, followed by another fisherman. He had a small gaff and volunteered to hook the salmon in the gills as I led him toward shore with the line. The water was ice cold, and the gaffer didn't want to get in over his boots. The shooter and Ann held hands, and he held the gaffer's hand while he leaned out, and gaffed the salmon. The salmon gave a mighty leap for safety, and took the first two men with him. Ann was smart enough to turn loose. I had to remain on the shore to keep tension on the line. The gaffer was standing in waist-deep, icy water, and was so angry he unsnapped his hunting knife, and stabbed the salmon in the head. This ended the battle.

When we had the salmon on the shore, we just stood and admired his size. I figured he must be at least four feet long. If this battle ever got out, none of us would ever be invited to join the Isaac Walton league. I thanked my partners in crime, and hoisted the salmon over my shoulder. He was so heavy, I unloaded and cleaned and washed him right there. I held the head at my waist, the body went over my shoulder and the tail was slapping me on the rear.

Ann and I had just returned to the car when a carload of trout fishermen arrived. They were all big-eyed as I deposited the monster fish in the trunk. I could tell they were dying to ask questions, so just before we pulled out, I commented out the window, "You should have seen the one that got away!"

FORTY-FOUR

The fishing trip proved to be the finale of Ann's fling. When I came through the roundhouse the next evening, I noticed an engine watchman job was up for bid at Portage. Normally an engine watchman was the lowest rung on the fireman ladder. He didn't go anywhere, all he had to do was lubricate the engine and keep steam up while the crew wasn't working. His pay started when the crew tied up, and ended when they resumed work. It did pay the same as a fireman.

I wouldn't have thought anything of it, except I knew the work train being put on this summer was only going to work forty hours a week—no overtime. There should have been two engine watchmen put up for bid. One engine watchman would be putting in an astronomical amount of overtime. Carl had screwed up, and if he didn't catch it, I was going to throw in a bid at the last second.

Carl didn't—I did, and when the selection was posted, all my friends and probably some enemies, thought I had cracked up. Here I was, sitting at the top of the fireman's seniority list with my choice of any run I wanted, leaving behind my cars, plane, and log cabin with sexy redhead installed, to bid in the lowest fireman's job—out of town! The latest thinking was I had a native girl tucked away at Portage, and I was spending the summer there for a change of pace. I explained to Ann how

I would be gone for months, and she reluctantly agreed to return to Seattle for the summer.

I lucked out on the engine. It was fresh out of the shop, and with a judicious amount of coal and water, it would sit and steam for twelve hours without attention. It took about a half hour to lube the engine, add coal and water, and I was free for eleven hours with pay.

The government was putting in a highway to Seward, next to the railroad, and Portage was the command and living area for the construction workers. They were a rough lot, mostly interested in booze and hookers. They lost two days work to get to Anchorage and back by train, and the foreman wasn't happy. One of the workers had been on the work train with me last year, and knew I had an airplane.

"Jack, if you will bring your plane out here, we will keep you busy flying."

"I'm not going to land on the tide flats."

"Where would you like the runway?"

"The strip between the railroad and highway would be nice."

The next day there was almost as much equipment working on the landing strip as there was on the highway.

I loaded the engine firebox with coal, and caught a ride into Anchorage with my former freight crew. I leveled with Denny, the engineer, who was also our union representative. He didn't know of any rule requiring time slips be turned in on a timely basis. Everyone just did it to get paid. I knew that the first month's slips would alert Carl that he had screwed up, and he would immediately add another engine watchman. Denny, who had bumped heads with Carl over union matters, thought it was a great joke on Carl, and agreed not to spill the beans.

He dropped me off at the market, where Ann was happily surprised to see me. It had been over a week. She took off from work early, and we headed for the cabin to catch up on our loving.

I explained the new twist, and that I would be in town a lot more than we had figured. Ann smiled happily and forgot Seattle.

I parked the Packard at the airport, and took off in the L-5 for Portage. The landing strip was great, and I parked the plane close to the outfit car, where I occasionally slept. All in all, it had been a busy day. I put sixteen hours on my time slip; actually, I went on overtime on

Wednesday, sixteen hours Thursday, sixteen Friday, twenty-four Saturday, and twenty-four Sunday. I knew when I turned in my time slips; Carl was probably going to have a heart attack!

I refueled the firebox of the steam engine, and my air shuttle service started immediately. I charged twenty dollars a head each way. Due to the limited width of the rear seat, a heavy-set worker had to find a slim one to fly with him. I told everyone up front I didn't have a commercial license, and if they admitted to the wrong person I was charging for the flights, my private license would be lifted and the shuttle would be over.

There was a sleazy bar close to the airport, which became the rendezvous place for return flights. With every flight in, I checked for returning passengers. It took about an hour for a round trip, and a tank of gas after every third one.

Finally the newness wore off during the week, and I was down to about three flights an evening. After the last flight in, I spent my time with Ann at the cabin until the bars closed, and I picked up my return passengers. I was clearing over two hundred a night, which was a lot more than the railroad was paying, even with the massive overtime. Saturday and Sunday were at least double that. At the rate I was going, I would pay for the airplane many times over. My only concern was the possibility of running into Carl in Anchorage, while I was being paid to engine watch at Portage.

The word must have spread about the horny construction workers at Portage, because I was being solicited at the bar by hookers for flights to Portage on the weekends. I told them if I didn't have immediate return passengers, I would take them. When they asked how much, I said if they had a profitable weekend to remember the pilot. They were usually good for fifty dollars. Ann wasn't too happy about that.

My financial bonanza continued most of the summer before a problem developed. The commercial pilots at the airport became very suspicious of the yellow L5 that kept appearing, and was buying more gasoline than all of them combined. They knew I was on to something, and they were jealous and suspicious of my legality. When they questioned the passengers, they just answered, "The pilot was a good guy who gave them a free ride."

The hookers weren't going to blow their transportation with a wrong answer.

Finally, while I was gassing up, a CAA man drove up in a big black car and asked to see my pilot's license. When I showed it to him he commented, "You know you can't carry passengers for pay with a private license."

"Yes sir, I do know that, but the construction workers at Portage were nice enough to build me a landing strip so I could commute to Anchorage. I figured the least I could do, would be to take them with me when I come and go."

"Seems there has been a lot of coming and going. Would you like to comment on that?"

I hung my head, "It's kind of embarrassing. I have an engine watchman job with the railroad at Portage that only requires I be there every six hours. I have this sexy redhead staying with me in Anchorage, who has my new Ford and needs lots of attention. I commute a lot."

"That wouldn't be a new, blue Ford, would it?"

"Why yes, it is."

"I've seen the Ford and the redhead; I can understand your problem. Don't get into trouble with the passengers. I'd hate to pull your license and leave the redhead all alone."

He got into his big black car and drove off. He hadn't said a word about more than one passenger in the back seat.

The weekend before the work train was to be pulled off; a massive air show was being put on at the Air Force Base above Anchorage. A famous Air Force precision jet team would be putting on a demonstration, as well as many others. Ann and I both wanted to see it—unfortunately, most of the construction workers did also. I started ferrying passengers very early in the morning and flew steadily until just before the show started. Ann was waiting when I came in, and drove my last passengers and me to the base.

When the show was over, I started ferrying them back again. Before the night was finished, I had collected over a thousand dollars. Summer was over and the work train was pulled off. I turned in four months of time slips, and waited for the explosion; it wasn't long in coming.

Carl was livid! "What in hell are you trying to pull, Kid? This is ridiculous, why that's more money than the general manager made this summer!"

"You put the job up for bid, Carl. All I did was bid on it. Those time slips are accurate."

"Yes, but you deliberately withheld the time slips so I wouldn't discover the mistake. I am going to pay you what you would have earned with two engine watchmen."

"Better think twice, Carl. I've already talked to the union and they say I have put in the time, and I have earned the pay. Denny said if there is any question, to come to him."

Carl was so angry that if he had a nail between his teeth, he would have bit it in half.

"All right, Kid. I'll pay it, but I'll tell you this—you will never be an engineer on this railroad!"

I laughed condescendingly, "Carl, if you pay your firemen this well—I don't want to be an engineer!"

I thought Carl was going to have a stroke right there as I turned and walked away.

Between the railroad and flying, I banked over twenty thousand for those four months.

FORTY-FIVE

I took a couple weeks off to spend with Ann and work around the cabin. I had bought the five acres between the cabin and the lake last year, and I wanted to finish selectively thinning it in such a way we would have a lake view. I was just completing this when I had a message from Paul, my former engineer. He was now the assistant road foreman of engines.

"Jack, get in here quick and take the engineer's exam. You are next on the list and when Carl went outside on vacation, he forgot to leave any instructions regarding you!"

When Carl returned, I had been promoted and was working the extra board. There is quite a change in job choices between the top of the fireman's seniority list and the bottom of the engineers. At twenty-three, I was the youngest locomotive engineer on the North American continent. I would have been second youngest, only Perry Bowery, the youngest, took a curve too fast, and dumped half the train into a ravine. They named it Bowery's fill, and fired him.

Paul warned me Carl was adamant about getting me fired. He thought Carl blamed me for the loss of the coal contract, as well as the censure he received over the work train fiasco. He said whenever I caught a run outside Anchorage; he had his roadmaster buddy follow in his single-seat, special built gas car, with the aluminum cab, heater, and recording speedometer. After Bower's fill there were speed limits on each section of railway, and Carl was determined to nail—and fire—me for speeding.

Winter arrived with a vengeance. We had more snow than usual. After the rotary plow passed through, it left a bare track with massive walls of snow on each side. The moose discovered this was a lot easier walking than bucking the drifts. The only problem was, once in the narrow corridor, they didn't want to get out.

I learned a lot about moose that winter. They are ill-tempered brutes that do not like being pushed. I pushed a big bull too hard, and he whirled and charged the engine. When his head hit the snowplow -they felt the shock in the caboose. Of course it killed him and then we were stuck with over a half-ton of dead moose. The fireman and I carved a notch in the wall of snow with the scoop and then nudged him into it with the snowplow mounted on the front of the engine. The head brakeman kept a machete in the cab, and he whacked off the hindquarter, which protruded. We manhandled it onto the tender, and dropped it off at the mess hall where we ate. The cook promised moose steaks when we came back through.

The worst possible scenario occurred when we came to a bridge. The moose would get about half way across and then his feet would fall between the ties. There would be a mad moose on his belly, and no way to ever get up. He had to be killed, and rolled over the side. Fish and Game wouldn't let us carry firearms, so the only way to dispatch him was to beat his head in with the heavy iron shaker bar. It was a bloody, sickening business, and I vowed to find a better way.

By trial and error, I found I could come up behind an angry moose, nudge him with the snowplow into the bank and get by him before he could recover. There was a narrow space between the engine and snow bank and if he remained still he was all right. The minute he moved he lost some hide on the passing cars. It was surprising how quickly the message got across. Of course, by the time we had passed, there was a very angry moose in the track.

Finally I got tired of having the roadmaster dogging our train. Just before we pulled into the railroad settlement where we ate, I deliberately antagonized a massive bull moose. The moose may have lost some skin with our passing. When I pulled up to let the train crew off at the mess hall, instead of going in, they motioned for me to back up. The conductor was really upset. He said a moose had knocked the roadmaster's gas car off the track and now was rearing back and beating the aluminum shell down around the roadmaster's ears with his front hoofs. He wanted me to back the caboose up to where the gas car was, and they would try to scare the moose off with flares.

I backed up, and the moose must have already fully vented his ire, because he took off when they popped the flares. Without the proper tools, it took half an hour to extract the roadmaster from the flattened cab of his gas car. I don't believe either would ever be quite the same again.

I unloaded them all at the mess hall again, and went in to eat. The roadmaster's face was as white as a sheet, and blood dripped from a torn ear. After the meal, I told the roadmaster to tell Carl to never, ever, send a gas car behind me again. I didn't care who heard what I said.

This story, of course, made the railroad rounds, and just added to my infamous reputation. I began to suspect my time on the railroad was limited.

FORTY-SIX

Spring came, and with it some real trouble. My kid sister arrived for the visit I had foolishly offered. Little did I know then, that at eighteen she would be so beautiful—and so out of control. Ann and I took a couple days off to show her around, and all this did was convince her that she was a valuable commodity here in Alaska. The dumb young men were making fools of themselves. She was sleeping on the sofa and driving the Packard when I was out of town. I refused to give her any more money, hoping this might get her headed home. Instead, she cashed in her return ticket, and got a job at the post exchange of the Air Force Base.

When I came home after a late night run, there would usually be some airman from the base, either looking for her, or crying because she never showed up for their date.

I had a frank talk with my sister, and told her if she was going to date servicemen, to at least pick pilots. When they got out, they could work for an airline, and make real money. She just laughed, and said the airmen were so cute.

I gave up, and contacted mother. She didn't have any better luck than I, and the next thing I knew, Mom arrived at my door. Ann and I gave mother and daughter the bedroom and we slept on the sofa bed, which didn't do much for our love life.

Mother discovered she liked Alaska, and when she realized her daughter was going to do as she damned well pleased anyway, she forgot the reason she was here and began to enjoy herself. Mother was in her early forties, and still a slim, attractive woman. She had married young and, I suspected, never had a fling. Now I was working weird hours, and had three women in my little bachelor cabin—in various stages of a fling!

Dad was getting upset without his wife, and when she wouldn't return, he chopped off her money. That didn't faze mom; she got a job at the local drug store, and developed a coterie of older gentlemen.

Ann had been very quiet lately, so I took her to our favorite restaurant and ordered wine with dinner. After the second glass her concerns came pouring out. Her mother was failing again and Ann's skin was starting to react to Alaska's long summer sun, even though she kept covered up. She knew she had to leave and it was tearing her up.

Ann said, "Jack, I think the time has come for us to check our hole card. You changed my life and gave me more than two wonderful years. I know I will think about you every night I live, but I am going back to Seattle. Matthew promised that if I marry him he will see mother has the very best of care, and will leave everything to me if he should die first."

"When would you leave?"

"Soon. It won't get any easier if we drag it out."

In a week, Ann was gone, and I felt alone—even with my mother and sister there.

The lake was warm enough for swimming. To distract me from my blues over losing Ann, I picked up a barbecue, a table with benches, pads and an umbrella, and installed them on my private, sandy beach. This became the entertainment center on the weekends. When I was there, I barbecued. Occasionally, mother's friends came out, and when my sister's friends from the air base found out, it became very popular indeed. This was one of the few sandy beaches in the Anchorage area on private land.

Lake Spenard was becoming popular for home sites, and the developers were moving in. My dirt road was graded, graveled and oiled—at no expense to me. Houses were being built on the adjoining properties, and they were expensive. Before long, my flattop log cabin would stick out like a sore thumb. At least I had the best beach on this side of the lake. My new neighbor was friendly, so I invited him to use the beach for swimming.

We became friends, and I discovered he was one of the principal developers in the area. He wanted to know what I planned to do with the ten acres. I told him that, for the time being, I planned to enjoy it. He said if the time came I wanted to sell, he would show me a way to make some money.

What happened next put me in a mood to discuss it with him. The Alaska Railroad converted to diesel in a matter of just weeks. There went the romance of railroading. No more listening to the steam burst up the stack with each stroke of the piston. The diesel engines were noisy, and smelly, and when the engineer pulled the whistle cord, instead of a melodic whistle—out came a loud blatt! I hated them.

What was even worse, the alcoholic engineers that had been "Rule G"ed off every road in the states was now being fired here. I was gaining seniority so rapidly, before long I might be locked into this as a career. It was time to talk to my neighbor. Without Ann's presence, Alaska had lost its charm.

I had just made this decision when mother received a letter from a friend in Sacramento. Enclosed was a picture and article from the front page of the Sacramento newspaper. The picture was of four drunken legionnaires, in their legion caps, in a jeep, parked in the lobby of the Senator Hotel. The hotel is across the street from the state capital, and is famous. It was Dad's jeep and he was the driver.

The American Legion held its convention in Sacramento, and Dad and three World War One buddies got canned up on ale, and decided to see if the jeep would climb the long series of steps to the hotel. The answer was yes. The article was written humorously.

The next morning, mom was on a plane home, and I had my bedroom back. Now, what would it take to get my sister on a plane?

FORTY-SEVEN

I invited Mike, my developer friend next door, to join me, and over a couple beers I asked for his recommendations. He looked the cabin over and said the land was too valuable for a flattop log cabin; it would drag down adjoining values.

"However Jack, if you put a conventional log cabin roof on it, it would have a romantic appeal and would be an asset."

"I hate to part with the flattop Mike, that foot of sawdust insulation keeps the cabin toasty warm in the winter."

We went outside to eyeball the situation.

"Hell, Jack, leave it there. Just trim off the overhang, remove the log that causes the roof and ceiling to slope, and put the new roof right over it. No one will be able to tell the difference. I have a builder who would do it for a thousand dollars. It would double the value of the property."

"What about the rest of the ten acres?"

"Jack, your property is a natural. The ten acres are a long rectangle, just the right width for slicing into one-acre parcels. You have the best swimming beach on the lake. Don't sell that acre. Deed a one-ninth undivided interest to each of the nine parcels you sell. That way, each buyer will always have access to the beach.

Your only expenses would be the survey, and the cost of a gravel road down one side. Next year, the building boom at Spenard will be in full swing. You should be able to get five thousand a bare parcel with deeded beach access, and twenty thousand for the one with the cabin. If you decide to put the road down our mutual property line, I'll furnish half the land and pay half the cost. It would be beneficial to both of us."

I decided not to fool around and ordered the new roof and survey. Mike said he would take care of the road, and I could pay my half when it was finished.

I had to deadhead to Fairbanks to temporarily take over the engineer job of my first run as a fireman. I was the only fireman who had lasted with that engineer over a month. Carl had finally got tired of losing every fireman assigned there and fired him for rule G. The man was an alcoholic and it was a wonder he hadn't caused a wreck.

The roundhouse foreman was still there and had apparently been following my infamous career with glee. I had to divulge the gory details of all my past encounters.

It was over two weeks before I returned to Anchorage, and when I reached home I almost didn't recognize the place. The new roof was installed, and the cabin looked like it belonged there. It blended in beautifully.

Mike's carpenter didn't fool around, and neither did his road builder. The new gravel road was installed, and I could see cars parked at the beach. It was the weekend, it was hot, and the beach was crowded with swimmers. I located my sister, reclining like a queen bee on a chaise lounge, surrounded by young men. One was barbecuing, another was bringing her a cold drink from a tub filled with ice, and the others were sitting around, looking at her adoringly.

Damn! It was going to take dynamite to ever get her out of Alaska.

Well, it was my beach—I might as well get a swim and some food and drink. I donned my swimsuit and waved at my sister as I passed. She looked so startled; I wondered what else she had been up to while I was away…

After the swim, I joined my sister and her following. The barbecuer fixed a hamburger for me just the way I liked it, and the drink server quickly supplied a cold beer. Being my sister's brother did have some benefits.

I finished the hamburger and was sipping the beer when I saw Mike, his attractive wife, and a young man arrive in swimsuits. They spread a blanket and I drifted over.

"Jack, you made it back." Mike smiled.

"I guess, for a while there, I thought I took a wrong turn; my flattop cabin disappeared."

"How do you like the finished product?"

"Mike, your carpenter is a genius. It looks like it was built that way from the beginning and fits in perfectly. I'm pleased with the road also."

"Jack I'd like you to meet my nephew, Martin. He is just out of college, and is going to be working with me in the land development business. He also likes log cabins."

Martin and I shook hands. He seemed a pleasant young man.

"Mr. Barnes, I was over there when the carpenter was putting on the new roof. Your sister was kind enough to give me a tour of the interior. It is everything I dreamed a log cabin could be."

Martin had a very wistful look. I wasn't sure if the cabin or my sister inspired it. Martin and I were probably only a couple years apart in age, but in experience it was a great deal more.

"Tell me, Mike, did the surveyor ever show up?"

"Not only did he show up, he has an iron stake in each corner of your acre parcels. He just finished the plat map and I have a copy with me. I thought you might arrive this weekend. It also shows our mutual road."

Mike pulled a copy out of the pocket of the shirt he was wearing over his swimsuit. I eagerly checked it out. Mike had penciled in the cabin and fortunately it was in the center of one of the parcels. Had it been on the line I would have lost another acre to sell it.

There was something exciting and satisfying about changing the boundaries of a parcel of land and greatly increasing its value and salability. Mike and Martin were definitely on to something. My total investment for the ten acres would be about ten thousand and if Mike's projections were accurate, I would be getting sixty thousand back. It beat shoveling coal!

I thanked Mike for all his help and invited him to come over to the cabin at his convenience, and we would settle up. He didn't seem worried.

My sister had taken off with her military entourage when he came over that evening. I popped a couple beers and wrote a check for my share of the road, roof, and survey. He had paid the surveyor for me. It came to twenty-two hundred and fifty dollars, total.

"Mike, you asked me to let you know if I ever had a change in plans. I guess I was more attached to the redhead that helped me fix the cabin up than I realized. Alaska hasn't been the same since she went back to Seattle—then the railroad switched to diesel engines, and took the fun out of being an engineer. I'm thinking about selling what's salable, listing the property with a real estate agent and going south before snow flies."

"Jack, I would truly hate to lose you as a neighbor and friend, but if you are bound and determined, we may be able to help each other. Martin needs a place of his own and is in love with your cabin. I would like him out of the house but still close. My older sister and her husband are well to do, and have offered to buy him a place. If we can get together on price, it should be a win-win for all three of us."

"You had mentioned twenty thousand when we talked about it earlier. Does that figure still seem reasonable?"

"Very much so, and by not going through a realtor you would save twelve hundred." I held out my hand and Mike shook it.

"Well I guess that takes care of that. Will you start the paper work? Now all I need to do is sell the new Ford and L-5. I'll keep the Packard till the last minute."

"Umm, Jack," Mike said with a sheepish expression on his face. "Ever since Martin saw your sister driving the Ford around, he has wanted one just like it, and he does need a car."

I laughed. Okay, tell Martin to check with the Ford dealer. I got it on a trade and they are very familiar with it. There are only about a thousand miles on the speedometer. Tell Martin to say that I want to know exactly what they would ask for it if they were selling it"

"Umm, Jack," Mike was laughing." What kind of shape is the L-5 in?"

"You got to be kidding!"

"No, I am really serious. I need a seaplane for my business and everyone says the L-5 has the best performance. I know where there is a pair of floats over across the lake, but I haven't located an L-5. I flew one once in the war when I was a bomber pilot, and never forgot it."

"This is the latest G model, Mike, with the droop ailerons and hundred and ninety horse. It was in mint condition when I bought it in California three years ago and flew it up the Alcan. I've babied it since. Among other things, I'm an aircraft mechanic. It has only a thousand hours total time and it just came out of the shop with a fresh annual and all new fabric."

I reluctantly admitted the reason for the new fabric and prop.

I could tell Mike was excited. He reminded me of myself when I was on the trail of an L-5.

"When can I see it?"

"Tomorrow, if I don't have a call. Come by in the morning and, if I'm free, I'll check you out."

Mike arrived early and drove us to the airport. I could see his eyes light up when he saw the plane. There is something about L-5s!

I parked him in the front seat and checked him out on the droop ailerons. The one Mike had flown had been an earlier model and didn't have them. After he completed a familiarity check on the other controls, I stuck a stick in the rear seat control, climbed in, and Mike taxied out for the takeoff.

I had mentioned the unexpected torque from the engine. Mike picked up on it and compensated right away. It only took a few minutes to convince me this fella could fly. Once we were over the inlet with altitude, he put the L-5 through its paces. When he pulled it up into a full power stall and all the L-5 did was dip its nose to pick up flying speed, I could sense his smile. Unstable aircraft have a tendency to do unstable things in a power stall. By the time he was finished, we were over Portage and I pointed out my private airstrip.

"Be a good place to shoot some touch and goes."

Mike smiled like a kid with a new toy. He touched down with a no-flap landing—a partial-flap landing—and on the last one he cranked down the droop ailerons, hung out the two barn-door flaps, and walked it in hanging on the prop. We only used a couple hundred feet of the runway as we coasted to a stop.

"Jack, this is the damnedest performance I ever heard of. No wonder the float boys were saying this is the only way to go."

"Hey, Mike, you're blowing it. That isn't the way a prospective buyer should be talking to a prospective seller, before a price is established."

He laughed. "Jack set your price. I'll pay it."

"What do you think about five thousand?"

"If you had said more, I would have agreed."

"I'd rather keep you as a close friend. Besides, this plane paid for itself four times over in four months last summer, right from this strip. It was one of those-once-in-a-lifetime situations. I can afford to be generous—especially as your real estate advice has already made me a bundle. It's going to cost you a check out, when you get the floats on. I've wondered how it would perform with floats."

We shook hands on the deal.

Back at the cabin, Mike returned my check and wrote me one for the balance. I located the title and signed it over to him. It hurt, parting with the L-5.

Mike had been eyeballing the cabin furnishings and appliances.

"Umm, Jack." We both burst out laughing. "What are you going to do with the furniture?"

I gave him a conspiratorial grin, "Tell Martin if he will keep my sister, I'll throw the furniture in free!"

That hit Mike's funny bone. "I'm sorry—I don't think Martin is up to your sister's speed."

"Damn, I was afraid you would say that. I guess I will have to feed her knockout drops and put her on an airplane home. Tell Martin; he can have the furniture and appliances for five hundred if he wants them. I'll even throw in my cold-weather gear."

"Consider it done. What are you going to do when you go outside?"

"That's the rub—I don't know. It won't be flying or railroading. I'll have about fifty-five thousand in cash and the value of the eight lots."

He hesitated, and then decided to proceed.

FORTY-EIGHT

"Jack, I'm going to share something that may be right up your alley. You have the funds and this could pay off—big-time!

A couple years ago, I was taking post-graduate studies at U.C.L.A., and blundered onto an unpublished projection done by a brilliant professor. It was a study of the motivational factors directing the population shift on the west coast—projected for the ten years following the war. We are three years into the study now, and so far it has been right on the money.

Basically, I know who is going to move where, and what they want when they get there. The professor factored in Alaska's coming statehood and gave the Anchorage area the early potential for land development. I was so convinced; I dropped my studies, took Milton's parents in as a partner, and started buying up property around Lake Spenard. Water is big as a motivational factor. It's working out even better than the projection."

"That's great, Mike, but it looks like you have things pretty well tied up here."

"That's true, and because I'm going to be involved here for years, I'll share the next coming hot spot—Southern Oregon!"

"Southern Oregon! —Why, that's mostly timber and farm land."

"Ah, that's where the projection comes in. California is already having some serious growing pains. People migrated there during the war to make big bucks in the aircraft factories and shipyards. They liked the climate and job opportunities and stayed. Before long, they invited all their friends and relatives. Add the Mexicans from below the border, and the immigrants from Europe and Asia, and some people are already feeling squeezed. The air around Los Angles is so bad you can hardly see the sun. People can't go south, they don't want to go back east, so guess where the only close, uncrowded area, with a mild climate, abundant water, and cheap land, exists?"

"Southern Oregon?"

Mike smiled. "Southern Oregon. Now, the projection adds that the government is going to build a four-lane freeway along the west coast from Canada to Mexico, and Southern Oregon will become an easy drive from California. Not only will the massive construction be a shot in the arm economically, but it will also expose Oregon's beauty, livability, abundant water, and reasonable land prices. I checked out the area before I settled on Alaska. It's a unique opportunity, Jack."

I could feel the excitement start to build.

"You were there with development in mind. Which part of Southern Oregon do you think has the most potential?"

"Two areas, the Rogue River and the Illinois River Valley. I am firmly committed to either streams or lakes on the property or close by. The Rogue is the most beautiful, but it already has had some development pressure.

The Illinois, which is a tributary of the Rogue, is an undiscovered gem. The Illinois Valley is about thirty miles long and five miles wide, with both forks and the main river running the length. Highway 199 also runs through the valley, with the ocean on one end and Grants Pass on the other. The new freeway will go through Grants Pass. With your finances you would get the biggest bang for a buck on the Illinois. It will be slow until the freeway is completed—then watch out!"

"Mike, if you were in my shoes, how would you proceed?"

He thought a moment. "I believe I would move to Cave Junction, in the Illinois Valley, and get an Oregon real estate license. That way I would have an income, and would be the first to know of any good buys.

I would also be assured my properties were shown first. I would invest in as much river frontage as I could swing, with a low down payment and release clauses. This way I could sell small parcels of the property at my price and get the owner to release title at an earlier agreed upon price per acre. In reality, the seller would be financing the project.

This way I could also tie up the largest amount of land, with the least amount of capital. When the river frontage is gone, I would move back into the logged over land, which is usually cheap, clean up the slash, and replant enough young trees for a cosmetic effect. A young growing forest has a lot of appeal.

The projection indicates the strongest demand will be for retirement home sites of five acres. I would choose properties that have good road access, for easy division. The larger the property, usually the lower cost per acre.

Jack, when I divide land down to a size people want—the mark up usually is five hundred percent! I would sell with a low down payment, easy monthly payments and ten percent interest on the balance—which fits most pocketbooks.

In essence, I would become a banker as well as a developer. They pay equally well. By the time the parcels are paid off, I would have received more than double the sale price, and the buyer would still be happy. Should the buyer want to pay it off before I pay off, I would exercise my release clause and deliver a deed."

"Mike, I think you have just solved my future career problem. This is something I would enjoy doing. I am really appreciative as I think you had this tucked away for yourself later. Thank you!"

Mike looked embarrassed and changed the subject.

The next night when I returned from work, my sister wasn't home and a young airman was waiting for me.

"Mr. Barnes, I'm really glad to see you. Your sister is in serious trouble. One of the airmen she has been playing games with has gone off the deep end. She refused his proposal and he is telling everyone if he can't have her, no one else will. He is packing a .45, and I believe he intends to shoot her and himself tonight!"

I halfway expected something like this.

"Where is she now?"

"She's at the movie with another airman. He's supposed to bring her back to the base to pick up her car. That would be the most dangerous time."

"Do you know when the movie lets out?"

The airman glanced at his wristwatch. "In about twenty minutes."

"Hop in the car. I'll be right with you," I said, as I quickly retrieved my pistol from the cabin.

We arrived in front of the theater just as the crowd started to come out. I thanked the young man, told him he probably saved my sister's life, and asked him to get out and keep an eye open for the rejected lover. As my sister came out with her date, I intercepted them and took her arm.

"There is an emergency," I told her date, "and I'm taking her home."

My sister started to protest, but as I painfully tightened my grip, she followed obediently. Her date took one look at the expression on my face and took off.

On the way to the cabin, I explained what she had waiting for her back at the car. When she saw the pistol, she got the message and started packing for the morning flight to Seattle where she would have a layover before continuing on home.

I was there early to buy a one-way plane ticket to Sacramento and heaved a huge sigh of relief as I watched the plane take off. The civilian airliners used the military airport, and there still had been the possibility of trouble.

Alaska's winter arrived; I cut my ties, except for eight lots, sold my airplane, log cabin and cars. I waited to board the airliner for Seattle with a very large cashier's check and a thousand dollars in my money belt. I kept my account open at the bank and made arrangements for the title company to deposit the checks from the lots as they sold.

I was sure Carl, the road foreman, would be heartbroken at my departure.

The weather was strange. A cold front moved in earlier and the temperature remained stuck in the low teens; suddenly a warm, Chinook rain rolled through, and shortly thereafter the temperature plummeted.

Ice formed everywhere: on the runway, on the wings, and the tail of the airplane. I waited for the crew to de-ice the plane, but instead they started to load the waiting passengers. Maybe they would de-ice after we were aboard. I chose a seat on a row with an escape hatch on the window side, and placed my coat on the aisle seat next to me. I had a bad feeling about this takeoff. The pilot taxied to the entrance of the runway and began his engine checks.

So much for de-icing!

As he ran up the first engine to check the magnetos, the plane began to rotate. The locked wheels were skidding on the icy runway. I knew this determined fool was going to try to take off, no matter what, so when the pretty, young stewardess came by, I asked her to quickly bring all the spare pillows she could find. She didn't ask why: from the fear in her expressive eyes, she already knew. She arrived with an armful of pillows just as the airplane began trundling down the runway—without any more engine checks!

When she reluctantly turned to start back toward her fragile, jump seat, I took her hand and tugged her into the empty aisle seat beside me; it didn't take much effort. She quickly buckled up while I shared the pillows.

We stacked the pillows in front of us to help absorb a sudden stop, and her hand found mine under the pillows. When we came to the normal point of rotation, the pilot pulled the nose up—and nothing happened. I knew it was way too late to try to stop, and all the fuel we had aboard would burst into flames when we hit something. It was a shame I wouldn't be able to invest the money I had saved, and this vital, young woman holding my hand would die before she really lived.

We felt the plane run off the end of the runway where the plateau ended, and then we were descending onto the city of Anchorage. The stewardess was squeezing my hand so hard, it hurt. I hoped the idiot pilot would at least try not to take out Main Street. We were almost downtown before the plane slowly began to climb.

When it finally became evident we were not going to crash, the stewardess released my hand, unfastened her seat belt, and began gathering up pillows. As I handed her my last one she looked into my eyes with the strangest gleam, and murmured. "Thank you. Thank you!"

The light came on to release seat belts and I headed for the steps to the upstairs bar of the double-decked airplane. I stayed right there until it was time to buckle up for the landing in Seattle.

I debated about waiting and punching the idiot pilot on the nose, but then decided he had probably sweat enough blood for one evening.

I collected my suitcase from the luggage area and was heading for the telephones, when I felt an arm tuck around my empty one. It was the pretty stewardess.

"I have a taxi waiting…"

She had that gleam in her eyes again!

The End

ABOUT THE AUTHOR

Jack H. Barnes Sr. was born in the early 1920's, raised in Placerville California. On a wet dark night in the spring of 1942, after breaking down, he hitched a ride that changed his life forever. Since coming back from the Alaska, Jack went on to work for the federal government as an airplane mechanic, and then became a real estate broker. He has been blessed with the chance to watch his children, his children's children, and his children's children's children come into the world. Today, Jack lives in California with his wife of 50+ years, and their dog Buddy.